Twelve M

GW01403192

Theodore Dreiser

Alpha Editions

This edition published in 2024

ISBN : 9789362511195

Design and Setting By
Alpha Editions
www.alphaedis.com
Email - info@alphaedis.com

Contents

Peter

In any group of men I have ever known, speaking from the point of view of character and not that of physical appearance, Peter would stand out as deliciously and irrefutably different. In the great waste of American intellectual dreariness he was an oasis, a veritable spring in the desert. He understood life. He knew men. He was free—spiritually, morally, in a thousand ways, it seemed to me.

As one drags along through this inexplicable existence one realizes how such qualities stand out; not the pseudo freedom of strong men, financially or physically, but the real, internal, spiritual freedom, where the mind, as it were, stands up and looks at itself, faces Nature unafraid, is aware of its own weaknesses, its strengths; examines its own and the creative impulses of the universe and of men with a kindly and non-dogmatic eye, in fact kicks dogma out of doors, and yet deliberately and of choice holds fast to many, many simple and human things, and rounds out life, or would, in a natural, normal, courageous, healthy way.

The first time I ever saw Peter was in St. Louis in 1892; I had come down from Chicago to work on the St. Louis *Globe-Democrat*, and he was a part of the art department force of that paper. At that time—and he never seemed to change later even so much as a hair's worth until he died in 1908—he was short, stocky and yet quick and even jerky in his manner, with a bushy, tramp-like "get-up" of hair and beard, most swiftly and astonishingly disposed of at times only to be regrown at others, and always, and intentionally, I am sure, most amusing to contemplate. In addition to all this he had an air of well-being, force and alertness which belied the other surface characteristics as anything more than a genial pose or bit of idle gayety.

Plainly he took himself seriously and yet lightly, usually with an air of suppressed gayety, as though saying, "This whole business of living is a great joke." He always wore good and yet exceedingly mussy clothes, at times bespattered with ink or, worse yet, even soup—an amazing grotesquery that was the dismay of all who knew him, friends and relatives especially. In addition he was nearly always liberally besprinkled with tobacco dust, the source of which he used in all forms: in pipe, cigar and plug, even cigarettes when he could obtain nothing more substantial. One of the things about him which most impressed me at that time and later was this love of the ridiculous or the grotesque, in himself or others, which would not let him take anything in a dull or conventional mood, would not even permit him to appear normal at times but urged him on to all sorts of nonsense, in an effort, I suppose, to entertain himself and make life seem less commonplace.

And yet he loved life, in all its multiform and multiplex aspects and with no desire or tendency to sniff, reform or improve anything. It was good just as he found it, excellent. Life to Peter was indeed so splendid that he was always very much wrought up about it, eager to live, to study, to do a thousand things. For him it was a workshop for the artist, the thinker, as well as the mere grubber, and without really criticizing any one he was "for" the individual who is able to understand, to portray or to create life, either feelingly and artistically or with accuracy and discrimination. To him, as I saw then and see even more clearly now, there was no high and no low. All things were only relatively so. A thief was a thief, but he had his place. Ditto the murderer. Ditto the saint. Not man but Nature was planning, or at least doing, something which man could not understand, of which very likely he was a mere tool. Peter was as much thrilled and entendered by the brawling strumpet in the street or the bagnio as by the virgin with her starry crown. The rich were rich and the poor poor, but all were in the grip of imperial forces whose ruthless purposes or lack of them made all men ridiculous, pathetic or magnificent, as you choose. He pitied ignorance and necessity, and despised vanity and cruelty for cruelty's sake, and the miserly hoarding of anything. He was liberal, material, sensual and yet spiritual; and although he never had more than a little money, out of the richness and fullness of his own temperament he seemed able to generate a kind of atmosphere and texture in his daily life which was rich and warm, splendid really in thought (the true reality) if not in fact, and most grateful to all. Yet also, as I have said, always he wished to *seem* the clown, the scapegrace, the wanton and the loon even, mouthing idle impossibilities at times and declaring his profoundest faith in the most fantastic things.

Do I seem to rave? I am dealing with a most significant person.

In so far as I knew he was born into a mid-Western family of Irish extraction whose habitat was southwest Missouri. In the town in which he was reared there was not even a railroad until he was fairly well grown—a fact which amused but never impressed him very much. Apropos of this he once told me of a yokel who, never having seen a railroad, entered the station with his wife and children long before train time, bought his ticket and waited a while, looking out of the various windows, then finally returned to the ticket-seller and asked, "When does this thing start?" He meant the station building itself. At the time Peter had entered upon art work he had scarcely prosecuted his studies beyond, if so far as, the conventional high or grammar school, and yet he was most amazingly informed and but little interested in what any school or college had to offer. His father, curiously enough, was an educated Irish-American, a lawyer by profession, and a Catholic. His mother was an American Catholic, rather strict and narrow. His brothers and sisters, of whom there were four, were, as I learned later, astonishingly virile and interesting Americans of a rather wild, unsettled type. They were all, in so far as I could judge from chance meetings, agnostic, tense, quick-moving—so vital that they weighed on one a little, as very intense temperaments are apt to do. One of the brothers, K——, who seemed to seek me out ever so often for Peter's sake, was so intense, nervous, rapid-talking, rapid-living, that he frightened me a little. He loved noisy, garish places. He liked to play the piano, stay up very late; he was a high liver, a "good dresser," as the denizens of the Tenderloin would say, an excellent example of the flashy, clever promoter. He was always representing a new company, introducing something—a table or laxative water, a shaving soap, a chewing gum, a safety razor, a bicycle, an automobile tire or the machine itself. He was here, there, everywhere—in Waukesha, Wisconsin; San Francisco; New York; New Orleans. "My, my! This is certainly interesting!" he would exclaim, with an air which would have done credit to a comedian and extending both hands. "Peter's pet friend, Dreiser! Well, well, well! Let's have a drink. Let's have something to eat. I'm only in town for a day. Maybe you'd like to go to a show—or hit the high places? Would you? Well, well, well! Let's make a night of it! What do you say?" and he would fix me with a glistening, nervous and what was intended no doubt to be a reassuring eye, but which unsettled me as thoroughly as the imminence of an earthquake. But I was talking of Peter.

The day I first saw him he was bent over a drawing-board illustrating a snake story for one of the Sunday issues of the *Globe-Democrat*, which apparently delighted in regaling its readers with most astounding concoctions of this kind, and the snake he was drawing was most disturbingly vital and reptilian, beady-eyed, with distended jaws, extended tongue, most fatefully coiled.

"My," I commented in passing, for I was in to see him about another matter, "what a glorious snake!"

"Yes, you can't make 'em too snaky for the snake-editor up front," he returned, rising and dusting tobacco from his lap and shirtfront, for he was in his shirt-sleeves. Then he expectorated not in but to one side of a handsome polished brass cuspidor which contained not the least evidence of use, the rubber mat upon which it stood being instead most disturbingly "decorated." I was most impressed by this latter fact although at the time I said nothing, being too new. Later, I may as well say here, I discovered why. This was a bit of his clowning humor, a purely manufactured and as it were mechanical joke or ebullience of soul. If any one inadvertently or through unfamiliarity attempted to expectorate in his "golden cuspidor," as he described it, he was always quick to rise and interpose in the most solemn, almost sepulchral manner, at the same time raising a hand. "Hold! Out—not in—to one side, on the mat! That cost me seven dollars!" Then he would solemnly seat himself and begin to draw again. I saw him do this to all but the chiefest of the authorities of the paper. And all, even the dullest, seemed to be amused, quite fascinated by the utter trumpery folly of it.

But I am getting ahead of my tale. In so far as the snake was concerned, he was referring to the assistant who had these snake stories in charge. "The fatter and more venomous and more scaly they are," he went on, "the better. I'd like it if we could use a little color in this paper—red for eyes and tongue, and blue and green for scales. The farmers upstate would love that. They like good but poisonous snakes." Then he grinned, stood back and, cocking his head to one side in a most examining and yet approving manner, ran his hand through his hair and beard and added, "A snake can't be too vital, you know, for this paper. We have to draw 'em strong, plenty of vitality, plenty of go." He grinned most engagingly.

I could not help laughing, of course. The impertinent air! The grand, almost condescending manner!

We soon became fast friends.

In the same office in close contact with him was another person, one D—— W———, also a newspaper artist, who, while being exceedingly interesting and special in himself, still as a character never seems to have served any greater purpose in my own mind than to have illustrated how emphatic and important Peter was. He had a thin, pale, Dantesque face, coal black, almost Indian-like hair most carefully parted in the middle and oiled and slicked down at the sides and back until it looked as though it had been glued. His eyes were small and black and querulous but not mean—petted eyes they were—and the mouth had little lines at each corner which seemed to say he had endured much, much pain, which of course he had not, but which nevertheless seemed to ask for, and I suppose earned him some, sympathy. Dick in his way was an actor, a tragedian of sorts, but with an element of humor, cynicism and insight which saved him from being utterly ridiculous. Like most actors, he was a great poseur. He invariably affected the long, loose flowing tie with a soft white or blue or green or brown linen shirt (would any American imitation of the "Quartier Latin" denizen have been without one at that date?), yellow or black gloves, a round, soft crush hat, very soft and limp and very *different*, patent leather pumps, betimes a capecoat, a slender cane, a boutonnière—all this in hard, smoky, noisy, commercial St. Louis, full of middle-West business men and farmers!

I would not mention this particular person save that for a time he, Peter and myself were most intimately associated. We temporarily constituted in our way a "soldiers three" of the newspaper world. For some years after we were more or less definitely in touch as a group, although later Peter and myself having drifted Eastward and hob-nobbing as a pair had been finding more and more in common and had more and more come to view Dick for what he was: a character of Dickensian, or perhaps still better, Cruikshankian, proportions and qualities. But in those days the three of us were all but inseparable; eating, working, playing, all but sleeping together. I had a studio of sorts in a more or less dilapidated factory section of St. Louis (Tenth near Market; now I suppose briskly commercial), Dick had one at Broadway and Locust, directly opposite the then famous Southern Hotel. Peter lived with his family on the South Side, a most respectable and homey-home neighborhood.

It has been one of my commonest experiences, and one of the most interesting to me, to note that nearly all of my keenest experiences intellectually, my most gorgeous *rapprochements* and swiftest developments mentally, have been by, to, and through men, not women, although there have been several exceptions to this. Nearly every turning point in my career has been signalized by my meeting some man of great force, to whom I owe some of the most ecstatic intellectual hours of my life, hours in which life seemed to bloom forth into new aspects, glowed as with the radiance of a gorgeous tropic day.

Peter was one such. About my own age at this time, he was blessed with a natural understanding which was simply Godlike. Although, like myself, he was raised a Catholic and still pretending in a boisterous, Rabelaisian way to have some reverence for that faith, he was amusingly sympathetic to everything good, bad, indifferent—"in case there might be something in it; you never can tell." Still he hadn't the least interest in conforming to the tenets of the church and laughed at its pretensions, preferring his own theories to any other. Apparently nothing amused him so much as the thought of confession and communion, of being shrived by some stout, healthy priest as worldly as himself, and preferably Irish, like himself. At the same time he had a hearty admiration for the Germans, all their ways, conservatisms, their breweries, food and such things, and finally wound up by marrying a German girl.

As far as I could make out, Peter had no faith in anything except Nature itself, and very little in that except in those aspects of beauty and accident and reward and terrors with which it is filled and for which he had an awe if not a reverence and in every manifestation of which he took the greatest delight. Life was a delicious, brilliant mystery to him, horrible in some respects, beautiful in others; a great adventure. Unlike myself at the time, he had not the slightest trace of any lingering Puritanism, and wished to live in a lush, vigorous, healthy, free, at times almost barbaric, way. The negroes, the ancient Romans, the Egyptians, tales of the Orient and the grotesque Dark Ages, our own vile slums and evil quarters—how he reveled in these! He was for nights of wandering, endless investigation, reading, singing, dancing, playing!

Apropos of this I should like to relate here that one of his seemingly gross but really innocent diversions was occasionally visiting a certain black house of prostitution, of which there were many in St. Louis. Here while he played a flute and some one else a tambourine or small drum, he would have two or three of the inmates dance in some weird savage way that took one instanter to the wilds of Central Africa. There was, so far as I know, no payment of any kind made in connection with this. He was a friend, in some crude, artistic or barbaric way. He satisfied, I am positive, some love of color, sound and the dance in these queer revels.

Nor do I know how he achieved these friendships, such as they were. I was never with him when he did. But aside from the satiation they afforded his taste for the strange and picturesque, I am sure they reflected no gross or sensual appetite. But I wish to attest in passing that the mere witnessing of these free scenes had a tonic as well as toxic effect on me. As I view myself now, I was a poor, spindling, prying fish, anxious to know life, and yet because of my very narrow training very fearsome of it, of what it might do to me, what dreadful contagion of thought or deed it might open me to! Peter was not so. To him all, positively *all*, life was good. It was a fascinating spectacle, to be studied or observed and rejoiced in as a spectacle. When I look back now on the shabby, poorly-lighted, low-ceiled room to which he led me "for fun," the absolutely black or brown girls with their white teeth and shiny eyes, the unexplainable, unintelligible love of rhythm and the dance displayed, the beating of a drum, the sinuous, winding motions of the body, I am grateful to him. He released my mind, broadened my view, lengthened my perspective. For as I sat with him, watching him beat his drum or play his flute, noted the gayety, his love of color and effect, and feeling myself *low*, a criminal, disgraced, the while I was staring with all my sight and enjoying it intensely, I realized that I was dealing with a man who was "bigger" than I was in many respects, saner, really more wholesome. I was a moral coward, and he was not losing his life and desires through fear—which the majority of us do. He was strong, vital, unafraid, and he made me so.

But, lest I seem to make him low or impossible to those who instinctively cannot accept life beyond the range of their own little routine world, let me hasten to his other aspects. He was not low but simple, brilliant and varied in his tastes. America and its point of view, religious and otherwise, was simply amusing to him, not to be taken seriously. He loved to contemplate man at his mysteries, rituals, secret schools. He loved better yet ancient history, medieval inanities and atrocities—a most singular, curious and wonderful mind. Already at this age he knew many historians and scientists (their work), a most astonishing and illuminating list to me—Maspero, Froude, Huxley, Darwin, Wallace, Rawlinson, Froissart, Hallam, Taine, Avebury! The list of painters, sculptors and architects with whose work he was familiar and books about whom or illustrated by whom he knew, is too long to be given here. His chief interest, in so far as I could make out, in these opening days, was Egyptology and the study of things natural and primeval—all the wonders of a natural, groping, savage world.

"Dreiser," he exclaimed once with gusto, his bright beady eyes gleaming with an immense human warmth, "you haven't the slightest idea of the fascination of some of the old beliefs. Do you know the significance of a scarab in Egyptian religious worship, for instance?"

"A scarab? What's a scarab? I never heard of one," I answered.

"A beetle, of course. An Egyptian beetle. You know what a beetle is, don't you? Well, those things burrowed in the earth, the mud of the Nile, at a certain period of their season to lay their eggs, and the next spring, or whenever it was, the eggs would hatch and the beetles would come up. Then the Egyptians imagined that the beetle hadn't died at all, or if it had that it also had the power of restoring itself to life, possessed immortality. So they thought it must be a god and began to worship it," and he would pause and survey me with those amazing eyes, bright as glass beads, to see if I were properly impressed.

"You don't say!"

"Sure. That's where the worship came from," and then he might go on and add a bit about monkey-worship, the Zoroastrians and the Parsees, the sacred bull of Egypt, its sex power as a reason for its religious elevation, and of sex worship in general; the fantastic orgies at Sidon and Tyre, where enormous images of the male and female sex organs were carried aloft before the multitude.

Being totally ignorant of these matters at the time, not a rumor of them having reached me as yet in my meagre reading, I knew that it must be so. It fired me with a keen desire to read—not the old orthodox emasculated histories of the schools but those other books and pamphlets to which I fancied he must have access. Eagerly I inquired of him where, how. He told me that in some cases they were outlawed, banned or not translated wholly or fully, owing to the puritanism and religiosity of the day, but he gave me titles and authors to whom I might have access, and the address of an old book-dealer or two who could get them for me.

In addition he was interested in ethnology and geology, as well as astronomy (the outstanding phases at least), and many, many phases of applied art: pottery, rugs, pictures, engraving, wood-carving, jewel-cutting and designing, and I know not what else, yet there was always room even in his most serious studies for humor of the bizarre and eccentric type, amounting to all but an obsession. He wanted to laugh, and he found occasion for doing so under the most serious, or at least semi-serious, circumstances. Thus I recall that one of the butts of his extreme humor was this same Dick, whom he studied with the greatest care for points worthy his humorous appreciation. Dick, in addition to his genuinely lively mental interests, was a most romantic person on one side, a most puling and complaining soul on the other. As a newspaper artist I believe he was only a fairly respectable craftsman, if so much, whereas Peter was much better, although he deferred to Dick in the most persuasive manner and seemed to believe at times, though I knew he did not, that Dick represented all there was to know in matters artistic.

Among other things at this time, the latter was, or pretended to be, immensely interested in all things pertaining to the Chinese and to know not only something of their language, which he had studied a little somewhere, but also their history—a vague matter, as we all know—and the spirit and significance of their art and customs. He sometimes condescended to take us about with him to one or two Chinese restaurants of the most beggarly description, and—as he wished to believe, because of the romantic titillation involved—the hang-outs of crooks and thieves and disreputable Tenderloin characters generally. (Of such was the beginning of the Chinese restaurant in America.) He would introduce us to a few of his Celestial friends, whose acquaintance apparently he had been most assiduously cultivating for some time past and with whom he was now on the best of terms. He had, as Peter pointed out to me, the happy knack of persuading himself that there was something vastly mysterious and superior about the whole Chinese race, that there was some Chinese organization known as the Six Companions, which, so far as I could make out from him, was ruling very nearly (and secretly, of course) the entire habitable globe. For one thing it had some governing connection with great constructive ventures of one kind and another in all parts of the world, supplying, as he said, thousands of Chinese laborers to any one who desired them, anywhere, and although they were employed by others, ruling them with a rod of iron, cutting their throats when they failed to perform their bounden duties and burying them head down in a basket of rice, then transferring their remains quietly to China in coffins made in China and brought for that purpose to the country in which they were. The Chinese who had worked for the builders of the Union Pacific had been supplied by this company, as I understood from Dick. In regard to all this Peter used to analyze and dispose of Dick's self-generated romance with the greatest gusto, laughing the while and yet pretending to accept it all.

But there was one phase of all this which interested Peter immensely. Were there on sale in St. Louis any bits of jade, silks, needlework, porcelains, basketry or figurines of true Chinese origin? He was far more interested in this than in the social and economic sides of the lives of the Chinese, and was constantly urging Dick to take him here, there and everywhere in order that he might see for himself what of these amazing wonders were locally extant, leading Dick in the process a merry chase and a dog's life. Dick was compelled to persuade nearly all of his boasted friends to produce all they had to show. Once, I recall, a collection of rare Chinese porcelains being shown at the local museum of art, there was nothing for it but that Dick must get one or more of his Oriental friends to interpret this, that and the other symbol in connection with this, that and the other vase—things which put him to no end of trouble and which led to nothing, for among all the local Chinese there was not one who knew anything about it, although they, Dick included, were not honest enough to admit it.

"You know, Dreiser," Peter said to me one day with the most delicious gleam of semi-malicious, semi-tender humor, "I am really doing all this just to torture Dick. He doesn't know a damned thing about it and neither do these Chinese, but it's fun to haul 'em out there and make 'em sweat. The museum sells an illustrated monograph covering all this, you know, with pictures of the genuinely historic pieces and explanations of the various symbols in so far as they are known, but Dick doesn't know that, and he's lying awake nights trying to find out what they're all about. I like to see his expression and that of those chinks when they examine those things." He subsided with a low chuckle all the more disturbing because it was so obviously the product of well-grounded knowledge.

Another phase of this same humor related to the grand artistic, social and other forms of life to which Dick was hoping to ascend via marriage and which led him, because of a kind of anticipatory eagerness, into all sorts of exaggerations of dress, manners, speech, style in writing or drawing, and I know not what else. He had, as I have said, a "studio" in Broadway, an ordinary large, square upper chamber of an old residence turned commercial but which Dick had decorated in the most, to him, recherché or *different* manner possible. In Dick's gilding imagination it was packed with the rarest and most carefully selected things, odd bits of furniture, objects of art, pictures, books—things which the ordinary antique shop provides in plenty but which to Dick, having been reared in Bloomington, Illinois, were of the utmost artistic import. He had vaulting ambitions and pretensions, literary and otherwise, having by now composed various rondeaus, triolets, quatrains, sonnets, in addition to a number of short stories over which he had literally slaved and which, being rejected by many editors, were kept lying idly and inconsequentially and seemingly inconspicuously about his place— the more to astonish the poor unsophisticated "outsider." Besides it gave him the opportunity of posing as misunderstood, neglected, depressed, as becomes all great artists, poets, and thinkers.

His great scheme or dream, however, was that of marriage to an heiress, one of those very material and bovine daughters of the new rich in the West end, and to this end he was bending all his artistic thought, writing, dressing, dreaming the thing he wished. I myself had a marked tendency in this direction, although from another point of view, and speaking from mine purely, there was this difference between us: Dick being an artist, rather remote and disdainful in manner and decidedly handsome as well as poetic and better positioned than I, as I fancied, was certain to achieve this gilded and crystal state, whereas I, not being handsome nor an artist nor sufficiently poetic perhaps, could scarcely aspire to so gorgeous a goal. Often, as around dinnertime he ambled from the office arrayed in the latest mode—dark blue suit, patent leather boots, a dark, round soft felt hat, loose tie blowing idly about his neck, a thin cane in his hand—I was already almost convinced that the anticipated end was at hand, this very evening perhaps, and that I should never see him more except as the husband of a very rich girl, never be permitted even to speak to him save as an almost forgotten friend, and in passing! Even now perhaps he was on his way to her, whereas I, poor oaf that I was, was moiling here over some trucky work. Would my ship never come in? my great day never arrive? my turn? Unkind heaven!

As for Peter he was the sort of person who could swiftly detect, understand and even sympathize with a point of view of this kind the while he must laugh at it and his mind be busy with some plan of making a fol-de-rol use of it. One day he came into the city-room where I was working and bending over my desk fairly bursting with suppressed humor announced, "Gee, Dreiser, I've just thought of a delicious trick to play on Dick! Oh, Lord!" and he stopped and surveyed me with beady eyes the while his round little body seemed to fairly swell with pent-up laughter. "It's too rich! Oh, if it just works out Dick'll be sore! Wait'll I tell you," he went on. "You know how crazy he is about rich young heiresses? You know how he's always 'dressing up' and talking and writing about marrying one of those girls in the West end?" (Dick was forever composing a short story in which some lorn but perfect and great artist was thus being received via love, the story being read to us nights in his studio.) "That's all bluff, that talk of his of visiting in those big houses out there. All he does is to dress up every night as though he were going to a ball, and walk out that way and moon around. Well, listen. Here's the idea. We'll go over to Mermod & Jaccards to-morrow and get a few sheets of their best monogrammed paper, sample sheets. Then we'll get up a letter and sign it with the most romantic name we can think of—Juanita or Cyrene or Doris—and explain who she is, the daughter of a millionaire living out there, and that she's been strictly brought up but that in spite of all that she's seen his name in the paper at the bottom of his pictures and wants to meet him, see? Then we'll have her suggest that he come out to the west gate of, say, Portland Place at seven o'clock and meet her. We'll have her describe herself, see, young and beautiful, and some attractive costume she's to wear, and we'll kill him. He'll fall hard. Then we'll happen by there at the exact time when he's waiting, and detain him, urge him to come into the park with us or to dinner. We'll look our worst so he'll be ashamed of us. He'll squirm and get wild, but we'll hang on and spoil the date for him, see? We'll insist in the letter that he must be alone, see, because she's timid and afraid of being recognized. My God, he'll be crazy! He'll think we've ruined his life—oh, ho, ho!" and he fairly writhed with inward joy.

The thing worked. It was cruel in its way, but when has man ever grieved over the humorous ills of others? The paper was secured, the letter written by a friend of Peter's in a nearby real estate office, after the most careful deliberation as to wording on our part. Extreme youth, beauty and a great mansion were all hinted at. The fascination of Dick as a romantic figure was touched upon. He would know her by a green silk scarf about her waist, for it was spring, the ideal season. Seven o'clock was the hour. She could give him only a moment or two then—but later—and she gave no address!

The letter was mailed in the West end, as was meet and proper, and in due season arrived at the office. Peter, working at the next easel, observed him, as he told me, out of the corner of his eye.

"You should have seen him, Dreiser," he exclaimed, hunting me up about an hour after the letter arrived. "Oh, ho! Say, you know I believe he thinks it's the real thing. It seemed to make him a little sick. He tried to appear nonchalant, but a little later he got his hat and went out, over to Deck's," a nearby saloon, "for a drink, for I followed him. He's all fussed up. Wait'll we heave into view that night! I'm going to get myself up like a joke, a hobo. I'll disgrace him. Oh, Lord, he'll be crazy! He'll think we've ruined his life, scared her off. There's no address. He can't do a thing. Oh, ho, ho, ho!"

On the appointed day—and it was a delicious afternoon and evening, aflame with sun and in May—Dick left off his work at three p.m., as Peter came and told me, and departed, and then we went to make our toilets. At six we met, took a car and stepped down not more than a short block from the point of meeting. I shall never forget the sweetness of the air, the something of sadness in the thought of love, even in this form. The sun was singing its evensong, as were the birds. But Peter—blessings or curses upon him!—was arrayed as only he could array himself when he wished to look absolutely disconcerting—more like an unwashed, uncombed tramp who had been sleeping out for weeks, than anything else. His hair was over his eyes and ears, his face and hands dirty, his shoes ditto. He had even blackened one tooth slightly. He had on a collarless shirt, and yet he was jaunty withal and carried a cane, if you please, assuming, as he always could and in the most aggravating way, to be totally unconscious of the figure he cut. At one angle of his multiplex character the man must have been a born actor.

We waited a block away, concealed by a few trees, and at the exact hour Dick appeared, hopeful and eager no doubt, and walking and looking almost all that he hoped—delicate, pale, artistic. The new straw hat! The pale green "artists'" shirt! His black, wide-buckled belt! The cane! The dark-brown low shoes! The boutonnière! He was plainly ready for any fate, his great moment.

And then, before he could get the feeling that his admirer might not be coming, we descended upon him in all our wretched nonchalance and unworthiness—out of hell, as it were. We were most brisk, familiar, affectionate. It was so fortunate to meet him so, so accidentally and peradventure. The night was so fine. We were out for a stroll in the park, to eat afterward. He must come along.

I saw him look at Peter in that hat and no collar, and wilt. It was too much. Such a friend—such friends (for on Peter's advice I was looking as ill as I might, an easy matter)! No, he couldn't come. He was waiting for some friends. We must excuse him.

But Peter was not to be so easily shaken off. He launched into the most brisk and serious conversation. He began his badger game by asking about some work upon which Dick had been engaged before he left the office, some order, how he was getting along with it, when it would be done; and, when Dick evaded and then attempted to dismiss the subject, took up another and began to expatiate on it, some work he himself was doing, something that had developed in connection with it. He asked inane questions, complimented Dick on his looks, began to tease him about some girl. And poor Dick—his nervousness, his despair almost, the sense of the waning of his opportunity! It was cruel. He was becoming more and more restless, looking about more and more wearily and anxiously and wishing to go or for us to go. He was horribly unhappy. Finally, after ten or fifteen minutes had gone and various girls had crossed the plaza in various directions, as well as carriages and saddle-horses—each one carrying his heiress, no doubt!—he seemed to summon all his courage and did his best to dispose of us. "You two'll have to excuse me," he exclaimed almost wildly. "I can't wait." Those golden moments! She could not approach! "My people aren't coming, I guess. I'll have to be going on."

He smiled weakly and made off, Peter half following and urging him to come back. Then, since he would not, we stood there on the exact spot of the rendezvous gazing smirkily after him. Then we went into the park a few paces and sat on a bench in full view, talking—or Peter was—most volubly. He was really choking with laughter. A little later, at seven-thirty, we went cackling into the park, only to return in five minutes as though we had changed our minds and were coming out—and saw Dick bustling off at our approach. It was sad really. There was an element of the tragic in it. But not to Peter. He was all laughter, all but apoplectic gayety. "Oh, by George!" he choked. "This is too much! Oh, ho! This is great! his poor heiress! And he came back! Har! Har! Har!"

"Peter, you dog," I said, "aren't you ashamed of yourself, to rub it in this way?"

"Not a bit, not a bit!" he insisted most enthusiastically. "Do him good. Why shouldn't he suffer? He'll get over it. He's always bluffing about his heiresses. Now he's lost a real one. Har! Har! Har!" and he fairly choked, and for days and weeks and months he laughed, but he never told. He merely chortled at his desk, and if any one asked him what he was laughing about, even Dick, he would reply, "Oh, something—a joke I played on a fellow once."

If Dick ever guessed he never indicated as much. But that lost romance! That faded dream!

Not so long after this, the following winter, I left St. Louis and did not see Peter for several years, during which time I drifted through various cities to New York. We kept up a more or less desultory correspondence which resulted eventually in his contributing to a paper of which I had charge in New York, and later, in part at least I am sure, in his coming there. I noticed one thing, that although Peter had no fixed idea as to what he wished to be— being able to draw, write, engrave, carve and what not—he was in no way troubled about it. "I don't see just what it is that I am to do best," he said to me once. "It may be that I will wind up as a painter or writer or collector— I can't tell yet. I want to study, and meantime I'm making a living—that's all I want now. I want to live, and I am living, in my way."

Some men are masters of cities, or perhaps better, of all the elements which enter into the making of them, and Peter was one. I think sometimes that he was born a writer of great force and charm, only as yet he had not found himself. I have known many writers, many geniuses even, but not one his superior in intellect and romantic response to life. He was a poet, thinker, artist, philosopher and master of prose, as a posthumous volume ("Wolf, the Autobiography of a Cave Dweller") amply proves, but he was not ready then to fully express himself, and it troubled him not at all. He loved life's every facet, was gay and helpful to himself and others, and yet always with an eye for the undercurrent of human misery, error and tragedy as well as comedy. Immediately upon coming to New York he began to examine and grasp it in a large way, its museums, public buildings, geography, politics, but after a very little while decided suddenly that he did not belong there and without a by-your-leave, although once more we had fallen into each other's ways, he departed without a word, and I did not hear from him for months. Temporarily at least he felt that he had to obtain more experience in a lesser field, and lost no time in so doing. The next I knew he was connected, at a comfortable salary, with the then dominant paper of Philadelphia.

It was after he had established himself very firmly in Philadelphia that we two finally began to understand each other fully, to sympathize really with each other's point of view as opposed to the more or less gay and casual nature of our earlier friendship. Also here perhaps, more than before, we felt the binding influence of having worked together in the West. It was here that I first noticed the ease with which he took hold of a city, the many-sidedness of his peculiar character which led him to reflect so many angles of it, which a less varied temperament would never have touched upon. For, first of all, wherever he happened to be, he was intensely interested in the age and history of his city, its buildings and graveyards and tombstones which pointed to its past life, then its present physical appearance, the chief characteristics of the region in which it lay, its rivers, lakes, parks and adjacent places and spots of interest (what rambles we took!), as well as its newest and finest things architecturally. Nor did any one ever take a keener interest in the current intellectual resources of a city—any city in which he happened to be—its museums, libraries, old bookstores, newspapers, magazines, and I know not what else. It was he who first took me into Leary's bookstore in Philadelphia, descanting with his usual gusto on its merits. Then and lastly he was keenly and wisely interested in various currents of local politics, society and finance, although he always considered the first a low mess, an arrangement or adjustment of many necessary things among the lower orders. He seemed to know or sense in some occult way everything that was going on in those various realms. His mind was so full and rich that merely to be with him was a delight. He gushed like a fountain, and yet not polemically, of all he knew, heard, felt, suspected. His thoughts were so rich at times that to me they were more like a mosaic of variegated and richly colored stones and jewels. I felt always as though I were in the presence of a great personage, not one who was reserved or pompous but a loose bubbling temperament, wise beyond his years or day, and so truly great that perhaps because of the intensity and immense variety of his interests he would never shine in a world in which the most intensive specialization, and that of a purely commercial character, was the grand rôle.

And yet I always felt that perhaps he might. He attracted people of all grades so easily and warmly. His mind leaped from one interest to another almost too swiftly, and yet the average man understood and liked him. While in a way he contemned their mental states as limited or bigoted, he enjoyed the conditions under which they lived, seemed to wish to immerse himself in them. And yet nearly all his thoughts were, from their point of view perhaps, dangerous. Among his friends he was always talking freely, honestly, of things which the average man could not or would not discuss, dismissing as trash illusion, lies or the cunning work of self-seeking propagandists, most of the things currently accepted as true.

He was constantly commenting on the amazing dullness of man, his prejudices, the astonishing manner in which he seized upon and clung savagely or pathetically to the most ridiculous interpretations of life. He was also forever noting that crass chance which wrecks so many of our dreams and lives,—its fierce brutalities, its seemingly inane indifference to wondrous things,—but never in a depressed or morbid spirit; merely as a matter of the curious, as it were. But if any one chanced to contradict him he was likely to prove liquid fire. At the same time he was forever reading, reading, reading— history, archæology, ethnology, geology, travel, medicine, biography, and descanting on the wonders and idiosyncrasies of man and nature which they revealed. He was never tired of talking of the intellectual and social conditions that ruled in Greece and Rome from 600 B.C. on, the philosophies, the travels, the art, the simple, natural pagan view of things, and regretting that they were no more. He grieved at times, I think, that he had not been of that world, might not have seen it, or, failing that, might not see all the shards of those extinct civilizations. There was something loving and sad in the manner in which at times, in one museum and another, he would examine ancient art designs, those of the Egyptians, Greeks and Romans, their public and private house plans, their statues, book rolls, inscriptions, flambeaux, boats, swords, chariots. Carthage, Rome, Greece, Phoenicia—their colonies, art and trade stuffs, their foods, pleasures and worships—how he raved! A book like Thaïs, Salammbo, Sonica, Quo Vadis, touched him to the quick.

At the same time, and odd as it may seem, he was seemingly in intimate contact with a circle of friends that rather astonished me by its catholicity. It included, for instance, and quite naïvely, real estate dealers, clerks, a bank cashier or two, some man who had a leather shop or cigar factory in the downtown section, a drummer, a printer, two or three newspaper artists and reporters—a list too long to catalogue here and seemingly not interesting, at least not inspiring to look at or live in contact with. Yet his relations with all of these were of a warm, genial, helpful, homely character, quite intimate. He used them as one might a mulch in which to grow things, or in other words he took them on their own ground; a thing which I could never quite understand, being more or less aloof myself and yet wishing always to be able so to do, to take life, as he did.

For he desired, and secured, their good will and drew them to him. He took a simple, natural pleasure in the kinds of things they were able to do, as well as the kinds of things he could do. With these, then, and a type of girl who might not be classed above the clerk or manicure class, he and they managed to eke out a social life, the outstanding phases of which were dances, "parties," dinners at one simple home and another, flirting, boating, and fishing expeditions in season, evenings out at restaurants or the theater, and I know not what else. He could sing (a very fair baritone), play the piano, cornet, flute, banjo, mandolin and guitar, but always insisted that his favorite instruments were the jews'-harp, the French harp (mouth organ) and a comb with a piece of paper over it, against which he would blow with fierce energy, making the most outrageous sounds, until stopped. At any "party" he was always talking, jumping about, dancing, cooking something—fudge, taffy, a rarebit, and insisting in the most mock-serious manner that all the details be left strictly to him. "Now just cut out of this, all of you, and leave this to your Uncle Dudley. Who's doing this? All I want is sugar, chocolate, a pot, a big spoon, and I'll show you the best fudge you ever ate." Then he would don an apron or towel and go to work in a manner which would rob any gathering of a sense of stiffness and induce a naturalness most intriguing, calculated to enhance the general pleasure an hundredfold.

Yes, Peter woke people up. He could convey or spread a sense of ease and good nature and give and take among all. Wise as he was and not so good-looking, he was still attractive to girls, very much so, and by no means unconscious of their beauty. He could always, and easily, break down their reserve, and was soon apparently on terms of absolute friendship, exchanging all sorts of small gossip and news with them about this, that and the other person about whom they knew. Indeed he was such a general favorite and so seemingly impartial that it was hard to say how he came close to any, and yet he did. At odd tête-à-tête moments he was always making confessions as to "nights" or "afternoons." "My God, Dreiser, I've found a peach! I can't tell you—but oh, wonderful! Just what I need. This world's a healthy old place, eh? Let's have another drink, what?" and he would order a stein or a half-schoppen of light German beer and pour it down, grinning like a gargoyle.

It was while he was in Philadelphia that he told me the beginnings of the love affair which eventually ended in his marrying and settling down into the homiest of home men I have ever seen and which for sheer naïveté and charm is one of the best love stories I know anything about. It appears that he was walking in some out-of-the-way factory realm of North Philadelphia one Saturday afternoon about the first or second year of his stay there, when, playing in the street with some other children, he saw a girl of not more than thirteen or fourteen who, as he expressed it to me, "came damned near being the prettiest thing I ever saw. She had yellow hair and a short blue dress and pink bows in her hair—and say, Dreiser, when I saw her I stopped flat and said 'me for that' if I have to wait fifteen years! Dutchy—you never saw the beat! And poor! Her shoes were clogs. She couldn't even talk English yet.

Neither could the other kids. They were all sausage—a regular German neighborhood.

"But, say, I watched her a while and then I went over and said, 'Come here, kid. Where do you live?' She didn't understand, and one of the other kids translated for her, and then she said, 'Ich sprech nicht English,'" and he mocked her. "That fixed her for me. One of the others finally told me who she was and where she lived—and, say, I went right home and began studying German. In three months I could make myself understood, but before that, in two weeks, I hunted up her old man and made him understand that I wanted to be friends with the family, to learn German. I went out Sundays when they were all at home. There are six children and I made friends with 'em all. For a long time I couldn't make Madchen (that's what they call her) understand what it was all about, but finally I did, and she knows now all right. And I'm crazy about her and I'm going to marry her as soon as she's old enough."

"How do you know that she'll have you?" I inquired.

"Oh, she'll have me. I always tell her I'm going to marry her when she's eighteen, and she says all right. And I really believe she does like me. I'm crazy about her."

Five years later, if I may anticipate a bit, after he had moved to Newark and placed himself rather well in the journalistic field and was able to carry out his plans in regard to himself, he suddenly returned to Philadelphia and married, preparing beforehand an apartment which he fancied would please her. It was a fortunate marriage in so far as love and home pleasures were concerned. I never encountered a more delightful atmosphere.

All along in writing this I feel as though I were giving but the thinnest portrait of Peter; he was so full and varied in his moods and interests. To me he illustrated the joy that exists, on the one hand, in the common, the so-called homely and what some might think ugly side of life, certainly the very simple and ordinarily human aspect of things; on the other, in the sheer comfort and satisfaction that might be taken in things truly intellectual and artistic, but to which no great expense attached—old books, prints, things connected with history and science in their various forms, skill in matters relating to the applied arts and what not, such as the coloring and firing of pottery and glass, the making of baskets, hammocks and rugs, the carving of wood, the collection and imitation of Japanese and Chinese prints, the art of embalming as applied by the Egyptians (which, in connection with an undertaker to whom he had attached himself, he attempted to revive or at least play with, testing his skill for instance by embalming a dead cat or two after the Egyptian manner). In all of these lines he trained himself after a fashion and worked with skill, although invariably he insisted that he was little more than a bungler, a poor follower after the art of some one else. But most of all, at this time and later, he was interested in collecting things Japanese and Chinese: netsukes, inros, censors, images of jade and porcelain, teajars, vases, prints; and it was while he was in Philadelphia and seemingly trifling about with the group I have mentioned and making love to his little German girl that he was running here and there to this museum and that and laying the foundations of some of those interesting collections which later he was fond of showing his friends or interested collectors. By the time he had reached Newark, as chief cartoonist of the leading paper there, he was in possession of a complete Tokaido (the forty views on the road between Tokio and Kyoto), various prints by Hokusai, Sesshiu, Sojo; a collection of one hundred inros, all of fifty netsukes, all of thirty censers, lacquered boxes and teajars, and various other exceedingly beautiful and valuable things—Mandarin skirts and coats, among other things—which subsequently he sold or traded around among one collector friend and another for things which they had. I recall his selling his completed Tokaido, a labor which had extended over four years, for over a thousand dollars. Just before he died he was trading netsukes for inros and getting ready to sell all these latter to a man, who in turn was going to sell his collection to a museum.

But in between was this other, this ultra-human side, which ran to such commonplaces as bowling, tennis-playing, golf, billiards, cards and gambling with the dice—a thing which always struck me as having an odd turn to it in connection with Peter, since he could be interested in so many other things, and yet he pursued these commonplaces with as much gusto at times as one possessed of a mania. At others he seemed not to miss or think of them. Indeed, you could be sure of him and all his interests, whatever they were, feeling that he had himself well in hand, knew exactly how far he was going, and that when the time came he could and would stop. Yet during the process of his momentary relaxation or satiation, in whatever field it might be, he would give you a sense of abandon, even ungovernable appetite, which to one who had not known him long might have indicated a mania.

Thus I remember once running over to Philadelphia to spend a Saturday and Sunday with him, visits of this kind, in either direction, being of the commonest occurrence. At that time he was living in some quiet-looking boarding-house in South Fourth Street, but in which dwelt or visited the group above-mentioned, and whenever I came there, at least, there was always an atmosphere of intense gaming or playing in some form, which conveyed to me nothing so much as a glorious sense of life and pleasure. A dozen or more men might be seated at or standing about a poker or dice table, in summer (often in winter) with their coats off, their sleeves rolled up, Peter always conspicuous among them. On the table or to one side would be money, a pitcher or a tin pail of beer, boxes of cigarettes or cigars, and there would be Peter among the players, flushed with excitement, his collar off, his hair awry, his little figure stirring about here and there or gesticulating or lighting a cigar or pouring down a glass of beer, shouting at the top of his voice, his eyes aglow, "That's mine!" "I say it's not!" "Two on the sixes!" "Three!" "Four!" "Ah, roll the bones! Roll the bones!" "Get off! Get off! Come on now, Spikes—cough up! You've got the money now. Pay back. No more loans if you don't." "Once on the fours—the fives—the aces!" "Roll the bones! Roll the bones! Come on!" Or, if he saw me, softening and saying, "Gee, Dreiser, I'm ahead twenty-eight so far!" or "I've lost thirty all told. I'll stick this out, though, to win or lose five more, and then I'll quit. I give notice, you fellows, five more, one way or the other, and then I'm through. See? Say, these damned sharks are always trying to turn a trick. And when they lose they don't want to pay. I'm offa this for life unless I get a better deal."

In the room there might be three or four girls—sisters, sweethearts, pals of one or other of the players—some dancing, some playing the piano or singing, and in addition the landlord and his wife, a slattern pair usually, about whose past and present lives Peter seemed always to know much. He had seduced them all apparently into a kind of rakish camaraderie which was literally amazing to behold. It thrilled, fascinated, at times frightened me, so thin and inadequate and inefficient seemed my own point of view and appetite for life. He was vigorous, charitable, pagan, gay, full of health and strength. He would play at something, anything, indoors or out as occasion offered, until he was fairly perspiring, when, throwing down whatever implement he had in hand—be it cards, a tennis-racket, a golf club—would declare, "That's enough! That's enough! I'm done now. I've licked-cha," or "I'm licked. No more. Not another round. Come on, Dreiser, I know just the place for us—" and then descanting on a steak or fish planked, or some new method of serving corn or sweet potatoes or tomatoes, he would lead the way somewhere to a favorite "rat's killer," as he used to say, or grill or Chinese den, and order enough for four or five, unless stopped. As he walked, and he always preferred to walk, the latest political row or scandal, the latest discovery, tragedy or art topic would get his keen attention. In his presence the whole world used to look different to me, more colorful, more hopeful, more gay. Doors seemed to open; in imagination I saw the interiors of a thousand realms—homes, factories, laboratories, dens, resorts of pleasure. During his day such figures as McKinley, Roosevelt, Hanna, Rockefeller, Rogers, Morgan, Peary, Harriman were abroad and active, and their mental states and points of view and interests—and sincerities and insincerities— were the subject of his wholly brilliant analysis. He rather admired the clever opportunist, I think, so long as he was not mean in view or petty, yet he scorned and even despised the commercial viewpoint or trade reactions of a man like McKinley. Rulers ought to be above mere commercialism. Once when I asked him why he disliked McKinley so much he replied laconically,

"The voice is the voice of McKinley, but the hands—are the hands of Hanna." Roosevelt seemed to amuse him always, to be a delightful if ridiculous and self-interested "grandstander," as he always said, "always looking out for Teddy, you bet," but good for the country, inspiring it with visions. Rockefeller was wholly admirable as a force driving the country on to autocracy, oligarchy, possibly revolution. Ditto Hanna, ditto Morgan, ditto Harriman, ditto Rogers, unless checked. Peary might have, and again might not have, discovered the North Pole. He refused to judge. Old "Doc" Cook, the pseudo discoverer, who appeared very shortly before he died, only drew forth chuckles of delight. "My God, the gall, the nerve! And that wreath of roses the Danes put around his neck! It's colossal, Dreiser. It's grand. Munchausen, Cook, Gulliver, Marco Polo—they'll live forever, or ought to!"

Some Saturday afternoons or Sundays, if he came to me or I to him in time, we indulged in long idle rambles, anywhere, either going first by streetcar, boat or train somewhere and then walking, or, if the mood was not so, just walking on and on somewhere and talking. On such occasions Peter was at his best and I could have listened forever, quite as the disciples of Plato and Aristotle must have to them, to his discourses on life, his broad and broadening conceptions of Nature—her cruelty, beauty, mystery. Once, far out somewhere beyond Camden, we were idling about an inlet where were boats and some fishermen and a trestle which crossed it. Just as we were crossing it some men in a boat below discovered the body of a possible suicide, in the water, days old and discolored, but still intact and with the clothes of a man of at least middle-class means. I was for leaving, being made a little sick by the mere sight. Not so Peter. He was for joining in the effort which brought the body to shore, and in a moment was back with the small group of watermen, speculating and arguing as to the condition and character of the dead man, making himself really one of the group. Finally he was urging the men to search the pockets while some one went for the police. But more than anything, with a hard and yet in its way humane realism which put any courage of mine in that direction to the blush, he was all for meditating on the state and nature of man, his chemical components—chlorine, sulphuric acid, phosphoric acid, potassium, sodium, calcium, magnesium, oxygen—and speculating as to which particular chemicals in combination gave the strange metallic blues, greens, yellows and browns to the decaying flesh! He had a great stomach for life. The fact that insects were at work shocked him not at all. He speculated as to *these*, their duties and functions! He asserted boldly that man was merely a chemical formula at best, that something much wiser than he had prepared him, for some not very brilliant purpose of his or its own perhaps, and that he or it, whoever or whatever he or it was, was neither good nor bad, as we imagined such things, but both. He at once went off into the mysteries—where, when with me at least, he seemed to prefer to dwell—talked of the divinations of the

Chaldeans, how they studied the positions of the stars and the entrails of dead animals before going to war, talked of the horrible fetiches of the Africans, the tricks and speculations of the priests of Greek and Roman temples, finally telling me the story of the ambitious eel-seller who anchored the dead horse in the stream in order to have plenty of eels every morning for market. I revolted. I declared he was sickening.

"My boy," he assured me, "you are too thin-skinned. You can't take life that way. It's all good to me, whatever happens. We're here. We're not running it. Why be afraid to look at it? The chemistry of a man's body isn't any worse than the chemistry of anything else, and we're eating the dead things we've killed all the time. A little more or a little less in any direction—what difference?"

Apropos of this same a little later—to shock me, of course, as he well knew he could—he assured me that in eating a dish of chop suey in a Chinese restaurant, a very low one, he had found and eaten a part of the little finger of a child, and that "it was very good—very good, indeed."

"Dog!" I protested. "Swine! Thou ghoula!" but he merely chuckled heartily and stuck to his tale!

But if I paint this side of him it is to round out his wonderful, to me almost incredible, figure. Insisting on such things, he was still and always warm and human, sympathetic, diplomatic and cautious, according to his company, so that he was really acceptable anywhere. Peter would never shock those who did not want to be shocked. A minute or two or five after such a discourse as the above he might be describing some marvelously beautiful process of pollination among the flowers, the history of some medieval trade guild or gazing at a beautiful scene and conveying to one by his very attitude his unspoken emotion.

After spending about two or three years in Philadelphia—which city came to reflect for me the color of Peter's interests and mood—he suddenly removed to Newark, having been nursing an arrangement with its principal paper for some time. Some quarrel or dissatisfaction with the director of his department caused him, without other notice, to paste some crisp quotation from one of the poets on his desk and depart! In Newark, a city to which before this I had paid not the slightest attention, he found himself most happy; and I, living in New York close at hand, felt that I possessed in it and him an earthly paradise. Although it contained no more than 300,000 people and seemed, or had, a drear factory realm only, he soon revealed it to me in quite another light, because he was there. Very swiftly he found a wondrous canal running right through it, under its market even, and we went walking along its banks, out into the woods and fields. He found or created out of an existing boardinghouse in a back street so colorful and gay a thing that after a time it seemed to me to outdo that one of Philadelphia. He joined a country club near Passaic, on the river of that name, on the veranda of which we often dined. He found a Chinese quarter with a restaurant or two; an amazing Italian section with a restaurant; a man who had a $40,000 collection of rare Japanese and Chinese curios, all in his rooms at the Essex County Insane Asylum, for he was the chemist there; a man who was a playwright and manager in New York; another who owned a newspaper syndicate; another who directed a singing society; another who was president of a gun club; another who owned and made or rather fired pottery for others. Peter was so restless and vital that he was always branching out in a new direction. To my astonishment he now took up the making and firing of pottery for himself, being interested in reproducing various Chinese dishes and vases of great beauty, the originals of which were in the Metropolitan Museum of Art. His plan was first to copy the design, then buy, shape or bake the clay at some pottery, then paint or decorate with liquid porcelain at his own home, and fire. In the course of six or eight months, working in his rooms Saturdays and Sundays and some mornings before going to the office, he managed to produce three or four which satisfied him and which he kept plates of real beauty. The others he gave away.

A little later, if you please, it was Turkish rug-making on a small scale, the frame and materials for which he slowly accumulated, and then providing himself with a pillow, Turkish-fashion, he crossed his legs before it and began slowly but surely to produce a rug, the colors and design of which were entirely satisfactory to me. As may be imagined, it was slow and tedious work, undertaken at odd moments and when there was nothing else for him to do, always when the light was good and never at night, for he maintained that the coloring required the best of light. Before this odd, homely, wooden machine, a combination of unpainted rods and cords, he would sit, cross-legged or on a bench at times, and pound and pick and tie and unravel—a most wearisome-looking task to me.

"For heaven's sake," I once observed, "couldn't you think of anything more interestingly insane to do than this? It's the slowest, most painstaking work I ever saw."

"That's just it, and that's just why I like it," he replied, never looking at me but proceeding with his weaving in the most industrious fashion. "You have just one outstanding fault, Dreiser. You don't know how to make anything out of the little things of life. You want to remember that this is an art, not a job. I'm discovering whether I can make a Turkish carpet or not, and it gives me pleasure. If I can get so much as one good spot of color worked out, one small portion of the design, I'll be satisfied. I'll know then that I can do it, the whole thing, don't you see? Some of these things have been the work of a lifetime of one man. You call that a small thing? I don't. The pleasure is in doing it, proving that you can, not in the rug itself." He clacked and tied, congratulating himself vastly. In due course of time three or four inches were finished, a soft and yet firm silky fabric, and he was in great glee over it, showing it to all and insisting that in time (how long? I often wondered) he would complete it and would then own a splendid carpet.

It was at this time that he built about him in Newark a structure of friendships and interests which, it seemed to me, promised to be for life. He interested himself intensely in the paper with which he was connected and although he was only the cartoonist, still it was not long before various departments and elements in connection with it seemed to reflect his presence and to be alive with his own good will and enthusiasm. Publisher, editor, art director, managing editor and business manager, were all in friendly contact with him. He took out life insurance for the benefit of the wife and children he was later to have! With the manager of the engraving department he was working out problems in connection with copperplate engraving and printing; with the official photographer, art photography; with the art director, some scheme for enlarging the local museum in some way. With his enduring love of the fantastic and ridiculous it was not long before he had successfully planned and executed a hoax of the most ridiculous character, a piece of idle drollery almost too foolish to think of, and yet which eventually succeeded in exciting the natives of at least four States and was telegraphed to and talked about in a Sunday feature way, by newspapers all over the country, and finally involved Peter as an actor and stage manager of the most vivid type imaginable. And yet it was all done really to amuse himself, to see if he could do it, as he often told me.

This particular hoax related to that silly old bugaboo of our boyhood days, the escaped and wandering wild man, ferocious, blood-loving, terrible. I knew nothing of it until Peter, one Sunday afternoon when we were off for a walk a year or two after he had arrived in Newark, suddenly announced apropos of nothing at all, "Dreiser, I've just hit upon a great idea which I am working out with some of the boys down on our paper. It's a dusty old fake, but it will do as well as any other, better than if it were a really decent idea. I'm inventing a wild man. You know how crazy the average dub is over anything strange, different,'terrible.' Barnum was right, you know. There's one born every minute. Well, I'm just getting this thing up now. It's as good as the sacred white elephant or the blood-sweating hippopotamus. And what's more, I'm going to stage it right here in little old Newark—and they'll all fall for it, and don't you think they won't," and he chuckled most ecstatically.

"For heaven's sake, what's coming now?" I sighed.

"Oh, very well. But I have it all worked out just the same. We're beginning to run the preliminary telegrams every three or four days—one from Ramblersville, South Jersey, let us say, another from Hohokus, twenty-five miles farther on, four or five days later. By degrees as spring comes on I'll bring him north—right up here into Essex County—a genuine wild man, see, something fierce and terrible. We're giving him long hair like a bison, red eyes, fangs, big hands and feet. He's entirely naked—or will be when he gets here. He's eight feet tall. He kills and eats horses, dogs, cattle, pigs, chickens. He frightens men and women and children. I'm having him bound across lonely roads, look in windows at night, stampede cattle and drive tramps and peddlers out of the country. But say, wait and see. As summer comes on we'll make a regular headliner of it. We'll give it pages on Sunday. We'll get the rubes to looking for him in posses, offer rewards. Maybe some one will actually capture and bring in some poor lunatic, a real wild man. You can do anything if you just stir up the natives enough."

I laughed. "You're crazy," I said. "What a low comedian you really are, Peter!"

Well, the weeks passed, and to mark progress he occasionally sent me clippings of telegrams, cut not from his pages, if you please, but from such austere journals as the *Sun* and *World* of New York, the *North American* of Philadelphia, the *Courant* of Hartford, recording the antics of his imaginary thing of the woods. Longish articles actually began to appear here and there, in Eastern papers especially, describing the exploits of this very elusive and moving demon. He had been seen in a dozen fairly widely distributed places within the month, but always coming northward. In one place he had killed three cows at once, in another two, and eaten portions of them raw! Old Mrs. Gorswitch of Dutchers Run, Pennsylvania, returning from a visit to her daughter-in-law, Annie A. Gorswitch, and ambling along a lonely road in Osgoroola County, was suddenly descended upon by a most horrific figure, half man, half beast, very tall and with long hair and red, all but bloody eyes who, looking at her with avid glance, made as if to seize her, but a wagon approaching along the road from another direction, he had desisted and fled, leaving old Mrs. Gorswitch in a faint upon the ground. Barns and haystacks had been fired here and there, lonely widows in distant cotes been made to abandon their homes through fear.... I marveled at the assiduity and patience of the man.

One day in June or July following, being in Newark and asking Peter quite idly about his wild man, he replied, "Oh, it's great, great! Couldn't be better! He'll soon be here now. We've got the whole thing arranged now for next Sunday or Saturday—depends on which day I can get off. We're going to photograph him. Wanto come over?"

"What rot!" I said. "Who's going to pose? Where?"

"Well," he chuckled, "come along and see. You'll find out fast enough. We've got an actual wild man. I got him. I'll have him out here in the woods. If you don't believe it, come over. You wouldn't believe me when I said I could get the natives worked up. Well, they are. Look at these," and he produced clippings from rival papers. The wild man was actually being seen in Essex County, not twenty-five miles from Newark. He had ravaged the property of people in five different States. It was assumed that he was a lunatic turned savage, or that he had escaped from a circus or trading-ship wrecked on the Jersey coast (suggestions made by Peter himself). His depredations, all told, had by now run into thousands, speaking financially. Staid residents were excited. Rewards for his capture were being offered in different places. Posses of irate citizens were, and would continue to be, after him, armed to the teeth, until he was captured. Quite remarkable developments might be expected at any time ... I stared. It seemed too ridiculous, and it was, and back of it all was smirking, chuckling Peter, the center and fountain of it!

"You dog!" I protested. "You clown!" He merely grinned.

Not to miss so interesting a dénouement as the actual capture of this prodigy of the wilds, I was up early and off the following Sunday to Newark, where in Peter's apartment in due time I found him, his rooms in a turmoil, he himself busy stuffing things into a bag, outside an automobile waiting and within it the staff photographer as well as several others, all grinning, and all of whom, as he informed me, were to assist in the great work of tracking, ambushing and, if possible, photographing the dread peril.

"Yes, well, who's going to be him?" I insisted.

"Never mind! Never mind! Don't be so inquisitive," chortled Peter. "A wild man has his rights and privileges, as well as any other. Remember, I caution all of you to be respectful in his presence. He's very sensitive, and he doesn't like newspapermen anyhow. He'll be photographed, and he'll be wild. That's all you need to know."

In due time we arrived at as comfortable an abode for a wild man as well might be. It was near the old Essex and Morris Canal, not far from Boonton. A charming clump of brush and rock was selected, and here a snapshot of a posse hunting, men peering cautiously from behind trees in groups and looking as though they were most eager to discover something, was made. Then Peter, slipping away—I suddenly saw him ambling toward us, hair upstanding, body smeared with black muck, daubs of white about the eyes, little tufts of wool about wrists and ankles and loins—as good a figure of a wild man as one might wish, only not eight feet tall.

"Peter!" I said. "How ridiculous! You loon!"

"Have a care how you address me," he replied with solemn dignity. "A wild man is a wild man. Our punctilio is not to be trifled with. I am of the oldest, the most famous line of wild men extant. Touch me not." He strode the grass with the air of a popular movie star, while he discussed with the art director and photographer the most terrifying and convincing attitudes of a wild man seen by accident and unconscious of his pursuers.

"But you're not eight feet tall!" I interjected at one point.

"A small matter. A small matter," he replied airily. "I will be in the picture. Nothing easier. We wild men, you know—"

Some of the views were excellent, most striking. He leered most terribly from arras of leaves or indicated fright or cunning. The man was a good actor. For years I retained and may still have somewhere a full set of the pictures as well as the double-page spread which followed the next week.

Well, the thing was appropriately discussed, as it should have been, but the wild man got away, as was feared. He went into the nearby canal and washed away all his terror, or rather he vanished into the dim recesses of Peter's memory. He was only heard of a few times more in the papers, his supposed body being found in some town in northeast Pennsylvania—or in the small item that was "telegraphed" from there. As for Peter, he emerged from the canal, or from its banks, a cleaner if not a better man. He was grinning, combing his hair, adjusting his tie.

"What a scamp!" I insisted lovingly. "What an incorrigible trickster!"

"Dreiser, Dreiser," he chortled, "there's nothing like it. You should not scoff. I am a public benefactor. I am really a creator. I have created a being as distinct as any that ever lived. He is in many minds—mine, yours. You know that you believe in him really. There he was peeking out from between those bushes only fifteen minutes ago. And he has made, and will make, thousands of people happy, thrill them, give them a new interest. If Stevenson can create a Jekyll and Hyde, why can't I create a wild man? I have. We have his picture to prove it. What more do you wish?"

I acquiesced. All told, it was a delightful bit of foolery and art, and Peter was what he was first and foremost, an artist in the grotesque and the ridiculous.

For some time thereafter peace seemed to reign in his mind, only now it was that the marriage and home and children idea began to grow. From much of the foregoing it may have been assumed that Peter was out of sympathy with the ordinary routine of life, despised the commonplace, the purely practical. As a matter of fact it was just the other way about. I never knew a man so radical in some of his viewpoints, so versatile and yet so wholly, intentionally and cravingly, immersed in the usual as Peter. He was all for creating, developing, brightening life along simple rather than outré lines, in so far as he himself was concerned. Nearly all of his arts and pleasures were decorative and homey. A good grocer, a good barber, a good saloon-keeper, a good tailor, a shoe maker, was just as interesting in his way to Peter as any one or anything else, if not a little more so. He respected their lines, their arts, their professions, and above all, where they had it, their industry, sobriety and desire for fair dealing. He believed that millions of men, especially those about him were doing the best they could under the very severe conditions which life offered. He objected to the idle, the too dull the swindlers and thieves as well as the officiously puritanic or dogmatic. He resented, for himself at least, solemn pomp and show. Little houses, little gardens, little porches, simple cleanly neighborhoods with their air of routine, industry, convention and order, fascinated him as apparently nothing else could. He insisted that they were enough. A man did not need a great house unless he was a public character with official duties.

"Dreiser," he would say in Philadelphia and Newark, if not before, "it's in just such a neighborhood as this that some day I'm going to live. I'm going to have my little *frau*, my seven children, my chickens, dog, cat, canary, best German style, my garden, my birdbox, my pipe; and Sundays, by God, I'll march 'em all off to church, wife and seven kids, as regular as clockwork, shined shoes, pigtails and all, and I'll lead the procession."

"Yes, yes," I said. "You talk."

"Well, wait and see. Nothing in this world means so much to me as the good old orderly home stuff. One ought to live and die in a family. It's the right way. I'm cutting up now, sowing my wild oats, but that's nothing. I'm just getting ready to eventually settle down and live, just as I tell you, and be an ideal orderly citizen. It's the only way. It's the way nature intends us to do. All this early kid stuff is passing, a sorting-out process. We get over it. Every fellow does, or ought to be able to, if he's worth anything, find some one woman that he can live with and stick by her. That makes the world that you and I like to live in, and you know it. There's a psychic call in all of us to it, I think. It's the genius of our civilization, to marry one woman and settle down. And when I do, no more of this all-night stuff with this, that and the other lady. I'll be a model husband and father, sure as you're standing there. Don't you think I won't. Smile if you want to—it's so. I'll have my garden. I'll be friendly with my neighbors. You can come over then and help us put the kids to bed."

"Oh, Lord! This is a new bug now! We'll have the vine-covered cot idea for a while, anyhow."

"Oh, all right. Scoff if you want to. You'll see."

Time went by. He was doing all the things I have indicated, living in a kind of whirl of life. At the same time, from time to time, he would come back to this thought. Once, it is true, I thought it was all over with the little yellow-haired girl in Philadelphia. He talked of her occasionally, but less and less. Out on the golf links near Passaic he met another girl, one of a group that flourished there. I met her. She was not unpleasing, a bit sensuous, rather attractive in dress and manners, not very well informed, but gay, clever, up-to-date; such a girl as would pass among other women as fairly satisfactory.

For a time Peter seemed greatly attracted to her. She danced, played a little, was fair at golf and tennis, and she was, or pretended to be, intensely interested in him. He confessed at last that he believed he was in love with her.

"So it's all day with Philadelphia, is it?" I asked.

"It's a shame," he replied, "but I'm afraid so. I'm having a hell of a time with myself, my alleged conscience, I tell you."

I heard little more about it. He had a fad for collecting rings at this time, a whole casket full, like a Hindu prince, and he told me once he was giving her her choice of them.

Suddenly he announced that it was "all off" and that he was going to marry the maid of Philadelphia. He had thrown the solitaire engagement ring he had given her down a sewer! At first he would confess nothing as to the reason or the details, but being so close to me it eventually came out. Apparently, to the others as to myself, he had talked much of his simple home plans, his future children—the good citizen idea. He had talked it to his new love also, and she had sympathized and agreed. Yet one day, after he had endowed her with the engagement ring, some one, a member of the golf club, came and revealed a tale. The girl was not "straight." She had been, mayhap was even then, "intimate" with other men—one anyhow. She was in love with Peter well enough, as she insisted afterward, and willing to undertake the life he suggested, but she had not broken with the old atmosphere completely, or if she had it was still not believed that she had. There were those who could not only charge, but prove. A compromising note of some kind sent to some one was involved, turned over to Peter.

"Dreiser," he growled as he related the case to me, "it serves me right. I ought to know better. I know the kind of woman I need. This one has handed me a damned good wallop, and I deserve it. I might have guessed that she wasn't suited to me. She was really too free—a life-lover more than a wife. That home stuff! She was just stringing me because she liked me. She isn't really my sort, not simple enough."

"But you loved her, I thought?"

"I did, or thought I did. Still, I used to wonder too. There were many ways about her that troubled me. You think I'm kidding about this home and family idea, but I'm not. It suits me, however flat it looks to you. I want to do that, live that way, go through the normal routine experience, and I'm going to do it."

"But how did you break it off with her so swiftly?" I asked curiously.

"Well, when I heard this I went direct to her and put it up to her. If you'll believe me she never even denied it. Said it was all true, but that she was in love with me all right, and would change and be all that I wanted her to be."

"Well, that's fair enough," I said, "if she loves you. You're no saint yourself, you know. If you'd encourage her, maybe she'd make good."

"Well, maybe, but I don't think so really," he returned, shaking his head. "She likes me, but not enough, I'm afraid. She wouldn't run straight, now that she's had this other. She'd mean to maybe, but she wouldn't. I feel it about her. And anyhow I don't want to take any chances. I like her—I'm crazy about her really, but I'm through. I'm going to marry little Dutchy if she'll have me, and cut out this old-line stuff. You'll have to stand up with me when I do."

In three months more the new arrangement was consummated and little Dutchy—or Zuleika, as he subsequently named her—was duly brought to Newark and installed, at first in a charming apartment in a conventionally respectable and cleanly neighborhood, later in a small house with a "yard," lawn front and back, in one of the homiest of home neighborhoods in Newark. It was positively entertaining to observe Peter not only attempting to assume but assuming the rôle of the conventional husband, and exactly nine months after he had been married, to the hour, a father in this humble and yet, in so far as his particular home was concerned, comfortable world. I have no space here for more than the barest outline. I have already indicated his views, most emphatically expressed and forecasted. He fulfilled them all to the letter, up to the day of his death. In so far as I could make out, he made about as satisfactory a husband and father and citizen as I have ever seen. He did it deliberately, in cold reason, and yet with a warmth and flare which puzzled me all the more since it *was* based on reason and forethought. I misdoubted. I was not quite willing to believe that it would work out, and yet if ever a home was delightful, with a charming and genuinely "happy" atmosphere, it was Peter's.

"Here she is," he observed the day he married her, "me *frau*—Zuleika. Isn't she a peach? Ever see any nicer hair than that? And these here, now, pink cheeks? What? Look at 'em! And her little Dutchy nose! Isn't it cute? Oh, Dutchy! And right here in me vest pocket is the golden band wherewith I am to be chained to the floor, the domestic hearth. And right there on her finger is my badge of prospective serfdom." Then, in a loud aside to me, "In six months I'll be beating her. Come now, Zuleika. We have to go through with this. You have to swear to be my slave."

And so they were married.

And in the home afterward he was as busy and helpful and noisy as any man about the house could ever hope to be. He was always fussing about after hours "putting up" something or arranging his collections or helping Zuleika wash and dry the dishes, or showing her how to cook something if she didn't know how. He was running to the store or bringing home things from the downtown market. Months before the first child was born he was declaring most shamelessly, "In a few months now, Dreiser, Zuleika and I are going to have our first calf. The bones roll for a boy, but you never can tell. I'm offering up prayers and oblations—both of us are. I make Zuleika pray every night. And say, when it comes, no spoiling-the-kid stuff. No bawling or rocking it to sleep nights permitted. Here's one kid that's going to be raised right. I've worked out all the rules. No trashy baby-foods. Good old specially brewed Culmbacher for the mother, and the kid afterwards if it wants it. This is one family in which law and order are going to prevail—good old 'dichtig, wichtig' law and order."

I used to chuckle the while I verbally denounced him for his coarse, plebeian point of view and tastes.

In a little while the child came, and to his immense satisfaction it was a boy. I never saw a man "carry on" so, make over it, take such a whole-souled interest in all those little things which supposedly made for its health and well-being. For the first few weeks he still talked of not having it petted or spoiled, but at the same time he was surely and swiftly changing, and by the end of that time had become the most doting, almost ridiculously fond papa that I ever saw. Always the child must be in his lap at the most unseemly hours, when his wife would permit it. When he went anywhere, or they, although they kept a maid the child must be carried along by him on his shoulder. He liked nothing better than to sit and hold it close, rocking in a rocking-chair American style and singing, or come tramping into my home in New York, the child looking like a woolen ball. At night if it stirred or whimpered he was up and looking. And the baby-clothes!—and the cradle!—and the toys!—colored rubber balls and soldiers the first or second or third week!

"What about that stern discipline that was to be put in force here—no rocking, no getting up at night to coddle a weeping infant?"

"Yes, I know. That's all good stuff before you get one. I've got one of my own now, and I've got a new light on this. Say, Dreiser, take my advice. Go through the routine. Don't try to escape. Have a kid or two or three. There's a psychic punch to it you can't get any other way. It's nature's way. It's a great scheme. You and your girl and your kid."

As he talked he rocked, holding the baby boy to his breast. It was wonderful.

And Mrs. Peter—how happy she seemed. There was light in that house, flowers, laughter, good fellowship. As in his old rooms so in this new home he gathered a few of his old friends around him and some new ones, friends of this region. In the course of a year or two he was on the very best terms of friendship with his barber around the corner, his grocer, some man who had a saloon and bowling alley in the neighborhood, his tailor, and then just neighbors. The milkman, the coal man, the druggist and cigar man at the next corner—all could tell you where Peter lived. His little front "yard" had two beds of flowers all summer long, his lot in the back was a garden—lettuce, onions, peas, beans. Peter was always happiest when he could be home working, playing with the baby, pushing him about in a go-cart, working in his garden, or lying on the floor making something—an engraving or print or a box which he was carving, the infant in some simple gingham romper crawling about. He was always busy, but never too much so for a glance or a mock-threatening, "Now say, not so much industry there. You leave my things alone," to the child. Of a Sunday he sat out on the front porch smoking, reading the Sunday paper, congratulating himself on his happy married life, and most of the time holding the infant. Afternoons he would carry it somewhere, anywhere, in his arms to his friends, the Park, New York, to see me. At breakfast, dinner, supper the heir presumptive was in a high-chair beside him.

"Ah, now, here's a rubber spoon. Beat with that. It's less destructive and less painful physically."

"How about a nice prust" (crust) "dipped in bravery" (gravy) "—heh? Do you suppose that would cut any of your teeth?"

"Zuleika, this son of yours seems to think a spoonful of beer or two might not hurt him. What do you say?"

Occasionally, especially of a Saturday evening, he wanted to go bowling and yet he wanted his heir. The problem was solved by fitting the latter into a tight little sweater and cap and carrying him along on his shoulder, into the bar for a beer, thence to the bowling alley, where young hopeful was fastened into a chair on the side lines while Peter and myself or some of his friends bowled. At ten or ten-thirty or eleven, as the case might be, he was ready to leave, but before that hour les ongfong might be sound asleep, hanging against Peter's scarf, his interest in his toes or thumbs having given out.

"Peter, look at that," I observed once. "Don't you think we'd better take him home?"

"Home nothing! Let him sleep. He can sleep here as well as anywhere, and besides I like to look at him." And in the room would be a great crowd, cigars, beers, laughter, and Peter's various friends as used to the child's presence and as charmed by it as he was. He was just the man who could do such things. His manner and point of view carried conviction. He believed in doing all that he wanted to do simply and naturally, and more and more as he went along people not only respected, I think they adored him, especially the simple homely souls among whom he chose to move and have his being.

About this time there developed among those in his immediate neighborhood a desire to elect him to some political position, that of councilman, or State assemblyman, in the hope or thought that he would rise to something higher. But he would none of it—not then anyhow. Instead, about this time or a very little later, after the birth of his second child (a girl), he devoted himself to the composition of a brilliant piece of prose poetry ("Wolf"), which, coming from him, did not surprise me in the least. If he had designed or constructed a great building, painted a great picture, entered politics and been elected governor or senator, I would have taken it all as a matter of course. He could have. The material from which anything may rise was there. I asked him to let me offer it to the publishing house with which I was connected, and I recall with interest the comment of the oldest and most experienced of the bookmen and salesmen among us. "You'll never make much, if anything, on this book. It's too good, too poetic. But whether it pays or not, I vote yes. I'd rather lose money on something like this than make it on some of the trash we do make it on."

Amen. I agreed then, and I agree now.

The last phase of Peter was as interesting and dramatic as any of the others. His married life was going forward about as he had planned. His devotion to his home and children, his loving wife, his multiplex interests, his various friends, was always a curiosity to me, especially in view of his olden days. One day he was over in New York visiting one of his favorite Chinese importing companies, through which he had secured and was still securing occasional objects of art. He had come down to me in my office at the Butterick Building to see if I would not come over the following Saturday as usual and stay until Monday. He had secured something, was planning something. I should see. At the elevator he waved me a gay "so long—see you Saturday!"

But on Friday, as I was talking with some one at my desk, a telegram was handed me. It was from Mrs. Peter and read: "Peter died today at two of pneumonia. Please come."

I could scarcely believe it. I did not know that he had even been sick. His little yellow-haired wife! The two children! His future! His interests! I dropped everything and hurried to the nearest station. En route I speculated on the mysteries on which he had so often speculated—death, dissolution, uncertainty, the crude indifference or cruelty of Nature. What would become of Mrs. Peter? His children?

I arrived only to find a home atmosphere destroyed as by a wind that puts out a light. There was Peter, stiff and cold, and in the other rooms his babies, quite unconscious of what had happened, prattling as usual, and Mrs. Peter practically numb and speechless. It had come so suddenly, so out of a clear sky, that she could not realize, could not even tell me at first. The doctor was there—also a friend of his, the nearest barber! Also two or three representatives from his paper, the owner of the bowling alley, the man who had the $40,000 collection of curios. All were stunned, as I was. As his closest friend, I took charge: wired his relatives, went to an undertaker who knew him to arrange for his burial, in Newark or Philadelphia, as his wife should wish, she having no connection with Newark other than Peter.

It was most distressing, the sense of dull despair and unwarranted disaster which hung over the place. It was as though impish and pagan forces, or malign ones outside life, had committed a crime of the ugliest character. On Monday, the day he saw me, he was well. On Tuesday morning he had a slight cold but insisted on running out somewhere without his overcoat, against which his wife protested. Tuesday night he had a fever and took quinine and aspirin and a hot whiskey. Wednesday morning he was worse and a doctor was called, but it was not deemed serious. Wednesday night he was still worse and pneumonia had set in. Thursday he was lower still, and by noon a metal syphon of oxygen was sent for, to relieve the sense of suffocation setting in. Thursday night he was weak and sinking, but expected to come round—and still, so unexpected was the attack, so uncertain the probability of anything fatal, that no word was sent, even to me. Friday morning he was no worse and no better. "If he was no worse by night he might pull through." At noon he was seized with a sudden sinking spell. Oxygen was applied by his wife and a nurse, and the doctor sent for. By one-thirty he was lower still, very low. "His face was blue, his lips ashen," his wife told me. "We put the oxygen tube to his mouth and I said 'Can you speak, Peter?' I was so nervous and frightened. He moved his head a little to indicate 'no.' 'Peter,' I said, 'you mustn't let go! You must fight! Think of me! Think of the babies!' I was a little crazy, I think, with fear. He looked at me very fixedly. He stiffened and gritted his teeth in a great effort. Then suddenly he collapsed and lay still. He was dead."

I could not help thinking of the force and energy—able at the last minute, when he could not speak—to "grit his teeth" and "fight," a minute before his death. What is the human spirit, or mind, that it can fight so, to the very last? I felt as though some one, something, had ruthlessly killed him, committed plain, unpunished murder—nothing more and nothing less.

And there were his cases of curios, his rug, his prints, his dishes, his many, many schemes, his book to come out soon. I gazed and marveled. I looked at his wife and babies, but could say nothing. It spelled, what such things always spell, in the face of all our dreams, crass chance or the willful, brutal indifference of Nature to all that relates to man. If he is to prosper he must do so without her aid.

That same night, sleeping in the room adjoining that in which was the body, a pale candle burning near it, I felt as though Peter were walking to and fro, to and fro, past me and into the room of his wife beyond, thinking and grieving. His imagined wraith seemed horribly depressed and distressed. Once he came over and moved his hand (something) over my face. I felt him walking into the room where were his wife and kiddies, but he could make no one see, hear, understand. I got up and looked at his *cadaver* a long time, then went to bed again.

The next day and the next and the next were filled with many things. His mother and sister came on from the West as well as the mother and brother of his wife. I had to look after his affairs, adjusting the matter of insurance which he left, his art objects, the burial of his body "in consecrated ground" in Philadelphia, with the consent and aid of the local Catholic parish rector, else no burial. His mother desired it, but he had never been a good Catholic and there was trouble. The local parish assistant refused me, even the rector. Finally I threatened the good father with an appeal to the diocesan bishop on the ground of plain common sense and courtesy to a Catholic family, if not charity to a tortured mother and wife—and obtained consent. All along I felt as if a great crime had been committed by some one, foul murder. I could not get it out of my mind, and it made me angry, not sad.

Two, three, five, seven years later, I visited the little family in Philadelphia. The wife was with her mother and father in a simple little home street in a factory district, secretary and stenographer to an architect. She was little changed—a little stouter, not so carefree, industrious, patient. His boy, the petted F——, could not even recall his father, the girl not at all of course. And in the place were a few of his prints, two or three Chinese dishes, pottered by himself, his loom with the unfinished rug. I remained for dinner and dreamed old dreams, but I was uncomfortable and left early. And Mrs. Peter, accompanying me to the steps, looked after me as though I, alone, was all that was left of the old life.

A Doer of the Word

Noank is a little played-out fishing town on the southeastern coast of Connecticut, lying half-way between New London and Stonington. Once it was a profitable port for mackerel and cod fishing. Today its wharves are deserted of all save a few lobster smacks. There is a shipyard, employing three hundred and fifty men, a yacht-building establishment, with two or three hired hands; a sail-loft, and some dozen or so shops or sheds, where the odds and ends of fishing life are made and sold. Everything is peaceful. The sound of the shipyard axes and hammers can be heard for miles over the quiet waters of the bay. In the sunny lane which follows the line of the shore, and along which a few shops struggle in happy-go-lucky disorder, may be heard the voices and noises of the workers at their work. Water gurgling about the stanchions of the docks, the whistle of some fisherman as he dawdles over his nets, or puts his fish ashore, the whirr of the single high-power sewing machine in the sail-loft, often mingle in a pleasant harmony, and invite the mind to repose and speculation.

I was in a most examining and critical mood that summer, looking into the nature and significance of many things, and was sitting one day in the shed of the maker of sailboats, where a half-dozen characters of the village were gathered, when some turn in the conversation brought up the nature of man. He is queer, he is restless; life is not so very much when you come to look upon many phases of it.

"Did any of you ever know a contented man?" I inquired idly, merely for the sake of something to say.

There was silence for a moment, and one after another met my roving glance with a thoughtful, self-involved and retrospective eye.

Old Mr. Main was the first to answer.

"Yes, I did. One."

"So did I," put in the sailboat maker, as he stopped in his work to think about it.

"Yes, and I did," said a dark, squat, sunny, little old fisherman, who sold cunners for bait in a little hut next door.

"Maybe you and me are thinking of the same one, Jacob," said old Mr. Main, looking inquisitively at the boat-builder.

"I think we've all got the same man in mind, likely," returned the builder.

"Who is he?" I asked.

"Charlie Potter," said the builder.

"That's the man!" exclaimed Mr. Main.

"Yes, I reckon Charlie Potter is contented, if anybody be," said an old fisherman who had hitherto been silent.

Such unanimity of opinion struck me forcibly. Charlie Potter—what a humble name; not very remarkable, to say the least. And to hear him so spoken of in this restless, religious, quibbling community made it all the more interesting.

"So you really think he is contented, do you?" I asked.

"Yes, sir! Charlie Potter is a contented man," replied Mr. Main, with convincing emphasis.

"Well," I returned, "that's rather interesting. What sort of a man is he?"

"Oh, he's just an ordinary man, not much of anybody. Fishes and builds boats occasionally," put in the boat-builder.

"Is that all? Nothing else?"

"He preaches now and then—not regularly," said Mr. Main.

A-ha! I thought. A religionist!

"A preacher is expected to set a good example," I said.

"He ain't a regular preacher," said Mr. Main, rather quickly. "He's just kind of around in religious work."

"What do you mean?" I asked curiously, not quite catching the import of this "around."

"Well," answered the boat builder, "he don't take any money for what he does. He ain't got anything."

"What does he live on then?" I persisted, still wondering at the significance of "around in religious work."

"I don't know. He used to fish for a living. Fishes yet once in a while, I believe."

"He makes models of yachts," put in one of the bystanders. "He sold the New Haven Road one for two hundred dollars here not long ago."

A vision of a happy-go-lucky Jack-of-all-trades arose before me. A visionary—a theorist.

"What else?" I asked, hoping to draw them out. "What makes you all think he is contented? What does he do that makes him so contented?"

"Well," said Mr. Main, after a considerable pause and with much of sympathetic emphasis in his voice, "Charlie Potter is just a good man, that's all. That's why he's contented. He does as near as he can what he thinks he ought to by other people—poor people."

"You won't find anybody with a kinder heart than Charlie Potter," put in the boat-builder. "That's the trouble with him, really. He's too good. He don't look after himself right, I say. A fellow has to look out for himself some in this world. If he don't, no one else will."

"Right you are, Henry," echoed a truculent sea voice from somewhere.

I was becoming both amused and interested, intensely so.

"If he wasn't that way, he'd be a darned sight better off than he is," said a thirty-year-old helper, from a far corner of the room.

"What makes you say that?" I queried. "Isn't it better to be kind-hearted and generous than not?"

"It's all right to be kind-hearted and generous, but that ain't sayin' that you've got to give your last cent away and let your family go hungry."

"Is that what Charlie Potter does?"

"Well, no, maybe he don't, but he comes mighty near to it at times. He and his wife and his adopted children have been pretty close to it at times."

You see, this was the center, nearly, for all village gossip and philosophic speculation, and many of the most important local problems, morally and intellectually speaking, were here thrashed put.

"There's no doubt but that's where Charlie is wrong," put in old Mr. Main a little later. "He don't always stop to think of his family."

"What did he ever do that struck you as being over-generous?" I asked of the young man who had spoken from the corner.

"That's all right," he replied in a rather irritated and peevish tone; "I ain't going to go into details now, but there's people around here that hang on him, and that he's give to, that he hadn't orter."

"I believe in lookin' out for Number One, that's what I believe in," interrupted the boat-maker, laying down his rule and line. "This givin' up everything and goin' without yourself may be all right, but I don't believe it. A man's first duty is to his wife and children, that's what I say."

"That's the way it looks to me," put in Mr. Main.

"Well, does Potter give up everything and go without things?" I asked the boat-maker.

"Purty blamed near it at times," he returned definitely, then addressing the company in general he added, "Look at the time he worked over there on Fisher's Island, at the Ellersbie farm—the time they were packing the ice there. You remember that, Henry, don't you?"

Mr. Main nodded.

"What about it?"

"What about it! Why, he give his rubber boots away, like a darned fool, to old drunken Jimmy Harper, and him loafin' around half the year drunk, and worked around on the ice without any shoes himself. He might 'a' took cold and died."

"Why did he do it?" I queried, very much interested by now.

"Oh, Charlie's naturally big-hearted," put in the little old man who sold cunners. "He believes in the Lord and the Bible. Stands right square on it, only he don't belong to no church like. He's got the biggest heart I ever saw in a livin' being."

"Course the other fellow didn't have any shoes for to wear," put in the boat-maker explanatorily, "but he never would work, anyhow."

They lapsed into silence while the latter returned to his measuring, and then out of the drift of thought came this from the helper in the corner:

"Yes, and look at the way Bailey used to sponge on him. Get his money Saturday night and drink it all up, and then Sunday morning, when his wife and children were hungry, go cryin' around Potter. Dinged if I'd 'a' helped him. But Potter'd take the food right off his breakfast table and give it to him. I saw him do it! I don't think that's right. Not when he's got four or five orphans of his own to care for."

"His own children?" I interrupted, trying to get the thing straight.

"No, sir; just children he picked up around, here and there."

Here is a curious character, sure enough, I thought—one well worth looking into.

Another lull, and then as I was leaving the room to give the matter a little quiet attention, I remarked to the boat-maker:

"Outside of his foolish giving, you haven't anything against Charlie Potter, have you?"

"Not a thing," he replied, in apparent astonishment. "Charlie Potter's one of the best men that ever lived. He's a good man."

I smiled at the inconsistency and went my way.

A day or two later the loft of the sail-maker, instead of the shed of the boat-builder, happened to be my lounging place, and thinking of this theme, now uppermost in my mind, I said to him:

"Do you know a man around here by the name of Charlie Potter?"

"Well, I might say that I do. He lived here for over fifteen years."

"What sort of a man is he?"

He stopped in his stitching a moment to look at me, and then said:

"How d'ye mean? By trade, so to speak, or religious-like?"

"What is it he has done," I said, "that makes him so popular with all you people? Everybody says he's a good man. Just what do you mean by that?"

"Well," he said, ceasing his work as though the subject were one of extreme importance to him, "he's a peculiar man, Charlie is. He believes in giving nearly everything he has away, if any one else needs it. He'd give the coat off his back if you asked him for it. Some folks condemn him for this, and for not giving everything to his wife and them orphans he has, but I always thought the man was nearer right than most of us. I've got a family myself—but, then, so's he, now, for that matter. It's pretty hard to live up to your light always."

He looked away as if he expected some objection to be made to this, but hearing none, he went on. "I always liked him personally very much. He ain't around here now any more—lives up in Norwich, I think. He's a man of his word, though, as truthful as kin be. He ain't never done nothin' for me, I not bein' a takin' kind, but that's neither here nor there."

He paused, in doubt apparently, as to what else to say.

"You say he's so good," I said. "Tell me one thing that he ever did that struck you as being preëminently good."

"Well, now, I can't say as I kin, exactly, offhand," he replied, "there bein' so many of them from time to time. He was always doin' things one way and another. He give to everybody around here that asked him, and to a good many that didn't. I remember once"—and a smile gave evidence of a genial memory—"he give away a lot of pork that he'd put up for the winter to some colored people back here—two or three barrels, maybe. His wife didn't object, exactly, but my, how his mother-in-law did go on about it. She was livin' with him then. She went and railed against him all around."

"She didn't like to give it to them, eh?"

"Well, I should say not. She didn't set with his views, exactly—never did. He took the pork, though—it was right in the coldest weather we had that winter—and hauled it back about seven miles here to where they lived, and handed it all out himself. Course they were awful hard up, but then they might 'a' got along without it. They do now, sometimes. Charlie's too good that way. It's his one fault, if you might so speak of it."

I smiled as the evidence accumulated. Houseless wayfarers, stopping to find food and shelter under his roof, an orphan child carried seven miles on foot from the bedside of a dead mother and cared for all winter, three children, besides two of his own, being raised out of a sense of affection and care for the fatherless.

One day in the local post office I was idling a half hour with the postmaster, when I again inquired:

"Do you know Charlie Potter?"

"I should think I did. Charlie Potter and I sailed together for something over eleven years."

"How do you mean sailed together?"

"We were on the same schooner. This used to be a great port for mackerel and cod. We were wrecked once together"

"How was that?"

"Oh, we went on rocks."

"Any lives lost?"

"No, but there came mighty near being. We helped each other in the boat. I remember Charlie was the last one in that time. Wouldn't get in until all the rest were safe."

A sudden resolution came to me.

"Do you know where he is now?"

"Yes, he's up in Norwich, preaching or doing missionary work. He's kind of busy all the time among the poor people, and so on. Never makes much of anything out of it for himself, but just likes to do it, I guess."

"Do you know how he manages to live?"

"No, I don't, exactly. He believes in trusting to Providence for what he needs. He works though, too, at one job and another. He's a carpenter for one thing. Got an idea the Lord will send 'im whatever he needs."

"Well, and does He?"

"Well, he lives." A little later he added:

"Oh, yes. There's nothing lazy about Charlie. He's a good worker. When he was in the fishing line here there wasn't a man worked harder than he did. They can't anybody lay anything like that against him."

"Is he very difficult to talk to?" I asked, meditating on seeking him out. I had so little to do at the time, the very idlest of summers, and the reports of this man's deeds were haunting me. I wanted to discover for myself whether he was real or not—whether the reports were true. The Samaritan in people is so easily exaggerated at times.

"Oh, no. He's one of the finest men that way I ever knew. You could see him, well enough, if you went up to Norwich, providing he's up there. He usually is, though, I think. He lives there with his wife and mother, you know."

I caught an afternoon boat for New London and Norwich at one-thirty, and arrived in Norwich at five. The narrow streets of the thriving little mill city were alive with people. I had no address, could not obtain one, but through the open door of a news-stall near the boat landing I called to the proprietor:

"Do you know any one in Norwich by the name of Charlie Potter?"

"The man who works around among the poor people here?"

"That's the man."

"Yes, I know him. He lives out on Summer Street, Number Twelve, I think. You'll find it in the city directory."

The ready reply was rather astonishing. Norwich has something like thirty thousand people.

I walked out in search of Summer Street and finally found a beautiful lane of that name climbing upward over gentle slopes, arched completely with elms. Some of the pretty porches of the cottages extended nearly to the sidewalk. Hammocks, rocking-chairs on verandas, benches under the trees—all attested the love of idleness and shade in summer. Only the glimpse of mills and factories in the valley below evidenced the grimmer life which gave rise mayhap to the need of a man to work among the poor.

"Is this Summer Street?" I inquired of an old darky who was strolling cityward in the cool of the evening. An umbrella was under his arm and an evening paper under his spectacled nose.

"Bress de Lord!" he said, looking vaguely around. "Ah couldn't say. Ah knows dat street—been on it fifty times—but Ah never did know de name. Ha, ha, ha!"

The hills about echoed his hearty laugh.

"You don't happen to know Charlie Potter?"

"Oh, yas, sah. Ah knows Charlie Potter. Dat's his house right ovah dar."

The house in which Charlie Potter lived was a two-story frame, overhanging a sharp slope, which descended directly to the waters of the pretty river below. For a mile or more, the valley of the river could be seen, its slopes dotted with houses, the valley itself lined with mills. Two little girls were upon the sloping lawn to the right of the house. A stout, comfortable-looking man was sitting by a window on the left side of the house, gazing out over the valley.

"Is this where Charlie Potter lives?" I inquired of one of the children.

"Yes, sir."

"Did he live in Noank?"

"Yes, sir."

Just then a pleasant-faced woman of forty-five or fifty issued from a vine-covered door.

"Mr. Potter?" she replied to my inquiry. "He'll be right out."

She went about some little work at the side of the house, and in a moment Charlie Potter appeared. He was short, thick-set, and weighed no less than two hundred pounds. His face and hands were sunburned and brown like those of every fisherman of Noank. An old wrinkled coat and a baggy pair of gray trousers clothed his form loosely. Two inches of a spotted, soft-brimmed hat were pulled carelessly over his eyes. His face was round and full, but slightly seamed. His hands were large, his walk uneven, and rather inclined to a side swing, or the sailor's roll. He seemed an odd, pudgy person for so large a fame.

"Is this Mr. Potter?"

"I'm the man."

"I live on a little hummock at the east of Mystic Island, off Noank."

"You do?"

"I came up to have a talk with you."

"Will you come inside, or shall we sit out here?"

"Let's sit on the step."

"All right, let's sit on the step."

He waddled out of the gate and sank comfortably on the little low doorstep, with his feet on the cool bricks below. I dropped into the space beside him, and was greeted by as sweet and kind a look as I have ever seen in a man's eyes. It was one of perfect courtesy and good nature—void of all suspicion.

"We were sitting down in the sailboat maker's place at Noank the other day, and I asked a half dozen of the old fellows whether they had ever known a contented man. They all thought a while, and then they said they had. Old Mr. Main and the rest of them agreed that Charlie Potter was a contented man. What I want to know is, are you?"

I looked quizzically into his eyes to see what effect this would have, and if there was no evidence of a mist of pleasure and affection being vigorously restrained I was very much mistaken. Something seemed to hold the man in helpless silence as he gazed vacantly at nothing. He breathed heavily, then drew himself together and lifted one of his big hands, as if to touch me, but refrained.

"Yes, brother," he said after a time, "I *am*."

"Well, that's good," I replied, taking a slight mental exception to the use of the word brother. "What makes you contented?"

"I don't know, unless it is that I've found out what I ought to do. You see, I need so very little for myself that I couldn't be very unhappy."

"What ought you to do?"

"I ought to love my fellowmen."

"And do you?"

"Say, brother, but I do," he insisted quite simply and with no evidence of chicane or make-believe—a simple, natural enthusiasm. "I love everybody. There isn't anybody so low or so mean but I love him. I love you, yes, I do. I love you."

He reached out and touched me with his hand, and while I was inclined to take exception to this very moral enthusiasm, I thrilled just the same as I have not over the touch of any man in years. There was something effective and electric about him, so very warm and foolishly human. The glance which accompanied it spoke, it seemed, as truthfully as his words. He probably did love me—or thought he did. What difference?

We lapsed into silence. The scene below was so charming that I could easily gaze at it in silence. This little house was very simple, not poor, by no means prosperous, but well-ordered—such a home as such a man might have. After a while I said:

"It is very evident that you think the condition of some of your fellowmen isn't what it ought to be. Tell me what you are trying to do. What method have you for improving their condition?"

"The way I reason is this-a-way," he began. "All that some people have is their feelings, nothing else. Take a tramp, for instance, as I often have. When you begin to sum up to see where to begin, you find that all he has in the world, besides his pipe and a little tobacco, is his feelings. It's all most people have, rich or poor, though a good many think they have more than that. I try not to injure anybody's feelings."

He looked at me as though he had expressed the solution of the difficulties of the world, and the wonderful, kindly eyes beamed in rich romance upon the scene.

"Very good," I said, "but what do you do? How do you go about it to aid your fellowmen?"

"Well," he answered, unconsciously overlooking his own personal actions in the matter, "I try to bring them the salvation which the Bible teaches. You know I stand on the Bible, from cover to cover."

"Yes, I know you stand on the Bible, but what do you do? You don't merely preach the Bible to them. What do you do?"

"No, sir, I don't preach the Bible at all. I stand on it myself. I try as near as I can to do what it says. I go wherever I can be useful. If anybody is sick or in trouble, I'm ready to go. I'll be a nurse. I'll work and earn them food. I'll give them anything I can—that's what I do."

"How can you give when you haven't anything? They told me in Noank that you never worked for money."

"Not for myself alone. I never take any money for myself alone. That would be self-seeking. Anything I earn or take is for the Lord, not me. I never keep it. The Lord doesn't allow a man to be self-seeking."

"Well, then, when you get money what do you do with it? You can't do and live without money."

He had been looking away across the river and the bridge to the city below, but now he brought his eyes back and fixed them on me.

"I've been working now for twenty years or more, and, although I've never had more money than would last me a few days at a time, I've never wanted for anything and I've been able to help others. I've run pretty close sometimes. Time and time again I've been compelled to say, 'Lord, I'm all out of coal,' or 'Lord, I'm going to have to ask you to get me my fare to New Haven tomorrow,' but in the moment of my need He has never forgotten me. Why, I've gone down to the depot time and time again, when it was necessary for me to go, without five cents in my pocket, and He's been there to meet me. Why, He wouldn't keep you waiting when you're about His work. He wouldn't forget you—not for a minute."

I looked at the man in open-eyed amazement.

"Do you mean to say that you would go down to a depot without money and wait for money to come to you?"

"Oh, brother," he said, with the softest light in his eyes, "if you only knew what it is to have faith!"

He laid his hand softly on mine.

"What is car-fare to New Haven or to anywhere, to Him?"

"But," I replied materially, "you haven't any car-fare when you go there— how do you actually get it? Who gives it to you? Give me one instance."

"Why, it was only last week, brother, that a woman wrote me from Maiden, Massachusetts, wanting me to come and see her. She's very sick with consumption, and she thought she was going to die. I used to know her in Noank, and she thought if she could get to see me she would feel better.

"I didn't have any money at the time, but that didn't make any difference.

"'Lord,' I said, 'here's a woman sick in Maiden, and she wants me to come to her. I haven't got any money, but I'll go right down to the depot, in time to catch a certain train,' and I went. And while I was standing there a man came up to me and said, 'Brother, I'm told to give you this,' and he handed me ten dollars."

"Did you know the man?" I exclaimed.

"Never saw him before in my life," he replied, smiling genially.

"And didn't he say anything more than that?"

"No."

I stared at him, and he added, as if to take the edge off my astonishment:

"Why, bless your heart, I knew he was from the Lord, just the moment I saw him coming."

"You mean to say you were standing there without a cent, expecting the Lord to help you, and He did?"

"'He shall call upon me, and I shall answer him,'" he answered simply, quoting the Ninety-first Psalm.

This incident was still the subject of my inquiry when a little colored girl came out of the yard and paused a moment before us.

"May I go down across the bridge, papa?" she asked.

"Yes," he answered, and then as she tripped away, said:

"She's one of my adopted children." He gazed between his knees at the sidewalk.

"Have you many others?"

"Three."

"Raising them, are you?"

"Yes."

"They seem to think, down in Noank, that living as you do and giving everything away is satisfactory to you but rather hard on your wife and children."

"Well, it is true that she did feel a little uncertain in the beginning, but she's never wanted for anything. She'll tell you herself that she's never been without a thing that she really needed, and she's been happy."

He paused to meditate, I presume, over the opinion of his former fellow townsmen, and then added:

"It's true, there have been times when we have been right where we had to have certain things pretty badly, before they came, but they never failed to come."

While he was still talking, Mrs. Potter came around the corner of the house and out upon the sidewalk. She was going to the Saturday evening market in the city below.

"Here she is," he said. "Now you can ask her."

"What is it?" she inquired, turning a serene and smiling face to me.

"They still think, down in Noank, that you're not very happy with me," he said. "They're afraid you want for something once in a while."

She took this piece of neighborly interference in better fashion than most would, I fancy.

"I have never wanted for anything since I have been married to my husband," she said. "I am thoroughly contented."

She looked at him and he at her, and there passed between them an affectionate glance.

"Yes," he said, when she had passed after a pleasing little conversation, "my wife has been a great help to me. She has never complained."

"People are inclined to talk a little," I said.

"Well, you see, she never complained, but she did feel a little bit worried in the beginning."

"Have you a mission or a church here in Norwich?"

"No, I don't believe in churches."

"Not in churches?"

"No. The sight of a minister preaching the word of God for so much a year is all a mockery to me."

"What do you believe in?"

"Personal service. Churches and charitable institutions and societies are all valueless. You can't reach your fellowman that way. They build up buildings and pay salaries—but there's a better way." (I was thinking of St. Francis and his original dream, before they threw him out and established monasteries and a costume or uniform—the thing he so much objected to.) "This giving of a few old clothes that the moths will get anyhow, that won't do. You've got to give something of yourself, and that's affection. Love is the only thing you can really give in all this world. When you give love, you give everything. Everything comes with it in some way or other."

"How do you say?" I queried. "Money certainly comes handy sometimes."

"Yes, when you give it with your own hand and heart—in no other way. It comes to nothing just contributed to some thing. Ah!" he added, with sudden animation, "the tangles men can get themselves into, the snarls, the wretchedness! Troubles with women, with men whom they owe, with evil things they say and think, until they can't walk down the street any more without peeping about to see if they are followed. They can't look you in die face; can't walk a straight course, but have got to sneak around corners. Poor, miserable, unhappy—they're worrying and crying and dodging one another!"

He paused, lost in contemplation of the picture he had conjured up.

"Yes," I went on catechistically, determined, if I could, to rout out this matter of giving, this actual example of the modus operandi of Christian charity. "What do you do? How do you get along without giving them money?"

"I don't get along without giving them some money. There are cases, lots of them, where a little money is necessary. But, brother, it is so little necessary at times. It isn't always money they want. You can't reach them with old clothes and charity societies," he insisted. "You've got to love them, brother.

- 47 -

You've got to go to them and love them, just as they are, scarred and miserable and bad-hearted."

"Yes," I replied doubtfully, deciding to follow this up later. "But just what is it you do in a needy case? One instance?"

"Why, one night I was passing a little house in this town," he went on, "and I heard a woman crying. I went right to the door and opened it, and when I got inside she just stopped and looked at me.

"'Madam,' I said, 'I have come to help you, if I can. Now you tell me what you're crying for.'

"Well, sir, you know she sat there and told me how her husband drank and how she didn't have anything in the house to eat, and so I just gave her all I had and told her I would see her husband for her, and the next day I went and hunted him up and said to him, 'Oh, brother, I wish you would open your eyes and see what you are doing. I wish you wouldn't do that any more. It's only misery you are creating.' And, you know, I got to telling about how badly his wife felt about it, and how I intended to work and try and help her, and bless me if he didn't up and promise me before I got through that he wouldn't do that any more. And he didn't. He's working today, and it's been two years since I went to him, nearly."

His eyes were alight with his appreciation of personal service.

"Yes, that's one instance," I said.

"Oh, there are plenty of them," he replied. "It's the only way. Down here in New London a couple of winters ago we had a terrible time of it. That was the winter of the panic, you know. Cold—my, but that was a cold winter, and thousands of people out of work—just thousands. It was awful. I tried to do what I could here and there all along, but finally things got so bad there that I went to the mayor. I saw they were raising some kind of a fund to help the poor, so I told him that if he'd give me a little of the money they were talking of spending that I'd feed the hungry for a cent-and-a-half a meal."

"A cent-and-a-half a meal!"

"Yes, sir. They all thought it was rather curious, not possible at first, but they gave me the money and I fed 'em."

"Good meals?"

"Yes, as good as I ever eat myself," he replied.

"How did you do it?" I asked.

"Oh, I can cook. I just went around to the markets, and told the market-men what I wanted—heads of mackerel, and the part of the halibut that's left after the rich man cuts off his steak—it's the poorest part that he pays for, you know. And I went fishing myself two or three times—borrowed a big boat and got men to help me—oh, I'm a good fisherman, you know. And then I got the loan of an old covered brickyard that no one was using any more, a great big thing that I could close up and build fires in, and I put my kettle in there and rigged up tables out of borrowed boards, and got people to loan me plates and spoons and knives and forks and cups. I made fish chowder, and fish dinners, and really I set a very fine table, I did, that winter."

"For a cent-and-a-half a meal!"

"Yes, sir, a cent-and-a-half a meal. Ask any one in New London. That's all it cost me. The mayor said he was surprised at the way I did it."

"Well, but there wasn't any particular personal service in the money they gave you?" I asked, catching him up on that point. "They didn't personally serve—those who gave you the money?"

"No, sir, they didn't," he replied dreamily, with unconscious simplicity. "But they gave through me, you see. That's the way it was. I gave the personal service. Don't you see? That's the way."

"Yes, that's the way," I smiled, avoiding as far as possible a further discussion of this contradiction, so unconscious on his part, and in the drag of his thought he took up another idea.

"I clothed 'em that winter, too—went around and got barrels and boxes of old clothing. Some of them felt a little ashamed to put on the things, but I got over that, all right. I was wearing them myself, and I just told them, 'Don't feel badly, brother. I'm wearing them out of the same barrel with you—I'm wearing them out of the same barrel.' Got my clothes entirely free for that winter."

"Can you always get all the aid you need for such enterprises?"

"Usually, and then I can earn a good deal of money when I work steadily. I can get a hundred and fifty dollars for a little yacht, you know, every time I find time to make one; and I can make a good deal of money out of fishing. I went out fishing here on the Fourth of July and caught two hundred blackfish—four and five pounds, almost, every one of them."

"That ought to be profitable," I said.

"Well, it was," he replied.

"How much did you get for them?"

"Oh, I didn't sell them," he said. "I never take money for my work that way. I gave them all away."

"What did you do?" I asked, laughing—"advertise for people to come for them?"

"No. My wife took some, and my daughters, and I took the rest and we carried them around to people that we thought would like to have them."

"Well, that wasn't so profitable, was it?" I commented amusedly.

"Yes, they were fine fish," he replied, not seeming to have heard me.

We dropped the subject of personal service at this point, and I expressed the opinion that his service was only a temporary expedient. Times changed, and with them, people. They forgot. Perhaps those he aided were none the better for accepting his charity.

"I know what you mean," he said. "But that don't make any difference. You just have to keep on giving, that's all, see? Not all of 'em turn back. It helps a lot. Money is the only dangerous thing to give—but I never give money—not very often. I give myself, rather, as much as possible. I give food and clothing, too, but I try to show 'em a new way—that's not money, you know. So many people need a new way. They're looking for it often, only they don't seem to know how. But God, dear brother, however poor or mean they are—He knows. You've got to reach the heart, you know, and I let Him help me. You've got to make a man over in his soul, if you want to help him, and money won't help you to do that, you know. No, it won't."

He looked up at me in clear-eyed faith. It was remarkable.

"Make them over?" I queried, still curious, for it was all like a romance, and rather fantastic to me. "What do you mean? How do you make them over?"

"Oh, in their attitude, that's how. You've got to change a man and bring him out of self-seeking if you really want to make him good. Most men are so tangled up in their own errors and bad ways, and so worried over their seekings, that unless you can set them to giving it's no use. They're always seeking, and they don't know what they want half the time. Money isn't the thing. Why, half of them wouldn't understand how to use it if they had it. Their minds are not bright enough. Their perceptions are not clear enough. All you can do is to make them content with themselves. And that, giving to others will do. I never saw the man or the woman yet who couldn't be happy if you could make them feel the need of living for others, of doing something for somebody besides themselves. It's a fact. Selfish people are never happy."

He rubbed his hands as if he saw the solution of the world's difficulties very clearly, and I said to him:

"Well, now, you've got a man out of the mire, and 'saved,' as you call it, and then what? What comes next?"

"Well, then he's saved," he replied. "Happiness comes next—content."

"I know. But must he go to church, or conform to certain rules?"

"No, no, no!" he replied sweetly. "Nothing to do except to be good to others. 'True religion and undefiled before our God and Father is this,'" he quoted, "'to visit the widow and the orphan in their affliction and to keep unspotted from the world. Charity is kind,' you know. 'Charity vaunteth not itself, is not puffed up, seeketh not its own.'"

"Well," I said, rather aimlessly, I will admit, for this high faith staggered me. (How high! How high!) "And then what?"

"Well, then the world would come about. It would be so much better. All the misery is in the lack of sympathy one with another. When we get that straightened out we can work in peace. There are lots of things to do, you know."

Yes, I thought, looking down on the mills and the driving force of self-interest—on greed, lust, love of pleasure, all their fantastic and yet moving dreams.

"I'm an ignorant man myself, and I don't know all," he went on, "and I'd like to study. My, but I'd like to look into all things, but I can't do it now. We can't stop until this thing is straightened out. Some time, maybe," and he looked peacefully away.

"By the way," I said, "whatever became of the man to whom you gave your rubber boots over on Fisher's Island?"

His face lit up as if it were the most natural thing that I should know about it.

"Say," he exclaimed, in the most pleased and confidential way, as if we were talking about a mutual friend, "I saw him not long ago. And, do you know, he's a good man now—really, he is. Sober and hard-working. And, say, would you believe it, he told me that I was the cause of it—just that miserable old pair of rubber boots—what do you think of that?"

I shook his hand at parting, and as we stood looking at each other in the shadow of the evening I asked him:

"Are you afraid to die?"

"Say, brother, but I'm not," he returned. "It hasn't any terror for me at all. I'm just as willing. My, but I'm willing."

He smiled and gripped me heartily again, and, as I was starting to go, said:

"If I die tonight, it'll be all right. He'll use me just as long as He needs me. That I know. Good-by."

"Good-by," I called back.

He hung by his fence, looking down upon the city. As I turned the next corner I saw him awakening from his reflection and waddling stolidly back into the house.

My Brother Paul

I like best to think of him as he was at the height of his all-too-brief reputation and success, when, as the author and composer of various American popular successes ("On the Banks of the Wabash," "Just Tell Them That You Saw Me," and various others), as a third owner of one of the most successful popular music publishing houses in the city and as an actor and playwright of some small repute, he was wont to spin like a moth in the white light of Broadway. By reason of a little luck and some talent he had come so far, done so much for himself. In his day he had been by turn a novitiate in a Western seminary which trained aspirants for the Catholic priesthood; a singer and entertainer with a perambulating cure-all oil troupe or wagon ("Hamlin's Wizard Oil") traveling throughout Ohio, Indiana and Illinois; both end- and middle-man with one, two or three different minstrel companies of repute; the editor or originator and author of a "funny column" in a Western small city paper; the author of the songs mentioned and a hundred others; a black-face monologue artist; a white-face ditto, at Tony Pastor's, Miner's and Niblo's of the old days; a comic lead; co-star and star in such melodramas and farces as "The Danger Signal," "The Two Johns," "A Tin Soldier," "The Midnight Bell," "A Green Goods Man" (a farce which he himself wrote, by the way), and others. The man had a genius for the kind of gayety, poetry and romance which may, and no doubt must be, looked upon as exceedingly middle-class but which nonetheless had as much charm as anything in this world can well have. He had at this time absolutely no cares or financial worries of any kind, and this plus his health, self-amusing disposition and talent for entertaining, made him a most fascinating figure to contemplate.

My first recollection of him is of myself as a boy often and he a man of twenty-five (my oldest brother). He had come back to the town in which we were then living solely to find his mother and help her. Six or seven years before he had left without any explanation as to where he was going, tired of or irritated by the routine of a home which for any genuine opportunity it offered him might as well never have existed. It was run dominantly by my father in the interest of religious and moral theories, with which this boy had little sympathy. He was probably not understood by any one save my mother, who understood or at least sympathized with us all. Placed in a school which was to turn him out a priest, he had decamped, and now seven years later was here in this small town, with fur coat and silk hat, a smart cane—a gentleman of the theatrical profession. He had joined a minstrel show somewhere and had become an "end-man." He had suspected that we were not as fortunate in this world's goods as might be and so had returned. His really great heart had called him.

But the thing which haunts me, and which was typical of him then as throughout life, was the spirit which he then possessed and conveyed. It was one of an agile geniality, unmarred by thought of a serious character but warm and genuinely tender and with a taste for simple beauty which was most impressive. He was already the author of a cheap songbook, "*The Paul Dresser Songster*" ("All the Songs Sung in the Show"), and some copies of this he had with him, one of which he gave me. But we having no musical instrument of any kind, he taught me some of the melodies "by ear." The home in which by force of poverty we were compelled to live was most unprepossessing and inconvenient, and the result of his coming could but be our request for, or at least the obvious need of, assistance. Still he was as much an enthusiastic part of it as though he belonged to it. He was happy in it, and the cause of his happiness was my mother, of whom he was intensely fond. I recall how he hung about her in the kitchen or wherever she happened to be, how enthusiastically he related all his plans for the future, his amusing difficulties in the past. He was very grand and youthfully self-important, or so we all thought, and still he patted her on the shoulder or put his arm about her and kissed her. Until she died years later she was truly his uppermost thought, crying with her at times over her troubles and his. He contributed regularly to her support and sent home all his cast-off clothing to be made over for the younger ones. (Bless her tired hands!)

As I look back now on my life, I realize quite clearly that of all the members of my family, subsequent to my mother's death, the only one who truly understood me, or, better yet, sympathized with my intellectual and artistic point of view, was, strange as it may seem, this same Paul, my dearest brother. Not that he was in any way fitted intellectually or otherwise to enjoy high forms of art and learning and so guide me, or that he understood, even in later years (long after I had written "Sister Carrie," for instance), what it was that I was attempting to do; he never did. His world was that of the popular song, the middle-class actor or comedian, the middle-class comedy, and such humorous æsthetes of the writing world as Bill Nye, Petroleum V. Nasby, the authors of the Spoopendyke Papers, and "Samantha at Saratoga." As far as I could make out—and I say this in no lofty, condescending spirit, by any means—he was entirely full of simple, middle-class romance, middle-class humor, middle-class tenderness and middle-class grossness, all of which I am very free to say early disarmed and won me completely and kept me so much his debtor that I should hesitate to try to acknowledge or explain all that he did for or meant to me.

Imagine, if you can, a man weighing all of three hundred pounds, not more than five feet ten-and-one-half inches in height and yet of so lithesome a build that he gave not the least sense of either undue weight or lethargy. His temperament, always ebullient and radiant, presented him as a clever, eager, cheerful, emotional and always highly illusioned person with so collie-like a warmth that one found him compelling interest and even admiration. Easily cast down at times by the most trivial matters, at others, and for the most part, he was so spirited and bubbly and emotional and sentimental that your fiercest or most gloomy intellectual rages or moods could scarcely withstand his smile. This tenderness or sympathy of his, a very human appreciation of the weaknesses and errors as well as the toils and tribulations of most of us, was by far his outstanding and most engaging quality, and gave him a very definite force and charm. Admitting, as I freely do, that he was very sensuous (gross, some people might have called him), that he had an intense, possibly an undue fondness for women, a frivolous, childish, horse-playish sense of humor at times, still he had other qualities which were absolutely adorable. Life seemed positively to spring up fountain-like in him. One felt in him a capacity to do (in his possibly limited field); an ability to achieve, whether he was doing so at the moment or not, and a supreme willingness to share and radiate his success—qualities exceedingly rare, I believe. Some people are so successful, and yet you know their success is purely selfish—exclusive, not inclusive; they never permit you to share in their lives. Not so my good brother. He was generous to the point of self-destruction, and that is literally true. He was the mark if not the prey of all those who desired much or little for nothing, those who previously might not have rendered him a service of any kind. He was all life and color, and thousands (I use the word with care) noted and commented on it.

When I first came to New York he was easily the foremost popular song-writer of the day and was the cause of my coming, so soon at least, having established himself in the publishing field and being so comfortably settled as to offer me a kind of anchorage in so troubled a commercial sea. I was very much afraid of New York, but with him here it seemed not so bad. The firm of which he was a part had a floor or two in an old residence turned office building, as so many are in New York, in Twentieth Street very close to Broadway, and here, during the summer months (1894-7) when the various theatrical road-companies, one of which he was always a part, had returned for the closed season, he was to be found aiding his concern in the reception and care of possible applicants for songs and attracting by his personality such virtuosi of the vaudeville and comedy stage as were likely to make the instrumental publications of his firm a success.

I may as well say here that he had no more business skill than a fly. At the same time, he was in no wise sycophantic where either wealth, power or fame was concerned. He considered himself a personage of sorts, and was. The minister, the moralist, the religionist, the narrow, dogmatic and self-centered in any field were likely to be the butt of his humor, and he could imitate so many phases of character so cleverly that he was the life of any idle pleasure-seeking party anywhere. To this day I recall his characterization of an old Irish washerwoman arguing; a stout, truculent German laying down the law; lean, gloomy, out-at-elbows actors of the Hamlet or classic school complaining of their fate; the stingy skinflint haggling over a dollar, and always with a skill for titillating the risibilities which is vivid to me even to this day. Other butts of his humor were the actor, the Irish day-laborer, the negro and the Hebrew. And how he could imitate them! It is useless to try to indicate such things in writing, the facial expression, the intonation, the gestures; these are not things of words. Perhaps I can best indicate the direction of his mind, if not his manner, by the following:

One night as we were on our way to a theater there stood on a nearby corner in the cold a blind man singing and at the same time holding out a little tin cup into which the coins of the charitably inclined were supposed to be dropped. At once my brother noticed him, for he had an eye for this sort of thing, the pathos of poverty as opposed to so gay a scene, the street with its hurrying theater crowds. At the same time, so inherently mischievous was his nature that although his sympathy for the suffering or the ill-used of fate was overwhelming, he could not resist combining his intended charity with a touch of the ridiculous.

"Got any pennies?" he demanded.

"Three or four."

Going over to an outdoor candystand he exchanged a quarter for pennies, then came back and waited until the singer, who had ceased singing, should begin a new melody. A custom of the singer's, since the song was of no import save as a means of attracting attention to him, was to interpolate a "Thank you" after each coin dropped in his cup and between the words of the song, regardless. It was this little idiosyncrasy which evidently had attracted my brother's attention, although it had not mine. Standing quite close, his pennies in his hand, he waited until the singer had resumed, then began dropping pennies, waiting each time for the "Thank you," which caused the song to go about as follows:

"Da-a-'ling" (Clink!—"Thank you!") "I am—" (Clink!—"Thank you!") "growing o-o-o-ld" (Clink!—"Thank you!"), "Silve-e-r—" (Clink!—"Thank you!") "threads among the—" (Clink!—"Thank you!") "go-o-o-ld—" (Clink! "Thank you!"). "Shine upon my-y" (Clink!—"Thank you!") "bro-o-ow toda-a-y" (Clink!—"Thank you!"), "Life is—" (Clink!—"Thank you!") "fading fast a-a-wa-a-ay" (Clink!—"Thank you!")—and so on ad infinitum, until finally the beggar himself seemed to hesitate a little and waver, only so solemn was his rôle of want and despair that of course he dared not but had to go on until the last penny was in, and until he was saying more "Thank yous" than words of the song. A passer-by noticing it had begun to "Haw-haw!", at which others joined in, myself included. The beggar himself, a rather sniveling specimen, finally realizing what a figure he was cutting with his song and thanks, emptied the coins into his hand and with an indescribably wry expression, half-uncertainty and half smile, exclaimed, "I'll have to thank you as long as you keep putting pennies in, I suppose. God bless you!"

My brother came away smiling and content.

However, it is not as a humorist or song-writer or publisher that I wish to portray him, but as an odd, lovable personality, possessed of so many interesting and peculiar and almost indescribable traits. Of all characters in fiction he perhaps most suggests Jack Falstaff, with his love of women, his bravado and bluster and his innate good nature and sympathy. Sympathy was really his outstanding characteristic, even more than humor, although the latter was always present. One might recite a thousand incidents of his generosity and out-of-hand charity, which contained no least thought of return or reward. I recall that once there was a boy who had been reared in one of the towns in which we had once lived who had never had a chance in his youth, educationally or in any other way, and, having turned out "bad" and sunk to the level of a bank robber, had been detected in connection with three other men in the act of robbing a bank, the watchman of which was subsequently killed in the mêlée and escape. Of all four criminals only this one had been caught. Somewhere in prison he had heard sung one of my brother's sentimental ballads, "The Convict and the Bird," and recollecting that he had known Paul wrote him, setting forth his life history and that now he had no money or friends.

At once my good brother was alive to the pathos of it. He showed the letter to me and wanted to know what could be done. I suggested a lawyer, of course, one of those brilliant legal friends of his—always he had enthusiastic admirers in all walks—who might take the case for little or nothing. There was the leader of Tammany Hall, Richard Croker, who could be reached, he being a friend of Paul's. There was the Governor himself to whom a plain recitation of the boy's unfortunate life might be addressed, and with some hope of profit.

All of these things he did, and more. He went to the prison (Sing Sing), saw the warden and told him the story of the boy's life, then went to the boy, or man, himself and gave him some money. He was introduced to the Governor through influential friends and permitted to tell the tale. There was much delay, a reprieve, a commutation of the death penalty to life imprisonment—the best that could be done. But he was so grateful for that, so pleased. You would have thought at the time that it was his own life that had been spared.

"Good heavens!" I jested. "You'd think you'd done the man an inestimable service, getting him in the penitentiary for life!"

"That's right," he grinned—an unbelievably provoking smile. "He'd better be dead, wouldn't he? Well, I'll write and ask him which he'd rather have."

I recall again taking him to task for going to the rescue of a "down and out" actor who had been highly successful and apparently not very sympathetic in his day, one of that more or less gaudy clan that wastes its substance, or so it seemed to me then, in riotous living. But now being old and entirely discarded and forgotten, he was in need of sympathy and aid. By some chance he knew Paul, or Paul had known him, and now because of the former's obvious prosperity—he was much in the papers at the time—he had appealed to him. The man lived with a sister in a wretched little town far out on Long Island. On receiving his appeal Paul seemed to wish to investigate for himself, possibly to indulge in a little lofty romance or sentiment. At any rate he wanted me to go along for the sake of companionship, so one dreary November afternoon we went, saw the pantaloon, who did not impress me very much even in his age and misery for he still had a few of his theatrical manners and insincerities, and as we were coming away I said, "Paul, why should you be the goat in every case?" for I had noted ever since I had been in New York, which was several years then, that he was a victim of many such importunities. If it was not the widow of a deceased friend who needed a ton of coal or a sack of flour, or the reckless, headstrong boy of parents too poor to save him from a term in jail or the reformatory and who asked for fine-money or an appeal to higher powers for clemency, or a wastrel actor or actress "down and out" and unable to "get back to New York" and requiring his or her railroad fare wired prepaid, it was the dead wastrel actor or actress who needed a coffin and a decent form of burial.

"Well, you know how it is, Thee" (he nearly always addressed me thus), "when you're old and sick. As long as you're up and around and have money, everybody's your friend. But once you're down and out no one wants to see you any more—see?" Almost amusingly he was always sad over those who had once been prosperous but who were now old and forgotten. Some of his silliest tender songs conveyed as much.

"Quite so," I complained, rather brashly, I suppose, "but why didn't he save a little money when he had it? He made as much as you'll ever make." The man had been a star. "He had plenty of it, didn't he? Why should he come to you?"

"Well, you know how it is, Thee," he explained in the kindliest and most apologetic way. "When you're young and healthy like that you don't think. I know how it is; I'm that way myself. We all have a little of it in us. I have; you have. And anyhow youth's the time to spend money if you're to get any good of it, isn't it? Of course when you're old you can't expect much, but still

I always feel as though I'd like to help some of these old people." His eyes at such times always seemed more like those of a mother contemplating a sick or injured child than those of a man contemplating life.

"But, Paul," I insisted on another occasion when he had just wired twenty-five dollars somewhere to help bury some one. (My spirit was not so niggardly as fearsome. I was constantly terrified in those days by the thought of a poverty-stricken old age for myself and him—why, I don't know. I was by no means incompetent.) "Why don't you save your money? Why should you give it to every Tom, Dick and Harry that asks you? You're not a charity organization, and you're not called upon to feed and clothe and bury all the wasters who happen to cross your path. If you were down and out how many do you suppose would help you?"

"Well, you know," and his voice and manner were largely those of mother, the same wonder, the same wistfulness and sweetness, the same bubbling charity and tenderness of heart, "I can't say I haven't got it, can I?" He was at the height of his success at the time. "And anyhow, what's the use being so hard on people? We're all likely to get that way. You don't know what pulls people down sometimes—not wasting always. It's thoughtlessness, or trying to be happy. Remember how poor we were and how mamma and papa used to worry." Often these references to mother or father or their difficulties would bring tears to his eyes. "I can't stand to see people suffer, that's all, not if I have anything," and his eyes glowed sweetly. "And, after all," he added apologetically, "the little I give isn't much. They don't get so much out of me. They don't come to me every day."

Another time—one Christmas Eve it was, when I was comparatively new to New York (my second or third year), I was a little uncertain what to do, having no connections outside of Paul and two sisters, one of whom was then out of the city. The other, owing to various difficulties of her own and a temporary estrangement from us—more our fault than hers—was therefore not available. The rather drab state into which she had allowed her marital affections to lead her was the main reason that kept us apart. At any rate I felt that I could not, or rather would not, go there. At the same time, owing to some difficulty or irritation with the publishing house of which my brother was then part owner (it was publishing the magazine which I was editing), we twain were also estranged, nothing very deep really—a temporary feeling of distance and indifference.

So I had no place to go except to my room, which was in a poor part of the town, or out to dine where best I might—some moderate-priced hotel, was my thought. I had not seen my brother in three or four days, but after I had strolled a block or two up Broadway I encountered him. I have always thought that he had kept an eye on me and had really followed me; was looking, in short, to see what I would do As usual he was most smartly and comfortably dressed.

"Where you going, Thee?" he called cheerfully.

"Oh, no place in particular," I replied rather suavely, I presume. "Just going up the street."

"Now, see here, sport," he began—a favorite expression of his, "sport"—with his face abeam, "what's the use you and me quarreling? It's Christmas Eve, ain't it? It's a shame! Come on, let's have a drink and then go out to dinner."

"Well," I said, rather uncompromisingly, for at times his seemingly extreme success and well-being irritated me, "I'll have a drink, but as for dinner I have another engagement."

"Aw, don't say that. What's the use being sore? You know I always feel the same even if we do quarrel at times. Cut it out. Come on. You know I'm your brother, and you're mine. It's all right with me, Thee. Let's make it up, will you? Put 'er there! Come on, now. We'll go and have a drink, see, something hot—it's Christmas Eve, sport. The old home stuff."

He smiled winsomely, coaxingly, really tenderly, as only he could smile. I "gave in." But now as we entered the nearest shining bar, a Christmas crowd buzzing within and without (it was the old Fifth Avenue Hotel), a new thought seemed to strike him.

"Seen E—— lately?" he inquired, mentioning the name of the troubled sister who was having a very hard time indeed. Her husband had left her and she was struggling over the care of two children.

"No," I replied, rather shamefacedly, "not in a week or two—maybe more."

He clicked his tongue. He himself had not been near her in a month or more. His face fell, and he looked very depressed.

"It's too bad—a shame really. We oughtn't to do this way, you know, sport. It ain't right. What do you say to our going around there," it was in the upper thirties, "and see how she's making out?—take her a few things, eh? Whaddya say?"

I hadn't a spare dollar myself, but I knew well enough what he meant by "take a few things" and who would pay for them.

"Well, we'll have to hurry if we want to get anything now," I urged, falling in with the idea since it promised peace, plenty and good will all around, and we rushed the drink and departed. Near at hand was a branch of one of the greatest grocery companies of the city, and near it, too, his then favorite hotel, the Continental. En route we meditated on the impossibility of delivery, the fact that we would have to carry the things ourselves, but he at last solved that by declaring that he could commandeer negro porters or bootblacks from the Continental. We entered, and by sheer smiles on his part and some blarney heaped upon a floor-manager, secured a turkey, sweet potatoes, peas, beans, a salad, a strip of bacon, a ham, plum pudding, a basket of luscious fruit and I know not what else—provender, I am sure, for a dozen meals. While it was being wrapped and packed in borrowed baskets, soon to be returned, he went across the way to the hotel and came back with three grinning darkies who for the tip they knew they would receive preceded us up Broadway, the nearest path to our destination. On the way a few additional things were picked up: holly wreaths, toys, candy, nuts—and then, really not knowing whether our plan might not mis-carry, we made our way through the side street and to the particular apartment, or, rather, flat-house, door, a most amusing Christmas procession, I fancy, wondering and worrying now whether she would be there.

But the door clicked in answer to our ring, and up we marched, the three darkies first, instructed to inquire for her and then insist on leaving the goods, while we lagged behind to see how she would take it.

The stage arrangement worked as planned. My sister opened the door and from the steps below we could hear her protesting that she had ordered nothing, but the door being open the negroes walked in and a moment or two afterwards ourselves. The packages were being piled on table and floor, while my sister, unable quite to grasp this sudden visitation and change of heart, stared.

"Just thought we'd come around and have supper with you, E———, and maybe dinner tomorrow if you'll let us," my brother chortled. "Merry Christmas, you know. Christmas Eve. The good old home stuff—see? Old sport here and I thought we couldn't stay away—tonight, anyhow."

He beamed on her in his most affectionate way, but she, suffering regret over the recent estrangement as well as the difficulties of life itself and the joy of this reunion, burst into tears, while the two little ones danced about, and he and I put our arms about her.

"There, there! It's all over now," he declared, tears welling in his eyes. "It's all off. We'll can this scrapping stuff. Thee and I are a couple of bums and we know it, but you can forgive us, can't you? We ought to be ashamed of ourselves, all of us, and that's the truth. We've been quarreling, too, haven't spoken for a week. Ain't that so, sport? But it's all right now, eh?"

There were tears in my eyes, too. One couldn't resist him. He had the power of achieving the tenderest results in the simplest ways. We then had supper, and breakfast the next morning, all staying and helping, even to the washing and drying of the dishes, and thereafter for I don't know how long we were all on the most affectionate terms, and he eventually died in this sister's home, ministered to with absolutely restless devotion by her for weeks before the end finally came.

But, as I have said, I always prefer to think of him at this, the very apex or tower window of his life. For most of this period he was gay and carefree. The music company of which he was a third owner was at the very top of its success. Its songs, as well as his, were everywhere. He had in turn at this time a suite at the Gilsey House, the Marlborough, the Normandie—always on Broadway, you see. The limelight district was his home. He rose in the morning to the clang of the cars and the honk of the automobiles outside; he retired at night as a gang of repair men under flaring torches might be repairing a track, or the milk trucks were rumbling to and from the ferries. He was in his way a public restaurant and hotel favorite, a shining light in the theater managers' offices, hotel bars and lobbies and wherever those flies of the Tenderloin, those passing lords and celebrities of the sporting, theatrical, newspaper and other worlds, are wont to gather. One of his intimates, as I now recall, was "Bat" Masterson, the Western and now retired (to Broadway!) bad man; Muldoon, the famous wrestler; Tod Sloan, the jockey; "Battling" Nelson; James J. Corbett; Kid McCoy; Terry McGovern—prize-fighters all. Such Tammany district leaders as James Murphy, "The" McManus, Chrystie and Timothy Sullivan, Richard Carroll, and even Richard Croker, the then reigning Tammany boss, were all on his visiting list. He went to their meetings, rallies and district doings generally to sing and play, and they came to his "office" occasionally. Various high and mighties of the Roman Church, "fathers" with fine parishes and good wine cellars, and judges of various municipal courts, were also of his peculiar world. He was always running to one or the other "to get somebody out," or they to him to get him to contribute something to something, or to sing and play or act, and betimes they were meeting each other in hotel grills or elsewhere and having a drink and telling "funny stories."

Apropos of this sense of humor of his, this love of horse-play almost, I remember that once he had a new story to tell—a vulgar one of course—and with it he had been making me and a dozen others laugh until the tears coursed down our cheeks. It seemed new to everybody and, true to his rather fantastic moods, he was determined to be the first to tell it along Broadway. For some reason he was anxious to have me go along with him, possibly because he found me at that time an unvarying fountain of approval and laughter, possibly because he liked to show me off as his rising brother, as he insisted that I was. At between six and seven of a spring or summer evening, therefore, we issued from his suite at the Gilsey House, whither he had returned to dress, and invading the bar below were at once centered among a group who knew him. A whiskey, a cigar, the story told to one, two, three, five, ten to roars of laughter, and we were off, over the way to Weber & Fields (the Musical Burlesque House Supreme of those days) in the same block, where to the ticket seller and house manager, both of whom he knew, it was told. More laughter, a cigar perhaps. Then we were off again, this time to the ticket seller of Palmer's Theater at Thirtieth Street, thence to the bar of the Grand Hotel at Thirty-first, the Imperial at Thirty-second, the Martinique at Thirty-third, a famous drug-store at the southwest corner of Thirty-fourth and Broadway, now gone of course, the manager of which was a friend of his. It was a warm, moony night, and he took a glass of vichy "for looks' sake," as he said.

Then to the quondam Hotel Aulic at Thirty-fifth and Broadway—the center and home of the then much-berated "Hotel Aulic or Actors' School of Philosophy," and a most impressive actors' rendezvous where might have been seen in the course of an evening all the "second leads" and "light comedians" and "heavies" of this, that and the other road company, all blazing with startling clothes and all explaining how they "knocked 'em" here and there: in Peoria, Pasadena, Walla-Walla and where not. My brother shone like a star when only one is in the sky.

Over the way then to the Herald Building, its owls' eyes glowing in the night, its presses thundering, the elevated thundering beside it. Here was a business manager whom he knew. Then to the Herald Square Theater on the opposite side of the street, ablaze with a small electric sign—among the newest in the city. In this, as in the business office of the *Herald* was another manager, and he knew them all. Thence to the Marlborough bar and lobby at Thirty-sixth, the manager's office of the Knickerbocker Theater at Thirty-eighth, stopping at the bar and lobby of the Normandie, where some blazing professional beauty of the stage waylaid him and exchanged theatrical witticisms with him—and what else? Thence to the manager's office of the Casino at Thirty-ninth, some bar which was across the street, another in Thirty-ninth west of Broadway, an Italian restaurant on the ground floor of the Metropolitan at Fortieth and Broadway, and at last but by no means least and by such slow stages to the very door of the then Mecca of Meccas of all theater- and sportdom, the sanctum sanctorum of all those sportively au fait, "wise," the "real thing"—the Hotel Metropole at Broadway and Forty-second Street, the then extreme northern limit of the white-light district. And what a realm! Rounders and what not were here ensconced at round tables, their backs against the leather-cushioned wall seats, the adjoining windows open to all Broadway and the then all but somber Forty-second Street.

It was wonderful, the loud clothes, the bright straw hats, the canes, the diamonds, the "hot" socks, the air of security and well-being, so easily assumed by those who gain an all too brief hour in this pretty, petty world of make-believe and pleasure and pseudo-fame. Among them my dearest brother was at his best. It was "Paul" here and "Paul" there—"Why, hello, Dresser, you're just in time! Come on in. What'll you have? Let me tell you something, Paul, a good one—". More drinks, cigars, tales—magnificent tales of successes made, "great shows" given, fights, deaths, marvelous winnings at cards, trickeries in racing, prize-fighting; the "dogs" that some people were, the magnificent, magnanimous "God's own salt" that others were. The oaths, stories of women, what low, vice-besmeared, crime-soaked ghoulas certain reigning beauties of the town or stage were—and so on and so on ad infinitum.

But his story?—ah, yes. I had all but forgotten. It was told in every place, not once but seven, eight, nine, ten times. We did not eat until we reached the Metropole, and it was ten-thirty when we reached it! The handshakes, the road stories—"This is my brother Theodore. He writes; he's a newspaper man." The roars of laughter, the drinks! "Ah, my boy, that's good, but let me tell you one—one that I heard out in Louisville the other day." A seedy, shabby ne'er-do-well of a song-writer maybe stopping the successful author in the midst of a tale to borrow a dollar. Another actor, shabby and distrait, reciting the sad tale of a year's misfortunes. Everywhere my dear brother was called to, slapped on the back, chuckled with. He was successful. One of his best songs was the rage, he had an interest in a going musical concern, he could confer benefits, favors.

Ah, me! Ah, me! That one could be so great, and that it should not last for ever and for ever!

Another of his outstanding characteristics was his love of women, a really amusing and at times ridiculous quality. He was always sighing over the beauty, innocence, sweetness, this and that, of young maidenhood in his songs, but in real life he seemed to desire and attract quite a different type— the young and beautiful, it is true, but also the old, the homely and the somewhat savage—a catholicity of taste I could never quite stomach. It was "Paul dearest" here and "Paul dearest" there, especially in his work in connection with the music-house and the stage. In the former, popular ballad singers of both sexes, some of the women most attractive and willful, were most numerous, coming in daily from all parts of the world apparently to find songs which they could sing on the American or even the English stage. And it was a part of his duty, as a member of the firm and the one who principally "handled" the so-called professional inquirers, to meet them and see that they were shown what the catalogue contained. Occasionally there was an aspiring female song-writer, often mere women visitors.

Regardless, however, of whether they were young, old, attractive or repulsive, male or female, I never knew any one whose manner was more uniformly winsome or who seemed so easily to disarm or relax an indifferent or irritated mood. He was positive sunshine, the same in quality as that of a bright spring morning. His blue eyes focused mellowly, his lips were tendrilled with smiles. He had a brisk, quick manner, always somehow suggestive of my mother, who was never brisk.

And how he fascinated them, the women! Their quite shameless daring where he was concerned! Positively, in the face of it I used to wonder what had become of all the vaunted and so-called "stabilizing morality" of the world. None of it seemed to be in the possession of these women, especially the young and beautiful. They were distant and freezing enough to all who did not interest them, but let a personality such as his come into view and they were all wiles, bending and alluring graces. It was so obvious, this fascination he had for them and they for him, that at times it took on a comic look.

"Get onto the hit he's making," one would nudge another and remark.

"Say, some tenderness, that!" This in reference to a smile or a melting glance on the part of a female.

"Nothing like a way with the ladies. Some baby, eh, boys?"—this following the flick of a skirt and a backward-tossed glance perhaps, as some noticeable beauty passed out.

"No wonder he's cheerful," a sour and yet philosophic vaudevillian, who was mostly out of a job and hung about the place for what free meals he could obtain, once remarked to me in a heavy and morose undertone. "If I had that many women crazy about me I'd be too."

And the results of these encounters with beauty! Always he had something most important to attend to, morning, noon or night, and whenever I encountered him after some such statement "the important thing" was, of course, a woman. As time went on and he began to look upon me as something more than a thin, spindling, dyspeptic and disgruntled youth, he began to wish to introduce me to some of his marvelous followers, and then I could see how completely dependent upon beauty in the flesh he was, how it made his life and world.

One day as we were all sitting in the office, a large group of vaudevillians, song-writers, singers, a chance remark gave rise to a subsequent practical joke at Paul's expense. "I'll bet," observed some one, "that if a strange man were to rush in here with a revolver and say, 'Where's the man that seduced my wife?' Paul would be the first to duck. He wouldn't wait to find out whether he was the one meant or not."

Much laughter followed, and some thought. The subject of this banter was, of course, not present at the time. There was one actor who hung about there who was decidedly skillful in make-up. On more than one occasion he had disguised himself there in the office for our benefit. Coöperating with us, he disguised himself now as a very severe and even savage-looking person of about thirty-five—side-burns, mustachios and goatee. Then, with our aid, timing his arrival to an hour when Paul was certain to be at his desk, he entered briskly and vigorously and, looking about with a savage air, demanded, "Where is Paul Dresser?"

The latter turned almost apprehensively, I thought, and at once seemed by no means captivated by the man's looks.

"That's Mr. Dresser there," explained one of the confederates most willingly.

The stranger turned and glared at him. "So you're the scoundrel that's been running around with my wife, are you?" he demanded, approaching him and placing one hand on his right hip.

Paul made no effort to explain. It did not occur to him to deny the allegation, although he had never seen the man before. With a rising and backward movement he fell against the rail behind him, lifting both hands in fright and exclaiming, "Why—why—Don't shoot!" His expression was one of guilt, astonishment, perplexity. As some one afterwards said, "As puzzled as if he was trying to discover which injured husband it might be." The shout that went up—for it was agreed beforehand that the joke must not be carried far—convinced him that a hoax had been perpetrated, and the removal by the actor of his hat, sideburns and mustache revealed the true character of the injured husband. At first inclined to be angry and sulky, later on he saw the humor of his own indefinite position in the matter and laughed as heartily as any. But I fancy it developed a strain of uncertainty in him also in regard to injured husbands, for he was never afterwards inclined to interest himself in the much-married, and gave such wives a wide berth.

But his great forte was of course his song-writing, and of this, before I speak of anything else, I wish to have my say. It was a gift, quite a compelling one, out of which, before he died, he had made thousands, all spent in the manner described. Never having the least power to interpret anything in a fine musical way, still he was always full of music of a tender, sometimes sad, sometimes gay, kind—that of the ballad-maker of a nation. He was constantly attempting to work them out of himself, not quickly but slowly, brooding as it were over the piano wherever he might find one and could have a little solitude, at times on the organ (his favorite instrument), improvising various sad or wistful strains, some of which he jotted down, others of which, having mastered, he strove to fit words to. At such times he preferred to be alone or with some one whose temperament in no way clashed but rather harmonized with his own. Living with one of my sisters for a period of years, he had a room specially fitted up for his composing work, a very small room for so very large a man, within which he would shut himself and thrum a melody by the hour, especially toward evening or at night. He seemed to have a peculiar fondness for the twilight hour, and at this time might thrum over one strain and another until over some particular one, a new song usually, he would be in tears!

And what pale little things they were really, mere bits and scraps of sentiment and melodrama in story form, most asinine sighings over home and mother and lost sweethearts and dead heroes such as never were in real life, and yet with something about them, in the music at least, which always appealed to me intensely and must have appealed to others, since they attained so wide a circulation. They bespoke, as I always felt, a wistful, seeking, uncertain temperament, tender and illusioned, with no practical knowledge of any side of life, but full of a true poetic feeling for the mystery and pathos of life and death, the wonder of the waters, the stars, the flowers, accidents of life, success, failure. Beginning with a song called "Wide Wings" (published by a small retail music-house in Evansville, Indiana), and followed by such national successes as "The Letter That Never Came," "I Believe It, For My Mother Told Me So" (!), "The Convict and the Bird," "The Pardon Came Too Late," "Just Tell Them That You Saw Me," "The Blue and the Grey," "On the Bowery," "On the Banks of the Wabash," and a number of others, he was never content to rest and never really happy, I think, save when composing. During this time, however, he was at different periods all the things I have described—a black-face monologue artist, an end- and at times a middle-man, a publisher, and so on.

I recall being with him at the time he composed two of his most famous successes: "Just Tell Them That You Saw Me," and "On the Banks of the Wabash," and noting his peculiar mood, almost amounting to a deep depression which ended a little later in marked elation or satisfaction, once he had succeeded in evoking something which really pleased him.

The first of these songs must have followed an actual encounter with some woman or girl whose life had seemingly if not actually gone to wreck on the shore of love or passion. At any rate he came into the office of his publishing house one gray November Sunday afternoon—it was our custom to go there occasionally, a dozen or more congenial souls, about as one might go to a club—and going into a small room which was fitted up with a piano as a "try-out" room (professionals desiring a song were frequently taught it in the office), he began improvising, or rather repeating over and over, a certain strain which was evidently in his mind. A little while later he came out and said, "Listen to this, will you, Thee?"

He played and sang the first verse and chorus. In the middle of the latter, so moved was he by the sentiment of it, his voice broke and he had to stop. Tears stood in his eyes and he wiped them away. A moment or two later he was able to go through it without wavering and I thought it charming for the type of thing it was intended to be. Later on (the following spring) I was literally astonished to see how, after those various efforts usually made by popular music publishers to make a song "go"—advertising it in the *Clipper* and *Mirror*, getting various vaudeville singers to sing it, and so forth—it suddenly began to sell, thousands upon thousands of copies being wrapped in great bundles under my very eyes and shipped express or freight to various parts of the country. Letters and telegrams, even, from all parts of the nation began to pour in—"Forward express today —— copies of Dresser's 'Tell Them That You Saw Me.'" The firm was at once as busy as a bee-hive, on "easy street" again, as the expression went, "in clover." Just before this there had been a slight slump in its business and in my brother's finances, but now once more he was his most engaging self. Every one in that layer of life which understands or takes an interest in popular songs and their creators knew of him and his song, his latest success. He was, as it were, a revivified figure on Broadway. His barbers, barkeepers, hotel clerks, theatrical box-office clerks, hotel managers and the stars and singers of the street knew of it and him. Some enterprising button firm got out a button on which the phrase was printed. Comedians on the stage, newspaper paragraphers, his bank teller or his tailor, even staid business men wishing to appear "up-to-date," used it as a parting salute. The hand-organs, the bands and the theater orchestras everywhere were using it. One could scarcely turn a corner or go into a cheap music hall or variety house without hearing a parody of it. It was wonderful, the enormous furore that it seemed to create, and of course my dear brother was privileged to walk about smiling and secure, his bank account large, his friends numerous, in the pink of health, and gloating over the fact that he was a success, well known, a genuine creator of popular songs.

It was the same with "On the Banks of the Wabash," possibly an even greater success, for it came eventually to be adopted by his native State as its State song, and in that region streets and a town were named after him. In an almost unintentional and unthinking way I had a hand in that, and it has always cheered me to think that I had, although I have never had the least talent for musical composition or song versification. It was one of those delightful summer Sunday mornings (1896, I believe), when I was still connected with his firm as editor of the little monthly they were issuing, and he and myself, living with my sister E——, that we had gone over to this office to do a little work. I had a number of current magazines I wished to examine; he was always wishing to compose something, to express that ebullient and emotional soul of his in some way.

"What do you suppose would make a good song these days?" he asked in an idle, meditative mood, sitting at the piano and thrumming while I at a nearby table was looking over my papers. "Why don't you give me an idea for one once in a while, sport? You ought to be able to suggest something."

"Me?" I queried, almost contemptuously, I suppose. I could be very lofty at times in regard to his work, much as I admired him—vain and yet more or less dependent snip that I was. "I can't write those things. Why don't you write something about a State or a river? Look at 'My Old Kentucky Home,' 'Dixie,' 'Old Black Joe'—why don't you do something like that, something that suggests a part of America? People like that. Take Indiana—what's the matter with it—the Wabash River? It's as good as any other river, and you were 'raised' beside it."

I have to smile even now as I recall the apparent zest or feeling with which all at once he seized on this. It seemed to appeal to him immensely. "That's not a bad idea," he agreed, "but how would you go about it? Why don't you write the words and let me put the music to them? We'll do it together!"

"But I can't," I replied. "I don't know how to do those things. You write it. I'll help—maybe."

After a little urging—I think the fineness of the morning had as much to do with it as anything—I took a piece of paper and after meditating a while scribbled in the most tentative manner imaginable the first verse and chorus of that song almost as it was published. I think one or two lines were too long or didn't rhyme, but eventually either he or I hammered them into shape, but before that I rather shamefacedly turned them over to him, for somehow I was convinced that this work was not for me and that I was rather loftily and cynically attempting what my good brother would do in all faith and feeling.

He read it, insisted that it was fine and that I should do a second verse, something with a story in it, a girl perhaps—a task which I solemnly rejected.

"No, you put it in. It's yours. I'm through."

Some time later, disagreeing with the firm as to the conduct of the magazine, I left—really was forced out—which raised a little feeling on my part; not on his, I am sure, for I was very difficult to deal with.

Time passed and I heard nothing. I had been able to succeed in a somewhat different realm, that of the magazine contributor, and although I thought a great deal of my brother I paid very little attention to him or his affairs, being much more concerned with my own. One spring night, however, the following year, as I was lying in my bed trying to sleep, I heard a quartette of boys in the distance approaching along the street in which I had my room. I could not make out the words at first but the melody at once attracted my attention. It was plaintive and compelling. I listened, attracted, satisfied that it was some new popular success that had "caught on." As they drew near my window I heard the words "On the Banks of the Wabash" most mellifluously harmonized.

I jumped up. They were my words! It was Paul's song! He had another "hit" then—"On the Banks of the Wabash," and they were singing it in the streets already! I leaned out of the window and listened as they approached and passed on, their arms about each other's shoulders, the whole song being sung in the still street, as it were, for my benefit. The night was so warm, delicious. A full moon was overhead. I was young, lonely, wistful. It brought back so much of my already spent youth that I was ready to cry—for joy principally. In three more months it was everywhere, in the papers, on the stage, on the street-organs, played by orchestras, bands, whistled and sung in the streets. One day on Broadway near the Marlborough I met my brother, gold-headed cane, silk shirt, a smart summer suit, a gay straw hat.

"Ah," I said, rather sarcastically, for I still felt peeved that he had shown so little interest in my affairs at the time I was leaving. "On the banks, I see."

"On the banks," he replied cordially. "You turned the trick for me, Thee, that time. What are you doing now? Why don't you ever come and see me? I'm still your brother, you know. A part of that is really yours."

"Cut that!" I replied most savagely. "I couldn't write a song like that in a million years. You know I couldn't. The words are nothing."

"Oh, all right. It's true, though, you know. Where do you keep yourself? Why don't you come and see me? Why be down on me? I live here, you know." He looked up at the then brisk and successful hotel.

"Well, maybe I will some time," I said distantly, but with no particular desire to mend matters, and we parted.

There was, however, several years later, a sequel to all this and one so characteristic of him that it has always remained in my mind as one of the really beautiful things of life, and I might as well tell it here and now. About five years later I had become so disappointed in connection with my work and the unfriendly pressure of life that I had suffered what subsequently appeared to have been a purely psychic breakdown or relapse, not physical, but one which left me in no mood or condition to go on with my work, or any work indeed in any form. Hope had disappeared in a sad haze. I could apparently succeed in nothing, do nothing mentally that was worth while. At the same time I had all but retired from the world, living on less and less until finally I had descended into those depths where I was in the grip of actual want, with no place to which my pride would let me turn. I had always been too vain and self-centered. Apparently there was but one door, and I was very close to it. To match my purse I had retired to a still sorrier neighborhood in B——, one of the poorest. I desired most of all to be let alone, to be to myself. Still I could not be, for occasionally I met people, and certain prospects and necessities drove me to various publishing houses. One day as I was walking in some street near Broadway (not on it) in New York, I ran into my brother quite by accident, he as prosperous and comfortable as ever. I think I resented him more than ever. He was of course astonished, shocked, as I could plainly see, by my appearance and desire not to be seen. He demanded to know where I was living, wanted me to come then and there and stay with him, wanted me to tell him what the trouble was—all of which I rather stubbornly refused to do and finally got away—not however without giving him my address, though with the caution that I wanted nothing.

The next morning he was there bright and early in a cab. He was the most vehement, the most tender, the most disturbed creature I have ever seen. He was like a distrait mother with a sick child more than anything else.

"For God's sake," he commented when he saw me, "living in a place like this—and at this number, too!" (130 it was, and he was superstitious as to the thirteen.) "I knew there'd be a damned thirteen in it!" he ejaculated. "And me over in New York! Jesus Christ! And you sick and run down this way! I might have known. It's just like you. I haven't heard a thing about you in I don't know when. Well, I'm not going back without you, that's all. You've got to come with me now, see? Get your clothes, that's all. The cabby'll take your trunk. I know just the place for you, and you're going there tomorrow or next day or next week, but you're coming with me now. My God, I should think you'd be ashamed of yourself, and me feeling the way I do about you!" His eyes all but brimmed.

I was so morose and despondent that, grateful as I felt, I could scarcely take his mood at its value. I resented it, resented myself, my state, life.

"I can't," I said finally, or so I thought. "I won't. I don't need your help. You don't owe me anything. You've done enough already."

"Owe, hell!" he retorted. "Who's talking about 'owe'? And you my brother— my own flesh and blood! Why, Thee, for that matter, I owe you half of 'On the Banks,' and you know it. You can't go on living like this. You're sick and discouraged. You can't fool me. Why, Thee, you're a big man. You've just got to come out of this! Damn it—don't you see—don't make me"—and he took out his handkerchief and wiped his eyes. "You can't help yourself now, but you can later, don't you see? Come on. Get your things. I'd never forgive myself if I didn't. You've got to come, that's all. I won't go without you," and he began looking about for my bag and trunk.

I still protested weakly, but in vain. His affection was so overwhelming and tender that it made me weak. I allowed him to help me get my things together. Then he paid the bill, a small one, and on the way to the hotel insisted on forcing a roll of bills on me, all that he had with him. I was compelled at once, that same day or the next, to indulge in a suit, hat, shoes, underwear, all that I needed. A bedroom adjoining his suite at the hotel was taken, and for two days I lived there, later accompanying him in his car to a famous sanitarium in Westchester, one in charge of an old friend of his, a well-known ex-wrestler whose fame for this sort of work was great. Here I was booked for six weeks, all expenses paid, until I should "be on my feet again," as he expressed it. Then he left, only to visit and revisit me until I returned to the city, fairly well restored in nerves if not in health.

But could one ever forget the mingled sadness and fervor of his original appeal, the actual distress written in his face, the unlimited generosity of his mood and deed as well as his unmerited self-denunciation? One pictures such tenderness and concern as existing between parents and children, but rarely between brothers. Here he was evincing the same thing, as soft as love itself, and he a man of years and some affairs and I an irritable, distrait and peevish soul.

Take note, ye men of satire and spleen. All men are not selfish or hard.

The final phase of course related to his untimely end. He was not quite fifty-five when he died, and with a slightly more rugged quality of mind he might have lasted to seventy. It was due really to the failure of his firm (internal dissensions and rivalries, in no way due to him, however, as I have been told) and what he foolishly deemed to be the end of his financial and social glory. His was one of those simple, confiding, non-hardy dispositions, warm and colorful but intensely sensitive, easily and even fatally chilled by the icy blasts of human difficulty, however slight. You have no doubt seen some animals, cats, dogs, birds, of an especially affectionate nature, which when translated to a strange or unfriendly climate soon droop and die. They have no spiritual resources wherewith to contemplate what they do not understand or know. Now his friends would leave him. Now that bright world of which he had been a part would know him no more. It was pathetic, really. He emanated a kind of fear. Depression and even despair seemed to hang about him like a cloak. He could not shake it off. And yet, literally, in his case there was nothing to fear, if he had only known.

And yet two years before he did die, I knew he would. Fantastic as it may seem, to be shut out from that bright world of which he deemed himself an essential figure was all but unendurable. He had no ready money now—not the same amount anyhow. He could not greet his old-time friends so gayly, entertain so freely. Meeting him on Broadway shortly after the failure and asking after his affairs, he talked of going into business for himself as a publisher, but I realized that he could not. He had neither the ability nor the talent for that, nor the heart. He was not a business man but a song-writer and actor, had never been anything but that. He tried in this new situation to write songs, but he could not. They were too morbid. What he needed was some one to buoy him up, a manager, a strong confidant of some kind, some one who would have taken his affairs in hand and shown him what to do. As it was he had no one. His friends, like winter-frightened birds, had already departed. Personally, I was in no position to do anything at the time, being more or less depressed myself and but slowly emerging from difficulties which had held me for a number of years.

About a year or so after he failed my sister E—— announced that Paul had been there and that he was coming to live with her. He could not pay so much then, being involved with all sorts of examinations of one kind and another, but neither did he have to. Her memory was not short; she gave him the fullness of her home. A few months later he was ostensibly connected with another publishing house, but by then he was feeling so poorly physically and was finding consolation probably in some drinking and the caresses of those feminine friends who have, alas, only caresses to offer. A little later I met a doctor who said, "Paul cannot live. He has pernicious anæmia. He is breaking down inside and doesn't know it. He can't last long. He's too depressed." I knew it was so and what the remedy was—money and success once more, the petty pettings and flattery of that little world of which he had been a part but which now was no more for him. Of all those who had been so lavish in their greetings and companionship earlier in his life, scarcely one, so far as I could make out, found him in that retired world to which he was forced. One or two pegged-out actors sought him and borrowed a little of the little that he had; a few others came when he had nothing at all. His partners, quarreling among themselves and feeling that they had done him an injustice, remained religiously away. He found, as he often told my sister, broken horse-shoes (a "bad sign"), met cross-eyed women, another "bad sign," was pursued apparently by the inimical number thirteen—and all these little straws depressed him horribly. Finally, being no longer strong enough to be about, he took to his bed and remained there days at a time, feeling well while in bed but weak when up. For a little while he would go "downtown" to see this, that and the other person, but would soon return. One day on coming back home he found one of his hats lying on his bed, accidentally put there by one of the children, and according to my sister, who was present at the time, he was all but petrified by the sight of it. To him it was the death-sign. Some one had told him so not long before!!!

Then, not incuriously, seeing the affectional tie that had always held us, he wanted to see me every day. He had a desire to talk to me about his early life, the romance of it—maybe I could write a story some time, tell something about him! (Best of brothers, here it is, a thin little flower to lay at your feet!) To please him I made notes, although I knew most of it. On these occasions he was always his old self, full of ridiculous stories, quips and slight *mots*, all in his old and best vein. He would soon be himself, he now insisted.

Then one evening in late November, before I had time to call upon him (I lived about a mile away), a hurry-call came from E——. He had suddenly died at five in the afternoon; a blood-vessel had burst in the head. When I arrived he was already cold in death, his soft hands folded over his chest, his face turned to one side on the pillow, that indescribable sweetness of expression about the eyes and mouth—the empty shell of the beetle. There were tears, a band of reporters from the papers, the next day obituary news articles, and after that a host of friends and flowers, flowers, flowers. It is amazing what satisfaction the average mind takes in standardized floral forms—broken columns and gates ajar!

Being ostensibly a Catholic, a Catholic sister-in-law and other relatives insistently arranged for a solemn high requiem mass at the church of one of his favorite rectors. All Broadway was there, more flowers, his latest song read from the altar. Then there was a carriage procession to a distant Catholic graveyard somewhere, his friend, the rector of the church, officiating at the grave. It was so cold and dreary there, horrible. Later on he was removed to Chicago.

But still I think of him as not there or anywhere in the realm of space, but on Broadway between Twenty-ninth and Forty-second Streets, the spring and summer time at hand, the doors of the grills and bars of the hotels open, the rout of actors and actresses ambling to and fro, his own delicious presence dressed in his best, his "funny" stories, his songs being ground out by the hand organs, his friends extending their hands, clapping him on the shoulder, cackling over the latest idle yarn.

Ah, Broadway! Broadway! And you, my good brother! Here is the story that you wanted me to write, this little testimony to your memory, a pale, pale symbol of all I think and feel. Where are the thousand yarns I have laughed over, the music, the lights, the song?

Peace, peace. So shall it soon be with all of us. It was a dream. It is. I am. You are. And shall we grieve over or hark back to dreams?

The County Doctor

How well I remember him—the tall, grave, slightly bent figure, the head like Plato's or that of Diogenes, the mild, kindly, brown-gray eyes peering, all too kindly, into the faces of dishonest men. In addition, he wore long, full, brown-gray whiskers, a long gray overcoat (soiled and patched toward the last) in winter, a soft black hat that hung darkeningly over his eyes. But what a doctor! And how simple and often non-drug-storey were so many of his remedies!

"My son, your father is very sick. Now, I'll tell you what you can do for me. You go out here along the Cheevertown road about a mile or two and ask any farmer this side of the creek to let you have a good big handful of peach sprigs—about so many, see? Say that Doctor Gridley said he was to give them to you for him. Then, Mrs. ——, when he brings them, you take a few, not more than seven or eight, and break them up and steep them in hot water until you have an amber-colored tea. Give Mr. —— about three or four tea-spoonfuls of that every three or four hours, and I hope we'll find he'll do better. This kidney case is severe, I know, but he'll come around all right."

And he did. My father had been very ill with gall stones, so weak at last that we thought he was sure to die. The house was so somber at the time. Over it hung an atmosphere of depression and fear, with pity for the sufferer, and groans of distress on his part. And then there were the solemn visits of the doctor, made pleasant by his wise, kindly humor and his hopeful predictions and ending in this seemingly mild prescription, which resulted, in this case, in a cure. He was seemingly so remote at times, in reality so near, and wholly thoughtful.

On this occasion I went out along the long, cold, country road of a March evening. I was full of thoughts of his importance as a doctor. He seemed so necessary to us, as he did to everybody. I knew nothing about medicine, or how lives were saved, but I felt sure that he did and that he would save my father in spite of his always conservative, speculative, doubtful manner. What a wonderful man he must be to know all these things—that peach sprouts, for instance, were an antidote to the agony of gall stones!

As I walked along, the simplicity of country life and its needs and deprivations were impressed upon me, even though I was so young. So few here could afford to pay for expensive prescriptions—ourselves especially— and Dr. Gridley knew that and took it into consideration, so rarely did he order anything from a drug-store. Most often, what he prescribed he took out of a case, compounded, as it were, in our presence.

A brisk wind had fluttered snow in the morning, and now the ground was white, with a sinking red sun shining across it, a sense of spring in the air. Being unknown to these farmers, I wondered if any one of them would really cut me a double handful of fresh young peach sprigs or suckers from their young trees, as the doctor had said. Did they really know him? Some one along the road—a home-driving farmer—told me of an old Mr. Mills who had a five-acre orchard farther on. In a little while I came to his door and was confronted by a thin, gaunt, bespectacled woman, who called back to a man inside:

"Henry, here's a little boy says Dr. Gridley said you were to cut him a double handful of peach sprigs."

Henry now came forward—a tall, bony farmer in high boots and an old wool-lined leather coat, and a cap of wool.

"Dr. Gridley sent cha, did he?" he observed, eyeing me most critically.

"Yes, sir."

"What's the matter? What does he want with 'em? Do ya know?"

"Yes, sir. My father's sick with kidney trouble, and Dr. Gridley said I was to come out here."

"Oh, all right. Wait'll I git my big knife," and back he went, returning later with a large horn-handled knife, which he opened. He preceded me out through the barn lot and into the orchard beyond.

"Dr. Gridley sent cha, did he, huh?" he asked as he went. "Well, I guess we all have ter comply with whatever the doctor orders. We're all apt ter git sick now an' ag'in," and talking trivialities of a like character, he cut me an armful, saying: "I might as well give ya too many as too few. Peach sprigs! Now, I never heered o' them bein' good fer anythin', but I reckon the doctor knows what he's talkin' about. He usually does—or that's what we think around here, anyhow."

In the dusk I trudged home with my armful, my fingers cold. The next morning, the tea having been brewed and taken, my father was better. In a week or two he was up and around, as well as ever, and during this time he commented on the efficacy of this tea, which was something new to him, a strange remedy, and which caused the whole incident to be impressed upon my mind. The doctor had told him that at any time in the future if he was so troubled and could get fresh young peach sprigs for a tea, he would find that it would help him. And the drug expense was exactly nothing.

In later years I came to know him better—this thoughtful, crusty, kindly soul, always so ready to come at all hours when his cases permitted, so anxious to see that his patients were not taxed beyond their financial resources.

I remember once, one of my sisters being very ill, so ill that we were beginning to fear death, one and another of us had to take turn sitting up with her at night to help and to give her her medicine regularly. During one of the nights when I was sitting up, dozing, reading and listening to the wind in the pines outside, she seemed persistently to get worse. Her fever rose, and she complained of such aches and pains that finally I had to go and call my mother. A consultation with her finally resulted in my being sent for Dr. Gridley—no telephones in those days—to tell him, although she hesitated so to do, how sister was and ask him if he would not come.

I was only fourteen. The street along which I had to go was quite dark, the town lights being put out at two a.m., for reasons of thrift perhaps. There was a high wind that cried in the trees. My shoes on the board walks, here and there, sounded like the thuds of a giant. I recall progressing in a shivery ghost-like sort of way, expecting at any step to encounter goblins of the most approved form, until finally the well-known outlines of the house of the doctor on the main street—yellow, many-roomed, a wide porch in front—came, because of a very small lamp in a very large glass case to one side of the door, into view.

Here I knocked, and then knocked more. No reply. I then made a still more forceful effort. Finally, through one of the red glass panels which graced either side of the door I saw the lengthy figure of the doctor, arrayed in a long white nightshirt, and carrying a small glass hand-lamp, come into view at the head of the stairs. His feet were in gray flannel slippers, and his whiskers stuck out most grotesquely.

"Wait! Wait!" I heard him call. "I'll be there! I'm coming! Don't make such a fuss! It seems as though I never get a real good night's rest any more."

He came on, opened the door, and looked out.

"Well," he demanded, a little fussily for him, "what's the matter now?"

"Doctor," I began, and proceeded to explain all my sister's aches and pains, winding up by saying that my mother said "wouldn't he please come at once?"

"Your mother!" he grumbled. "What can I do if I do come down? Not a thing. Feel her pulse and tell her she's all right! That's every bit I can do. Your mother knows that as well as I do. That disease has to run its course." He looked at me as though I were to blame, then added, "Calling me up this way at three in the morning!"

"But she's in such pain, Doctor," I complained.

"All right—everybody has to have a little pain! You can't be sick without it."

"I know," I replied disconsolately, believing sincerely that my sister might die, "but she's in such awful pain, Doctor."

"Well, go on," he replied, turning up the light. "I know it's all foolishness, but I'll come. You go back and tell your mother that I'll be there in a little bit, but it's all nonsense, nonsense. She isn't a bit sicker than I am right this minute, not a bit—" and he closed the door and went upstairs.

To me this seemed just the least bit harsh for the doctor, although, as I reasoned afterwards, he was probably half-asleep and tired—dragged out of his bed, possibly, once or twice before in the same night. As I returned home I felt even more fearful, for once, as I was passing a woodshed which I could not see, a rooster suddenly flapped his wings and crowed—a sound which caused me to leap all of nineteen feet Fahrenheit, sidewise. Then, as I walked along a fence which later by day I saw had a comfortable resting board on top, two lambent golden eyes surveyed me out of inky darkness! Great Hamlet's father, how my heart sank! Once more I leaped to the cloddy roadway and seizing a cobblestone or hunk of mud hurled it with all my might, and quite involuntarily. Then I ran until I fell into a crossing ditch. It was an amazing—almost a tragic—experience, then.

In due time the doctor came—and I never quite forgave him for not making me wait and go back with him. He was too sleepy, though, I am sure. The seizure was apparently nothing which could not have waited until morning. However, he left some new cure, possibly clear water in a bottle, and left again. But the night trials of doctors and their patients, especially in the country, was fixed in my mind then.

One of the next interesting impressions I gained of the doctor was that of seeing him hobbling about our town on crutches, his medicine case held in one hand along with a crutch, visiting his patients, when he himself appeared to be so ill as to require medical attention. He was suffering from some severe form of rheumatism at the time, but this, apparently, was not sufficient to keep him from those who in his judgment probably needed his services more than he did his rest.

One of the truly interesting things about Dr. Gridley, as I early began to note, was his profound indifference to what might be called his material welfare. Why, I have often asked myself, should a man of so much genuine ability choose to ignore the gauds and plaudits and pleasures of the gayer, smarter world outside, in which he might readily have shone, to thus devote himself and all his talents to a simple rural community? That he was an extremely able physician there was not the slightest doubt. Other physicians from other towns about, and even so far away as Chicago, were repeatedly calling him into consultation. That he knew life—much of it—as only a priest or a doctor of true wisdom can know it, was evident from many incidents, of which I subsequently learned, and yet here he was, hidden away in this simple rural world, surrounded probably by his Rabelais, his Burton, his Frazer, and his Montaigne, and dreaming what dreams—thinking what thoughts?

"Say," an old patient, friend and neighbor of his once remarked to me years later, when we had both moved to another city, "one of the sweetest recollections of my life is to picture old Dr. Gridley, Ed Boulder who used to run the hotel over at Sleichertown, Congressman Barr, and Judge Morgan, sitting out in front of Boulder's hotel over there of a summer's evening and haw-hawing over the funny stories which Boulder was always telling while they were waiting for the Pierceton bus. Dr. Gridley's laugh, so soft to begin with, but growing in force and volume until it was a jolly shout. And the green fields all around. And Mrs. Calder's drove of geese over the way honking, too, as geese will whenever people begin to talk or laugh. It was delicious."

One of the most significant traits of his character, as may be inferred, was his absolute indifference to actual money, the very cash, one would think, with which he needed to buy his own supplies. During his life, his wife, who was a thrifty, hard-working woman, used frequently, as I learned after, to comment on this, but to no result. He could not be made to charge where he did not need to, nor collect where he knew that the people were poor.

"Once he became angry at my uncle," his daughter once told me, "because he offered to collect for him for three per cent, dunning his patients for their debts, and another time he dissolved a partnership with a local physician who insisted that he ought to be more careful to charge and collect."

This generosity on his part frequently led to some very interesting results. On one occasion, for instance, when he was sitting out on his front lawn in Warsaw, smoking, his chair tilted back against a tree and his legs crossed in the fashion known as "jack-knife," a poorly dressed farmer without a coat came up and after saluting the doctor began to explain that his wife was sick and that he had come to get the doctor's advice. He seemed quite disturbed, and every now and then wiped his brow, while the doctor listened with an occasional question or gently accented "uh-huh, uh-huh," until the story was all told and the advice ready to be received. When this was given in a low, reassuring tone, he took from his pocket his little book of blanks and wrote out a prescription, which he gave to the man and began talking again. The latter took out a silver dollar and handed it to the doctor, who turned it idly between his fingers for a few seconds, then searched in his pocket for a mate to it, and playing with them a while as he talked, finally handed back the dollar to the farmer.

"You take that," he said pleasantly, "and go down to the drug-store and have the prescription filled. I think your wife will be all right."

When he had gone the doctor sat there a long time, meditatively puffing the smoke from his cob pipe, and turning his own dollar in his hand. After a time he looked up at his daughter, who was present, and said:

"I was just thinking what a short time it took me to write that prescription, and what a long time it took him to earn that dollar. I guess he needs the dollar more than I do."

In the same spirit of this generosity he was once sitting in his yard of a summer day, sunning himself and smoking, a favorite pleasure of his, when two men rode up to his gate from opposite directions and simultaneously hailed him. He arose and went out to meet them. His wife, who was sewing just inside the hall as she usually was when her husband was outside, leaned forward in her chair to see through the door, and took note of who they were. Both were men in whose families the doctor had practiced for years. One was a prosperous farmer who always paid his "doctor's bills," and the other was a miller, a "ne'er-do-well," with a delicate wife and a family of sickly children, who never asked for a statement and never had one sent him, and who only occasionally and at great intervals handed the doctor a dollar in payment for his many services. Both men talked to him a little while and then rode away, after which he returned to the house, calling to Enoch, his old negro servant, to bring his horse, and then went into his study to prepare his medicine case. Mrs. Gridley, who was naturally interested in his financial welfare, and who at times had to plead with him not to let his generosity stand wholly in the way of his judgment, inquired of him as he came out:

"Now, Doctor, which of those two men are you going with?"

"Why, Miss Susan," he replied—a favorite manner of addressing his wife, of whom he was very fond—the note of apology in his voice showing that he knew very well what she was thinking about, "I'm going with W——."

"I don't think that is right," she replied with mild emphasis. "Mr. N—— is as good a friend of yours as W——, and he always pays you."

"Now, Miss Susan," he returned coaxingly, "N—— can go to Pierceton and get Doctor Bodine, and W—— can't get any one but me. You surely wouldn't have him left without any one?"

What the effect of such an attitude was may be judged when it is related that there was scarcely a man, woman or child in the entire county who had not at some time or other been directly or indirectly benefited by the kindly wisdom of this Samaritan. He was nearly everybody's doctor, in the last extremity, either as consultant or otherwise. Everywhere he went, by every lane and hollow that he fared, he was constantly being called into service by some one—the well-to-do as well as by those who had nothing; and in both cases he was equally keen to give the same degree of painstaking skill, finding something in the very poor—a humanness possibly—which detained and fascinated him and made him a little more prone to linger at their bedsides than anywhere else.

"He was always doing it," said his daughter, "and my mother used to worry over it. She declared that of all things earthly, papa loved an unfortunate person; the greater the misfortune, the greater his care."

In illustration of his easy and practically controlling attitude toward the very well-to-do, who were his patients also, let me narrate this:

In our town was an old and very distinguished colonel, comparatively rich and very crotchety, who had won considerable honors for himself during the Civil War. He was a figure, and very much looked up to by all. People were, in the main, overawed by and highly respectful of him. A remote, stern soul, yet to Dr. Gridley he was little more than a child or schoolboy—one to be bossed on occasion and made to behave. Plainly, the doctor had the conviction that all of us, great and small, were very much in need of sympathy and care, and that he, the doctor, was the one to provide it. At any rate, he had known the colonel long and well, and in a public place—at the principal street corner, for instance, or in the postoffice where we school children were wont to congregate—it was not at all surprising to hear him take the old colonel, who was quite frail now, to task for not taking better care of himself—coming out, for instance, without his rubbers, or his overcoat, in wet or chilly weather, and in other ways misbehaving himself.

"There you go again!" I once heard him call to the colonel, as the latter was leaving the postoffice and he was entering (there was no rural free delivery in those days) "—walking around without your rubbers, and no overcoat! You want to get me up in the night again, do you?"

"It didn't seem so damp when I started out, Doctor."

"And of course it was too much trouble to go back! You wouldn't feel that way if you couldn't come out at all, perhaps!"

"I'll put 'em on! I'll put 'em on! Only, please don't fuss, Doctor. I'll go back to the house and put 'em on."

The doctor merely stared after him quizzically, like an old schoolmaster, as the rather stately colonel marched off to his home.

Another of his patients was an old Mr. Pegram, a large, kind, big-hearted man, who was very fond of the doctor, but who had an exceedingly irascible temper. He was the victim of some obscure malady which medicine apparently failed at times to relieve. This seemed to increase his irritability a great deal, so much so that the doctor had at last discovered that if he could get Mr. Pegram angry enough the malady would occasionally disappear. This seemed at times as good a remedy as any, and in consequence he was occasionally inclined to try it.

Among other things, this old gentleman was the possessor of a handsome buffalo robe, which, according to a story that long went the rounds locally, he once promised to leave to the doctor when he died. At the same time all reference to death both pained and irritated him greatly—a fact which the doctor knew. Finding the old gentleman in a most complaining and hopeless mood one night, not to be dealt with, indeed, in any reasoning way, the doctor returned to his home, and early the next day, without any other word, sent old Enoch, his negro servant, around to get, as he said, the buffalo robe—a request which would indicate, of course that the doctor had concluded that old Mr. Pegram had died, or was about to—a hopeless case. When ushered into the latter's presence, Enoch began innocently enough:

"De doctah say dat now dat Mr. Peg'am hab subspired, he was to hab dat ba—ba—buffalo robe."

"What!" shouted the old irascible, rising and clambering out of his bed. "What's that? Buffalo robe! By God! You go back and tell old Doc Gridley that I ain't dead yet by a damned sight! No, sir!" and forthwith he dressed himself and was out and around the same day.

Persons who met the doctor, as I heard years later from his daughter and from others who had known him, were frequently asking him, just in a social way, what to do for certain ailments, and he would as often reply in a humorous and half-vagrom manner that if he were in their place he would do or take so-and-so, not meaning really that they should do so but merely to get rid of them, and indicating of course any one of a hundred harmless things—never one that could really have proved injurious to any one. Once, according to his daughter, as he was driving into town from somewhere, he met a man on a lumber wagon whom he scarcely knew but who knew him well enough, who stopped and showed him a sore on the upper tip of his ear, asking him what he would do for it.

"Oh," said the doctor, idly and jestingly, "I think I'd cut it off."

"Yes," said the man, very much pleased with this free advice, "with what, Doctor?"

"Oh, I think I'd use a pair of scissors," he replied amusedly, scarcely assuming that his jesting would be taken seriously.

The driver jogged on and the doctor did not see or hear of him again until some two months later when, meeting him in the street, the driver smilingly approached him and enthusiastically exclaimed:

"Well, Doc, you see I cut 'er off, and she got well!"

"Yes," replied the doctor solemnly, not remembering anything about the case but willing to appear interested, "—what was it you cut off?"

"Why, that sore on my ear up here, you know. You told me to cut it off, and I did."

"Yes," said the doctor, becoming curious and a little amazed, "with what?"

"Why, with a pair of scissors, Doc, just like you said."

The doctor stared at him, the whole thing coming gradually back to him.

"But didn't you have some trouble in cutting it off?" he inquired, in disturbed astonishment.

"No, no," said the driver, "I made 'em sharp, all right. I spent two days whettin' 'em up, and Bob Hart cut 'er off fer me. They cut, all right, but I tell you she hurt when she went through the gristle."

He smiled in pleased remembrance of his surgical operation, and the doctor smiled also, but, according to his daughter, he decided to give no more idle advice of that kind.

In the school which I attended for a period were two of his sons, Fred and Walter. Both were very fond of birds, and kept a number of one kind or another about their home—not in cages, as some might, but inveigled and trained as pets, and living in the various open bird-houses fixed about the yard on poles. The doctor himself was intensely fond of these and all other birds, and, according to his daughter and his sons, always anticipated the spring return of many of diem—black-birds, blue jays, wrens and robins—with a hopeful, "Well, now, they'll soon be here again." During the summer, according to her, he was always an interested spectator of their gyrations in the air, and when evening would come was never so happy as when standing and staring at them gathering from all directions to their roosts in the trees or the birdhouses. Similarly, when the fall approached and they would begin their long flight Southward, he would sometimes stand and scan the sky and trees in vain for a final glimpse of his feathered friends, and when in the gathering darkness they were no longer to be seen would turn away toward the house, saying sadly to his daughter:

"Well, Dollie, the blackbirds are all gone. I am sorry. I like to see them, and I am always sorry to lose them, and sorry to know that winter is coming."

"Usually about the 25th or 26th of December," his daughter once quaintly added to me, "he would note that the days were beginning to get longer, and cheer up, as spring was certain to follow soon and bring them all back again."

One of the most interesting of his bird friendships was that which existed between him and a pair of crows he and his sons had raised, "Jim" and "Zip" by name. These crows came to know him well, and were finally so humanly attached to him that, according to his family, they would often fly two or three miles out of town to meet him and would then accompany him, lighting on fences and trees by the way, and cawing to him as he drove along! Both of them were great thieves, and would steal anything from a bit of thread up to a sewing machine, if they could have carried it. They were always walking about the house, cheerfully looking for what they might devour, and on one occasion carried off a set of spoons, which they hid about the eaves of the house. On another occasion they stole a half dozen tin-handled pocket knives, which the doctor had bought for the children and which the crows seemed to like for the brightness of the metal. They were recovered once by the children, stolen again by the crows, recovered once more, and so on, until at last it was a question as to which were the rightful owners.

The doctor was sitting in front of a store one day in the business-heart of town, where also he liked to linger in fair weather, when suddenly he saw one of his crows flying high overhead and bearing something in its beak, which it dropped into the road scarcely a hundred feet away. Interested to see what it was the bird had been carrying, he went to the spot where he saw it fall and found one of the tin-handled knives, which the crow had been carrying to a safe hiding-place. He picked it up and when he returned home that night asked one of his boys if he could lend him a knife.

"No," said his son. "Our knives are all lost. The crows took them."

"I knew that," said the doctor sweetly, "and so, when I met Zip uptown just now, I asked her to lend me one, and she did. Here it is."

He pulled out the knife and handed it to the boy and, when the latter expressed doubt and wonder, insisted that the crow had loaned it to him; a joke which ended in his always asking one of the children to run and ask Zip if she would lend him a knife, whenever he chanced to need one.

Although a sad man at times, as I understood, the doctor was not a pessimist, and in many ways, both by practical jokes and the humoring of odd characters, sought relief from the intense emotional strain which the large practice of his profession put upon him. One of his greatest reliefs was the carrying out of these little practical jokes, and he had been known to go to much trouble at times to work up a good laugh.

One of the, to him, richest jokes, and one which he always enjoyed telling, related to a country singing school which was located in the neighborhood of Pierceton, in which reading (the alphabet, at least), spelling, geography, arithmetic, rules of grammar, and so forth, were still taught by a process of singing. The method adopted in this form of education was to have the scholar memorize all knowledge by singing it. Thus in the case of geography the students would sing the name of the country, then its mountains, then the highest peaks, cities, rivers, principal points of interest, and so on, until all information about that particular country had been duly memorized in song or rhyme. Occasionally they would have a school-day on which the local dignitaries would be invited, and on a number of these occasions the doctor was, for amusement's sake merely, a grave and reverent listener. On one occasion, however, he was merely passing the school, when hearing "Africa-a, Africa-a, mountains of the moo-oo-oon" drawled out of the windows, he decided to stop in and listen a while. Having tethered his horse outside he knocked at the door and was received by the little English singing teacher who, after showing him to a seat, immediately called upon the class for an exhibition of their finest wisdom. When they had finished this the teacher turned to him and inquired if there was anything he would especially like them to sing.

"No," said the doctor gravely, and no doubt with an amused twinkle in his eye, "I had thought of asking you to sing the Rocky Mountains, but as the mountains are so high, and the amount of time I have so limited, I have decided that perhaps it will be asking too much."

"Oh, not at all, not at all" airily replied the teacher, and turning to his class, he exclaimed with a very superior smile: "Now, ladies and gentlemen, 'ere is a scientific gentleman who thinks it is 'arder to sing of 'igh mountings than it is to sing of low mountings," and forthwith the class began to demonstrate that in respect to vocalization there was no difference at all.

Only those, however, who knew Dr. Gridley in the sickroom, and knew him well, ever discovered the really finest trait of his character: a keen, unshielded sensibility to and sympathy for all human suffering, that could not bear to inflict the slightest additional pain. He was really, in the main, a man of soft tones and unctuous laughter, of gentle touch and gentle step, and a devotion to duty that carried him far beyond his interests or his personal well-being. One of his chiefest oppositions, according to his daughter, was to telling the friends or relatives of any stricken person that there was no hope. Instead, he would use every delicate shade of phrasing and tone in imparting the fateful words, in order if possible to give less pain. "I remember in the case of my father," said one of his friends, "when the last day came. Knowing the end was near, he was compelled to make some preliminary discouraging remark, and I bent over with my ear against my father's chest and said,

- 85 -

'Doctor Gridley, the disease is under control, I think. I can hear the respiration to the bottom of the lungs.'

"'Yes, yes,' he answered me sadly, but now with an implication which could by no means be misunderstood, 'it is nearly always so. The failure is in the recuperative energy. Vitality runs too low.' It meant from the first, 'Your father will not live.'"

In the case of a little child with meningitis, the same person was sent to him to ask what of the child—better or worse. His answer was: "He is passing as free from pain as ever I knew a case of this kind."

In yet another case of a dying woman, one of her relatives inquired: "Doctor, is this case dangerous?" "Not in the nature of the malady, madam," was his sad and sympathetic reply, "but fatal in the condition it meets. Hope is broken. There is nothing to resist the damage."

One of his patients was a farmer who lived in an old-time log house a few miles out from Silver Lake, who while working about his barn met with a very serious accident which involved a possible injury to the gall bladder. The main accident was not in itself fatal, but the possible injury to the gall bladder was, and this, if it existed, would show as a yellow tint in the eyeball on the tenth day. Fearing the danger of this, he communicated the possibility to the relatives, saying that he could do little after that time but that he would come just the same and make the patient as comfortable as possible. For nine days he came, sitting by the bedside and whiling away many a weary hour for the sufferer, until the tenth morning. On this day, according to his daughter, who had it from the sick man's relatives, his face but ill concealed the anxiety he felt. Coming up to the door, he entered just far enough to pretend to reach for a water bucket. With this in his hand he turned and gave one long keen look in the eye of the sick man, then walked down the yard to a chair under a tree some distance from the house, where he sat, drooping and apparently grieved, the certainty of the death of the patient affecting him as much as if he were his own child.

"There was no need for words," said one of them. "Every curve and droop of his figure, as he walked slowly and with bent head, told all of us who saw him that hope was gone and that death had won the victory."

One of his perpetual charges, as I learned later, was a poor old unfortunate by the name of Id Logan, who had a little cabin and an acre of ground a half dozen miles west of Warsaw, and who existed from year to year heaven only knows how.

Id never had any money, friends or relatives, and was always troubled with illness or hunger in some form or other, and yet the doctor always spoke of him sympathetically as "Poor old Id Logan" and would often call out there on his rounds to see how he was getting along. One snowy winter's evening as he was traveling homeward after a long day's ride, he chanced to recollect the fact that he was in the neighborhood of his worthless old charge, and fancying that he might be in need of something turned his horse into the lane which led up to the door. When he reached the house he noticed that no smoke was coming from the chimney and that the windows were slightly rimmed with frost, as if there were no heat within. Rapping at the door and receiving no response, he opened it and went in. There he found his old charge, sick and wandering in his mind, lying upon a broken-down bed and moaning in pain. There was no fire in the fireplace. The coverings with which the bed was fitted were but two or three old worn and faded quilts, and the snow was sifting in badly through the cracks where the chinking had fallen out between the logs, and under the doors and windows.

Going up to the sufferer and finding that some one of his old, and to the doctor well-known, maladies had at last secured a fatal grip upon him, he first administered a tonic which he knew would give him as much strength as possible, and then went out into the yard, where, after putting up his horse, he gathered chips and wood from under the snow and built a roaring fire. Having done this, he put on the kettle, trimmed the lamp, and after preparing such stimulants as the patient could stand, took his place at the bedside, where he remained the whole night long, keeping the fire going and the patient as comfortable as possible. Toward morning the sufferer died and when the sun was well up he finally returned to his family, who anxiously solicited him as to his whereabouts.

"I was with Id Logan," he said.

"What's ailing him now?" his daughter inquired.

"Nothing now," he returned. "It was only last night," and for years afterward he commented on the death of "poor old Id," saying always at the conclusion of his remarks that it must be a dreadful thing to be sick and die without friends.

His love for his old friends and familiar objects was striking, and he could no more bear to see an old friend move away than he could to lose one of his patients. One of his oldest friends was a fine old Christian lady by the name of Weeks, who lived down in Louter Creek bottoms and in whose household he had practiced for nearly fifty years. During the latter part of his life, however, this family began to break up, and finally when there was no one left but the mother she decided to move over into Whitley County, where she could stay with her daughter. Just before going, however, she expressed a wish to see Doctor Gridley, and he called in upon her. A little dinner had been prepared in honor of his coming. After it was over and the old times were fully discussed he was about to take his leave when Mrs. Weeks disappeared from the room and then returned, bearing upon her arm a beautiful yarn spread which she held out before her and, in her nervous, feeble way getting the attention of the little audience, said:

"Doctor, I am going up to Whitley now to live with my daughter, and I don't suppose I will get to see you very often any more. Like myself, you are getting old, and it will be too far for you to come. But I want to give you this spread that I have woven with my own hands since I have been sixty years of age. It isn't very much, but it is meant for a token of the love and esteem I bear you, and in remembrance of all that you have done for me and mine."

Her eyes were wet and her voice quivering as she brought it forward. The doctor, who had been wholly taken by surprise by this kindly manifestation of regard, had arisen during her impromptu address and now stood before her, dignified and emotionally grave, his own eyes wet with tears of appreciation.

Balancing the homely gift upon his extended hands, he waited until the force of his own sentiment had slightly subsided, when he replied:

"Madam, I appreciate this gift with which you have chosen to remember me as much as I honor the sentiment which has produced it. There are, I know, threads of feeling woven into it stronger than any cords of wool, and more enduring than all the fabrics of this world. I have been your physician now for fifty years, and have been a witness of your joys and sorrows. But, as much as I esteem you, and as highly as I prize this token of your regard, I can accept it but upon one condition, and that is, Mrs. Weeks, that you promise me that no matter how dark the night, how stormy the sky, or how deep the waters that intervene, you will not fail to send for me in your hour of need. It is both my privilege and my pleasure, and I should not rest content unless I knew it were so."

When the old lady had promised, he took his spread and going out to his horse, rode away to his own home, where he related this incident, and ended with, "Now I want this put on my bed."

His daughter, who lovingly humored his every whim, immediately complied with his wish, and from that day to the hour of his death the spread was never out of his service.

One of the most pleasing incidents to me was one which related to his last illness and death. Always, during his later years, when he felt the least bit ill, he refused to prescribe for himself, saying that a doctor, if he knew anything at all, was never such a fool as to take any of his own medicine. Instead, and in sequence to this humorous attitude, he would always send for one of the younger men of the vicinity who were beginning to practice here, one, for instance, who having other merits needed some assurance and a bit of superior recognition occasionally to help him along. On this occasion he called in a very sober young doctor, one who was greatly admired but had very little practice as yet, and saying, "Doctor, I'm sick today," lay back on his bed and waited for further developments.

The latter, owing to Dr. Gridley's great repute and knowledge, was very much flustered, so much so that he scarcely knew what to do.

"Well, Doctor," he finally said, after looking at his tongue, taking his pulse and feeling his forehead, "you're really a better judge of your own condition than I am, I'm sure. What do you think I ought to give you?"

"Now, Doctor," replied Gridley sweetly, "I'm your patient, and you're my doctor. I wouldn't prescribe for myself for anything in the world, and I'm going to take whatever you give me. That's why I called you in. Now, you just give me what you think my condition requires, and I'll take it."

The young doctor, meditating on all that was new or faddistic, decided at last that just for variation's sake he would give the doctor something of which he had only recently heard, a sample of which he had with him and which had been acclaimed in the medical papers as very effective. Without asking the doctor whether he had ever heard of it, or what he thought, he merely prescribed it.

"Well, now, I like that," commented Gridley solemnly. "I never heard of that before in my life, but it sounds plausible. I'll take it, and we'll see. What's more, I like a young doctor like yourself who thinks up ways of his own—" and, according to his daughter, he did take it, and was helped, saying always that what young doctors needed to do was to keep abreast of the latest medical developments, that medicine was changing, and perhaps it was just as well that old doctors died! He was so old and feeble, however, that he did not long survive, and when the time came was really glad to go.

One of the sweetest and most interesting of all his mental phases was, as I have reason to know, his attitude toward the problem of suffering and death, an attitude so full of the human qualities of wonder, sympathy, tenderness, and trust, that he could scarcely view them without exhibiting the emotion he felt. He was a constant student of the phenomena of dissolution, and in one instance calmly declared it as his belief that when a man was dead he was dead and that was the end of him, consciously. At other times he modified his view to one of an almost prayerful hope, and in reading Emily Brontë's somewhat morbid story of "Wuthering Heights," his copy of which I long had in my possession, I noted that he had annotated numerous passages relative to death and a future life with interesting comments of his own. To one of these passages, which reads:

"I don't know if it be a peculiarity with me, but I am seldom otherwise than happy while watching in the chamber of death, provided no frenzied or despairing mourner shares the duty with me. I see a repose that neither earth nor hell can break, and I feel an assurance of the endless and shadowless hereafter—the eternity they have entered— where life is boundless in its duration, and love in its sympathy, and joy in its fullness,"

he had added on the margin:

"How often I have felt this very emotion. How natural I know it to be. And what a consolation in the thought!"

Writing a final prescription for a young clergyman who was dying, and for whom he had been most tenderly solicitous, he added to the list of drugs he had written in Latin, the lines:

"In life's closing hour, when the trembling soul fliesAnd death stills the heart's last emotion,Oh, then may the angel of mercy ariseLike a star on eternity's ocean!"

When he himself was upon his death-bed he greeted his old friend Colonel Dyer—he of the absent overcoat and over-shoes—with:

"Dyer, I'm almost gone. I am in the shadow of death. I am standing upon the very brink. I cannot see clearly, I cannot speak coherently, the film of death obstructs my sight. I know what this means. It is the end, but all is well with me. I have no fear. I have said and done things that would have been better left unsaid and undone, but I have never willfully wronged a man in my life. I have no concern for myself. I am concerned only for those I leave behind. I never saved money, and I die as poor as when I was born. We do not know what there is in the future now shut out from our view by a very thin veil. It seems to me there is a hand somewhere that will lead us safely across, but I cannot tell. No one can tell."

This interesting speech, made scarcely a day before he closed his eyes in death, was typical of his whole generous, trustful, philosophical point of view.

"If there be green fields and placid waters beyond the river that he so calmly crossed," so ran an editorial in the local county paper edited by one of his most ardent admirers, "reserved for those who believe in and practice upon the principle of 'Do unto others as you would have them do unto you,' then this Samaritan of the medical profession is safe from all harm. If there be no consciousness, but only a mingling of that which was gentleness and tenderness here with the earth and the waters, then the greenness of the one and the sparkling limpidity of the other are richer for that he lived, and wrought, and returned unto them so trustingly again."

Culhane, the Solid Man

I met him in connection with a psychic depression which only partially reflected itself in my physical condition. I might almost say that I was sick spiritually. At the same time I was rather strongly imbued with a contempt for him and his cure. I had heard of him for years. To begin with, he was a wrestler of repute, or rather ex-wrestler, retired undefeated champion of the world. As a boy I had known that he had toured America with Modjeska as Charles, the wrestler, in "As You Like It." Before or after that he had trained John L. Sullivan, the world's champion prize fighter of his day, for one of his most successful fights, and that at a time when Sullivan was unfitted to fight any one. Before that, in succession, from youth up, he had been a peasant farmer's son in Ireland, a scullion in a ship's kitchen earning his way to America, a "beef slinger" for a packing company, a cooks' assistant and waiter in a Bowery restaurant, a bouncer in a saloon, a rubber down at prize fights, a policeman, a private in the army during the Civil War, a ticket-taker, exhibition wrestler, "short-change man" with a minstrel company, later a circus, until having attained his greatest fame as champion wrestler of the world, and as trainer of John L. Sullivan, he finally opened a sporting sanitarium in some county in upper New York State which later evolved into the great and now decidedly fashionable institution in Westchester, near New York.

It has always been interesting to me to see in what awe men of this type or profession are held by many in the more intellectual walks of life as well as by those whose respectful worship is less surprising,—those who revere strength, agility, physical courage, so-called, brute or otherwise. There is a kind of retiring worshipfulness, especially in men and children of the lower walks, for this type, which must be flattering in the extreme.

However, in so far as Culhane was concerned at this time, the case was different. Whatever he had been in his youth he was not that now, or at least his earlier rawness had long since been glazed over by other experiences. Self-education, an acquired politeness among strangers and a knowledge of the manners and customs of the better-to-do, permitted him to associate with them and to accept if not copy their manners and to a certain extent their customs in his relations with them. Literally, he owned hundreds of the best acres of the land about him, in one of the most fashionable residence sections of the East. He had already given away to some Sisters of Mercy a great estate in northern New York. His stables contained every type of fashionable vehicle and stalled and fed sixty or seventy of the worst horses, purposely so chosen, for the use of his "guests." Men of all professions visited his place, paid him gladly the six hundred dollars in advance which he asked for the course of six weeks' training, and brought, or attempted to, their own cars and retinues, which they lodged in the vicinity but could not use. I myself was introduced or rather foisted upon him by my dear brother, whose friend if not crony—if such a thing could have been said to exist in his life—he was. I was taken to him in a very somber and depressed mood and left; he rarely if ever received guests in person or at once. On the way, and before I had been introduced, I was instructed by my good brother as to his moods, methods, airs and tricks, supposed or rumored to be so beneficial in so many cases. They were very rough—purposely so.

The day I arrived, and before I saw him, I was very much impressed with the simplicity yet distinction of the inn or sanitarium or "repair shop," as subsequently I learned he was accustomed to refer to it, perched upon a rise of ground and commanding a quite wonderful panorama. It was spring and quite warm and bright. The cropped enclosure which surrounded it, a great square of green fenced with high, well-trimmed privet, was good to look upon, level and smooth. The house, standing in the center of this, was large and oblong and gray, with very simple French windows reaching to the floor and great wide balustraded balconies reaching out from the second floor, shaded with awnings and set with rockers. The land on which this inn stood sloped very gradually to the Sound, miles away to the southeast, and the spires of churches and the gables of villages rising in between, as well as various toy-like sails upon the water, were no small portion of its charm. To the west for a score of miles the green-covered earth rose and fell in undulating beauty, and here again the roofs and spires of nearby villages might in fair weather be seen nestling peacefully among the trees. Due south there was a suggestion of water and some peculiar configuration, which by day seemed to have no significance other than that which attached to the vague outlines of a distant landscape. By night, however, the soft glow emanating from myriads of lights identified it as the body and length of the merry, night-reveling New York. Northward the green waves repeated themselves unendingly until they passed into a dim green-blue haze.

Interiorly, as I learned later, this place was most cleverly and sensibly arranged for the purpose for which it was intended. It was airy and well-appointed, with, on the ground floor, a great gymnasium containing, outside of an alcove at one end where hung four or five punching bags, only medicine balls. At the other end was an office or receiving-room, baggage or store-room, and locker and dining-room. To the east at the center extended a wing containing a number of shower-baths, a lounging room and sun parlor. On the second floor, on either side of a wide airy hall which ran from an immense library, billiard and smoking-room at one end to Culhane's private suite at the other, were two rows of bedrooms, perhaps a hundred all told, which gave in turn, each one, upon either side, on to the balconies previously mentioned. These rooms were arranged somewhat like the rooms of a passenger steamer, with its center aisle and its outer decks and doors opening upon it. In another wing on the ground floor were kitchens, servants' quarters, and what not else! Across the immense lawn or campus to the east, four-square to the sanitarium, stood a rather grandiose stable, almost as impressive as the main building. About the place, and always more or less in evidence, were servants, ostlers, waiting-maids and always a decidedly large company of men of practically all professions, ages, and one might almost say nationalities. That is as nationalities are represented in America, by first and second generations.

The day I arrived I did not see my prospective host or manager or trainer for an hour or two after I came, being allowed to wait about until the very peculiar temperament which he possessed would permit him to come and see me. When he did show up, a more savage and yet gentlemanly-looking animal in clothes *de rigueur* I have never seen. He was really very princely in build and manner, shapely and grand, like those portraits that have come down to us of Richelieu and the Duc de Guise—fawn-colored riding trousers, bright red waistcoat, black-and-white check riding coat, brown leather riding boots and leggings with the essential spurs, and a riding quirt. And yet really, at that moment he reminded me not so much of a man, in his supremely well-tailored riding costume, as of a tiger or a very ferocious and yet at times purring cat, beautifully dressed, as in our children's storybooks, a kind of tiger in collar and boots. He was so lithe, silent, cat-like in his tread. In his hard, clear, gray animal eyes was that swift, incisive, restless, searching glance which sometimes troubles us in the presence of animals. It was hard to believe that he was all of sixty, as I had been told. He looked the very well-preserved man of fifty or less. The short trimmed mustache and goatee which he wore were gray and added to his grand air. His hair, cut a close pompadour, the ends of his heavy eyebrow hairs turned upward, gave him a still more distinguished air. He looked very virile, very intelligent, very indifferent, intolerant and even threatening.

"Well," he exclaimed on sight, "you wish to see me?"

I gave him my name.

"Yes, that's so. Your brother spoke to me about you. Well, take a seat. You will be looked after."

He walked off, and after an hour or so I was still waiting, for what I scarcely knew—a room, something to eat possibly, some one to speak a friendly word to me, but no one did.

While I was waiting in this rather nondescript antechamber, hung with hats, caps, riding whips and gauntlets, I had an opportunity to study some of the men with whom presumably I was to live for a number of weeks. It was between two and three in the afternoon, and many of them were idling about in pairs or threes, talking, reading, all in rather commonplace athletic costumes—soft woolen shirts, knee trousers, stockings and running or walking shoes. They were in the main evidently of the so-called learned professions or the arts—doctors, lawyers, preachers, actors, writers, with a goodly sprinkling of merchants, manufacturers and young and middle-aged society men, as well as politicians and monied idlers, generally a little the worse for their pleasures or weaknesses. A distinguished judge of one of the superior courts of New York and an actor known everywhere in the English-speaking world were instantly recognized by me. Others, as I was subsequently informed, were related by birth or achievement to some one fact or another of public significance. The reason for the presence of so many people rather above than under the average in intellect lay, as I came to believe later, in their ability or that of some one connected with them to sincerely appreciate or to at least be amused and benefited by the somewhat different theory of physical repair which the lord of the manor had invented, or for which at least he had become famous.

I have remarked that I was not inclined to be impressed. Sanitariums with their isms and theories did not appeal to me. However, as I was waiting here an incident occurred which stuck in my mind. A smart conveyance drove up, occupied by a singularly lean and haughty-looking individual, who, after looking about him, expecting some one to come out to him no doubt, clambered cautiously out, and after seeing that his various grips and one trunk were properly deposited on the gravel square outside, paid and feed his driver, then walked in and remarked:

"Ah—where is Mr. Culhane?"

"I don't know, sir," I replied, being the only one present. "He was here, but he's gone. I presume some one will show up presently."

He walked up and down a little while, and then added: "Um—rather peculiar method of receiving one, isn't it? I wired him I'd be here." He walked restlessly and almost waspishly to and fro, looking out of the window at times, at others commenting on the rather casual character of it all. I agreed.

Thus, some fifteen minutes having gone by without any one approaching us, and occasional servants or "guests" passing through the room or being seen in the offing without even so much as vouchsafing a word or appearing to be interested in us, the new arrival grew excited.

"This is very unusual," he fumed, walking up and down. "I wired him only three hours ago. I've been here now fully three-quarters of an hour! A most unheard-of method of doing business, I should say!"

Presently our stern, steely-eyed host returned. He seemed to be going somewhere, to be nowise interested in us. Yet into our presence, probably into the consciousness of this new "guest," he carried that air of savage strength and indifference, eyeing the stranger quite sharply and making no effort to apologize for our long wait.

"You wish to see me?" he inquired brusquely once more.

Like a wasp, the stranger was vibrant with rage. Plainly he felt himself insulted or terribly underrated.

"Are you Mr. Culhane?" he asked crisply.

"Yes."

"I am Mr. Squiers," he exclaimed. "I wired you from Buffalo and ordered a room," this last with an irritated wave of the hand.

"Oh, no, you didn't order any room," replied the host sourly and with an obvious desire to show his indifference and contempt even. "You wired to know if you *could engage* a room."

He paused. The temperature seemed to drop perceptibly. The prospective guest seemed to realize that he had made a mistake somewhere, had been misinformed as to conditions here.

"Oh! Um—ah! Yes! Well, have you a room?"

"I don't know. I doubt it. We don't take every one." His eyes seemed to bore into the interior of his would-be guest.

"Well, but I was told—my friend, Mr. X——," the stranger began a rapid, semi-irritated, semi-apologetic explanation of how he came to be here.

"I don't know anything about your friend or what he told you. If he told you you could order a room by telegraph, he's mistaken. Anyhow, you're not dealing with him, but with me. Now that you're here, though, if you want to sit down and rest yourself a little I'll see what I can do for you. I can't decide now whether I can let you stay. You'll have to wait a while." He turned and walked off.

The other stared. "Well," he commented to me after a time, walking and twisting, "if a man wants to come here I suppose he has to put up with such things, but it's certainly unusual, isn't it?" He sat down, wilted, and waited.

Later a clerk in charge of the registry book took us in hand, and then I heard him explaining that his lungs were not in good shape. He had come a long way—Denver, I believe. He had heard that all one needed to do was to wire, especially one in his circumstances.

"Some people think that way," solemnly commented the clerk, "but they don't know Mr. Culhane. He does about as he pleases in these matters. He doesn't do this any more to make money but rather to amuse himself, I think. He always has more applicants than he accepts."

I began to see a light. Perhaps there was something to this place after all. I did not even partially sense the drift of the situation, though, until bedtime when, after having been served a very frugal meal and shown to my very simple room, a kind of cell, promptly at nine o'clock lights were turned off. I lit a small candle and was looking over some things which I had placed in a grip, when I heard a voice in the hall outside: "Candles out, please! Candles out! All guests in bed!" Then it came to me that a very rigorous régime was being enforced here.

The next morning as I was still soundly sleeping at five-thirty a loud rap sounded at my door. The night before I had noticed above my bed a framed sign which read: "Guests must be dressed in running trunks, shoes and sweater, and appear in the gymnasium by six sharp." "Gymnasium at six! Gymnasium at six!" a voice echoed down the hall. I bounced out of bed. Something about the very air of the place made me feel that it was dangerous to attempt to trifle with the routine here. The tiger-like eyes of my host did not appeal to me as retaining any softer ray in them for me than for others. I had paid my six hundred ... I had better earn it. I was down in the great room in my trunks, sweater, dressing-gown, running shoes in less than five minutes.

And that room! By that time as odd a company of people as I have ever seen in a gymnasium had already begun to assemble. The leanness! the osseosity! the grandiloquent whiskers parted in the middle! the mustachios! the goatees! the fat, Hoti-like stomachs! the protuberant knees! the thin arms! the bald or semi-bald pates! the spectacles or horn glasses or pince-nezes!—laid aside a few moments later, as the exercises began. Youth and strength in the pink of condition, when clad only in trunks, a sweater and running shoes, are none too acceptable—but middle age! And out in the world, I reflected rather sadly, they all wore the best of clothes, had their cars, servants, city and country houses perhaps, their factories, employees, institutions. Ridiculous! Pitiful! As lymphatic and flabby as oysters without their shells, myself included. It was really painful.

Even as I meditated, however, I was advised, by many who saw that I was a stranger, to choose a partner, any partner, for medicine ball practice, for it might save me being taken or called by *him*. I hastened so to do. Even as we were assembling or beginning to practice, keeping two or three light medicine balls going between each pair, our host entered—that iron man, that mount of brawn. In his cowled dressing-gown he looked more like some great monk or fighting abbot of the medieval years than a trainer. He walked to the center, hung up his cowl and revealed himself lithe and lion-like and costumed like ourselves. But how much more attractive as he strode about, his legs lean and sturdy, his chest full, his arms powerful and graceful! At once he seized a large leather-covered medicine ball, as had all the others, and calling a name to which responded a lean whiskerando with a semi-bald pate, thin legs and arms, and very much caricatured, I presume, by the wearing of trunks and sweater. Taking his place opposite the host, he was immediately made the recipient of a volley of balls and brow-beating epithets.

"Hurry up now! Faster! Ah, come on! Put the ball back to me! Put the ball back! Do you want to keep it all day? Great God! What are you standing there for? What are you standing there for? What do you think you're doing—drinking tea? Come on! I haven't all morning for you alone. Move! Move, you ham! You call yourself an editor! Why, you couldn't edit a handbill! You can't even throw a ball straight! Throw it straight! Throw it straight! For Christ's sake where do you think I am—out in the office? Throw it straight! Hell!" and all the time one and another ball, grabbed from anywhere, for the floor was always littered with them, would be thrown in the victim's direction, and before he could well appreciate what was happening to him he was being struck, once in the neck and again on the chest by the rapidly delivered six ounce air-filled balls, two of which at least he and the host were supposed to keep in constant motion between them. Later, a ball striking him in the stomach, he emitted a weak "Ooph!" and laying his hands over the affected part ceased all effort. At this the master of the situation only smirked on him leoninely and holding up a ball as if to throw it continued, "What's the matter with you now? Come on! What do you want to stop for? What do you want to stand there for? You're not hurt. How do you expect to get anywhere if you can't keep two silly little balls like these going between us?" (There had probably been six or eight.) "Here I am sixty and you're forty, and you can't even keep up with me. And you pretend to give the general public advice on life! Well, go on; God pity the public, is all I say," and he dismissed him, calling out another name.

Now came a fat, bald soul, with dewlaps and a protruding stomach, who later I learned was a manufacturer of clothing—six hundred employees under him—down in health and nerves, really all "shot to pieces" physically. Plainly nervous at the sound of his name, he puffed quickly into position, grabbing wildly after the purposely eccentric throws which his host made and which kept him running to left and right in an all but panicky mood.

"Move! Move!" insisted our host as before, and, if anything, more irritably. "Say, you work like a crab! What a motion! If you had more head and less guts you could do this better. A fine specimen you are! This is what comes of riding about in taxis and eating midnight suppers instead of exercising.

Wake up! Wake up! A belt would have kept your stomach in long ago. A little less food and less sleep, and you wouldn't have any fat cheeks. Even your hair might stay on! Wake up! Wake up! What do you want to do—die?" and as he talked he pitched the balls so quickly that his victim looked at times as though he were about to weep. His physical deficiencies were all too plain in every way. He was generally obese and looked as though he might drop, his face a flaming red, his hands trembling and missing, when a "Well, go on," sounded and a third victim was called. This time it was a well-known actor who responded, a star, rather spry and well set up, but still nervous, for he realized quite well what was before him. He had been here for weeks and was in pretty fair trim, but still he was plainly on edge. He ran and began receiving and tossing as swiftly as he could, but as with the others so it was his turn now to be given such a grilling and tongue-lashing as falls to few of us in this world, let alone among the successful in the realm of the footlights. "Say, you're not an actor—you're a woman! You're a stewed onion! Move! Move! Come on! Come on! Look at those motions now, will you? Look at that one arm up! Where do you suppose the ball is? On the ceiling? It's not a lamp! Come on! Come on! It's a wonder when you're killed as Hamlet that you don't stay dead. You are. You're really dead now, you know. Move! Move!" and so it would go until finally the poor thespian, no match for his master and beset by flying balls, landing upon his neck, ear, stomach, finally gave up and cried:

"Well, I can't go any faster than I can, can I? I can't do any more than I can!"

"Ah, go on! Go back into the chorus!" called his host, who now abandoned him. "Get somebody from the baby class to play marbles with you," and he called another.

By now, as may well be imagined, I was fairly stirred up as to the probabilities of the situation. He might call me! The man who was playing opposite me— a small, decayed person who chose me, I think, because he knew I was new, innocuous and probably awkward—seemed to realize my thoughts as well as his own. By lively exercise with me he was doing his utmost to create an impression of great and valuable effort here. "Come on, let's play fast so he won't notice us," he said most pathetically at one point. You would have thought I had known him all my life.

But he didn't call us—not this morning at any rate. Whether owing to our efforts or the fact that I at least was too insignificant, too obscure, we escaped. He did reach me, however, on the fourth or fifth day, and no spindling failure could have done worse. I was struck and tripped and pounded until I all but fell prone upon the floor, half convinced that I was being killed, but I was not. I was merely sent stumbling and drooping back to the sidelines to recover while he tortured some one else. But the names he called me! The comments on my none too smoothly articulated bones—and my alleged mind! As in my schooldays when, a laggard in the fierce and seemingly malevolent atmosphere in which I was taught my ABC's, I crept shamefacedly and beaten from the scene.

It was in the adjoining bathroom, where the host daily personally superintended the ablutions of his guests, that even more of his remarkable method was revealed. Here a goodly portion of the force of his method was his skill in removing any sense of ability, agility, authority or worth from those with whom he dealt. Apparently to him, in his strength and energy, they were all children, weaklings, failures, numbskulls, no matter what they might be in the world outside. They had no understanding of the most important of their possessions, their bodies. And here again, even more than in the gymnasium, they were at the disadvantage of feeling themselves spectacles, for here they were naked. However grand an osseous, leathery lawyer or judge or doctor or politician or society man may look out in the world addressing a jury or a crowd or walking in some favorite place, glistening in his raiment, here, whiskered, thin of legs, arms and neck, with bulging brow and stripped not only of his gown but everything else this side of his skin—well, draw your own conclusion. For after performing certain additional exercises—one hundred times up on your toes, one hundred times (if you could) squatting to your knees, one hundred times throwing your arms out straight before you from your chest or up from your shoulders or out at right angles, right and left from your body and back to your hips until your fingers touched and the sweat once more ran—you were then ready to be told (for once in your life) how to swiftly and agilely take a bath.

"Well, now, you're ready, are you?" this to a noble jurist who, like myself perhaps, had arrived only the day before. "Come on, now. Now you have just ten seconds in which to jump under the water and get yourself wet all over, twenty seconds in which to jump out and soap yourself thoroughly, ten seconds in which to get back in again and rinse off all the soap, and twenty seconds in which to rub and dry your skin thoroughly—now start!"

The distinguished jurist began, but instead of following the advice given him for rapid action huddled himself in a shivering position under the water and stood all but inert despite the previous explanation of the host that the sole method of escaping the weakening influence of cold water was by counteracting it with activity, when it would prove beneficial.

He was such a noble, stalky, bony affair, his gold eyeglasses laid aside for the time being, his tweeds and carefully laundered linen all dispensed with during his stay here. As he came, meticulously and gingerly and quite undone by his efforts, from under the water, where he had been most roughly urged by Culhane, I hoped that he and not I would continue to be seized upon by this savage who seemed to take infinite delight in disturbing the social and intellectual poise of us all.

"Soap yourself!" exclaimed the latter most harshly now that the bather was out in the room once more. "Soap your chest! Soap your stomach! Soap your arms, damn it! Soap your arms! And don't rub them all day either! Now soap your legs, damn it! Soap your legs! Don't you know how to soap your legs! Don't stand there all day! Soap your legs! Now turn round and soap your back—soap your back! For Christ's sake, soap your back! Do it quick—quick! Now come back under the water again and see if you can get it off. Don't act as though you were cold molasses! Move! Move! Lord, you act as though you had all day—as though you had never taken a bath in your life! I never saw such an old poke. You come up here and expect me to do some things for you, and then you stand around as though you were made of bone! Quick now, move!"

The noble jurist did as demanded—that is, as quickly as he could—only the mental inadequacy and feebleness which he displayed before all the others, of course, was the worst of his cruel treatment here, and in this as in many instances it cut deep. So often it was the shock to one's dignity more than anything else which hurt so, to be called an old poke when one was perhaps a grave and reverent senior, or to be told that one was made of bone when one was a famous doctor or merchant. Once under the water this particular specimen had begun by nervously rubbing his hands and face in order to get the soap off, and when shouted at and abused for that had then turned his attention to one other spot—the back of his left forearm.

Mine host seemed enraged. "Well, well!" he exclaimed irascibly, watching him as might a hawk. "Are you going to spend all day rubbing that one spot? For God's sake, don't you know enough to rub your whole body and get out from under the water? Move! Move! Rub your chest! Rub your belly! Hell, rub your back! Rub your toes and get out!"

When routed from the ludicrous effort of vigorously rubbing one spot he was continually being driven on to some other, as though his body were some vast complex machine which he had never rightly understood before. He was very much flustered of course and seemed wholly unable to grasp how it was done, let alone please his exacting host.

"Come on!" insisted the latter finally and wearily. "Get out from under the water. A lot you know about washing yourself! For a man who has been on the bench for fifteen years you're the dullest person I ever met. If you bathe like that at home, how do you keep clean? Come on out and dry yourself!"

The distinguished victim, drying himself rather ruefully on an exceedingly rough towel, looked a little weary and disgusted. "Such language!" some one afterwards said he said to some one else. "He's not used to dealing with gentlemen, that's plain. The man talks like a blackguard. And to think we pay for such things! Well, well! I'll not stand it, I'm afraid. I've had about enough. It's positively revolting, positively revolting!" But he stayed on, just the same—second thoughts, a good breakfast, his own physical needs. At any rate weeks later he was still there and in much better shape physically if not mentally.

About the second or third day I witnessed another such spectacle, which made me laugh—only not in my host's presence—nay, verily! For into this same chamber had come another distinguished personage, a lawyer or society man, I couldn't tell which, who was washing himself rather leisurely, as was *not* the prescribed way, when suddenly he was spied by mine host, who was invariably instructing some one in this swift one-minute or less system. Now he eyed the operation narrowly for a few seconds, then came over and exclaimed:

"Wash your toes, can't you? Wash your toes! Can't you wash your toes?"

The skilled gentleman, realizing that he was now living under very different conditions from those to which presumably he was accustomed, reached down and began to rub the tops of his toes but without any desire apparently to widen the operation.

"Here!" called the host, this time much more sharply, "I said wash your toes, not the outside of them! Soap them! Don't you know how to wash your toes yet? You're old enough, God knows! Wash between 'em! Wash under 'em!"

"Certainly I know how to wash my toes," replied the other irritably and straightening up, "and what's more, I'd like you to know that I am a gentleman."

"Well, then, if you're a gentleman," retorted the other, "you ought to know how to wash your toes. Wash 'em—and don't talk back!"

"Pah!" exclaimed the bather now, looking twice as ridiculous as before. "I'm not used to having such language addressed to me."

"I can't help that," said Culhane. "If you knew how to wash your toes perhaps you wouldn't have to have such language addressed to you."

"Oh, hell!" fumed the other. "This is positively outrageous! I'll leave the place, by George!"

"Very well," rejoined the other, "only before you go you'll have to wash your toes!"

And he did, the host standing by and calmly watching the performance until it was finally completed.

It was just this atmosphere which made the place the most astonishing in which I have ever been. It seemed to be drawing the celebrated and the successful as a magnet might iron, and yet it offered conditions which one might presume they would be most opposed to. No one here was really any one, however much he might be outside. Our host was all. He had a great blazing personality which dominated everybody, and he did not hesitate to show before one and all that he did so do.

Breakfast here consisted of a cereal, a chop and coffee—plentiful but very plain, I thought. After breakfast, between eight-thirty and eleven, we were free to do as we chose: write letters, pack our bags if we were leaving, do up our laundry to be sent out, read, or merely sit about. At eleven, or ten-thirty, according to the nature of the exercise, one had to join a group, either one that was to do the long or short block, as they were known here, or one that was to ride horseback, all exercises being so timed that by proper execution one would arrive at the bathroom door in time to bathe, dress and take ten minutes' rest before luncheon. These exercises were simple enough in themselves, consisting, as they did in the case of the long and the short blocks (the long block seven, the short four miles in length), of our walking, or walking and running betimes, about or over courses laid up hill and down dale, over or through unpaved mudroads in many instances, along dry or wet beds of brooks or streams, and across stony or weedy fields, often still damp with dew or the spring rains. But in most cases, when people had not taken any regular exercise for a long time, this was by no means easy. The first day I thought I should never make it, and I was by no means a poor walker. Others, the new ones especially, often gave out and had to be sent for, or came in an hour late to be most severely and irritatingly ragged by the host. He seemed to all but despise weakness and had apparently a thousand disagreeable ways of showing it.

"If you want to see what poor bags of mush some people can become," he once said in regard to some poor specimen who had seemingly had great difficulty in doing the short block, "look at this. Here comes a man sent out to do four measly country miles in fifty minutes, and look at him. You'd think he was going to die. He probably thinks so himself. In New York he'd do seventeen miles in a night running from barroom to barroom or one lobster palace to another—that's a good name for them, by the way—and never say a word. But out here in the country, with plenty of fresh air and a night's rest and a good breakfast, he can't even do four miles in fifty minutes! Think of it! And he probably thinks of himself as a man—boasts before his friends, or his wife, anyhow. Lord!"

A day or two later there arrived here a certain major of the United States Army, a large, broad-chested, rather pompous person of about forty-eight or-nine, who from taking his ease in one sinecure and another had finally reached the place where he was unable to endure certain tests (or he thought so) which were about to be made with a view to retiring certain officers grown fat in the service. As he explained to Culhane, and the latter was always open and ribald afterward in his comments on those who offered explanations of any kind, his plan was to take the course here in order to be able to make the difficult tests later.

Culhane resented this, I think. He resented people using him or his methods to get anywhere, do anything more in life than he could do, and yet he received them. He felt, and I think in the main that he was right, that they looked down on him because of his lowly birth and purely material and mechanical career, and yet having attained some distinction by it he could not forego this work which raised him, in a way, to a position of dominance over these people. Now the sight of presumably so efficient a person in need of aid or exercise, to be built up, was all that was required to spur him on to the most waspish or wolfish attitude imaginable. In part at least he argued, I think (for in the last analysis he was really too wise and experienced to take any such petty view, although there is a subconscious "past-lack" motivating impulse in all our views), that here he was, an ex-policeman, ex-wrestler, ex-prize fighter, ex-private, ex-waiter, beef-carrier, bouncer, trainer; and here was this grand major, trained at West Point, who actually didn't know any more about life or how to take care of his body than to be compelled to come here, broken down at forty-eight, whereas he, because of his stamina and Spartan energy, had been able to survive in perfect condition until sixty and was now in a position to rebuild all these men and wastrels and to control this great institution. And to a certain extent he was right, although he seemed to forget or not to know that he was not the creator of his own great strength, by any means, impulses and tendencies over which he had no control having arranged for that.

However that may be, here was the major a suppliant for his services, and here was he, Culhane, and although the major was paying well for his minute room and his probably greatly decreased diet, still Culhane could not resist the temptation to make a show of him, to picture him as the more or less pathetic example that he was, in order perhaps that he, Culhane, might shine by contrast. Thus on the first day, having sent him around the short block with the others, it was found at twelve, when the "joggers" were expected to return, and again at twelve-thirty when they were supposed to take their places at the luncheon table, that the heavy major had not arrived. He had been seen and passed by all, of course. After the first mile or two probably he had given out and was making his way as best he might up hill and down dale, or along some more direct road, to the "shop," or maybe he had dropped out entirely, as some did, via a kindly truck or farmer's wagon, and was on his way to the nearest railway station.

At any rate, as Culhane sat down at his very small private table, which stood in the center of the dining-room and far apart from the others (a vantage point, as it were), he looked about and, not seeing the new guest, inquired, "Has any one seen that alleged army officer who arrived here this morning?"

No one could say anything more than that they had left him two or three miles back.

"I thought so," he said tersely. "There you have a fine example of the desk general and major—we had 'em in the army—men who sit in a swivel chair all day, wear a braided uniform and issue orders to other people. You'd think a man like that who had been trained at West Point and seen service in the Philippines would have sense enough to keep himself in condition. Not at all. As soon as they get a little way up in their profession they want to sit around hotel grills or society ballrooms and show off, tell how wonderful they are. Here's a man, an army officer, in such rotten shape that if I sent a good horse after him now it's ten to one he couldn't get on him. I'll have to send a truck or some such thing."

He subsided. About an hour later the major did appear, much the worse for wear. A groom with a horse had been sent out after him, and, as the latter confided to some one afterward, he "had to help the major on." From that time on, on the short block and the long, as well as on those horseback tours which every second or third morning we were supposed to take, the major was his especial target. He loved to pick on him, to tell him that he was "nearly all guts"—a phrase which literally sickened me at that time—to ask him how he expected to stay in the army if he couldn't do this or that, what good was he to the army, how could any soldier respect a thing like him, and so on *ad infinitum* until, while at first I pitied the major, later on I admired his pluck. Culhane foisted upon him his sorriest and boniest nag, the meanest animal he could find, yet he never complained; and although he forced on him all the foods he knew the major could not like, still there was no complaint; he insisted that he should be out and around of an afternoon when most of us lay about, allowed him no drinks whatever, although he was accustomed to them. The major, as I learned afterwards, stayed not six but twelve weeks and passed the tests which permitted him to remain in the army.

But to return to Culhane himself. The latter's method always contained this element of nag and pester which, along with his brazen reliance on and pride in his brute strength at sixty, made all these others look so puny and ineffectual. They might have brains and skill but here they were in his institution, more or less undone nervously and physically, and here he was, cold, contemptuous, not caring much whether they came, stayed or went, and laughing at them even as they raged. Now and then it was rumored that he found some single individual in whom he would take an interest, but not often. In the main I think he despised them one and all for the puny machines they were. He even despised life and the pleasures and dissipations or swinish indolence which, in his judgment, characterized most men. I recall once, for instance, his telling us how as a private in the United States Army when the division of which he was a unit was shut up in winter quarters, huddled about stoves, smoking (as he characterized them) "filthy pipes" or chewing tobacco and spitting, actually lousy, and never changing their clothes for weeks on end—how he, revolting at all this and the disease and fevers ensuing, had kept out of doors as much as possible, even in the coldest weather, and finding no other way of keeping clean the single shift of underwear and the one uniform he possessed he had, every other day or so, washed all, uniform and underwear, with or without soap as conditions might compel, in a nearby stream, often breaking the ice to get to the water, and dancing about naked in the cold, running and jumping, while they dried on bushes or the branch of a tree.

"Those poor rats," he added most contemptuously, "used to sit inside and wonder at me or laugh and jeer, hovering over their stoves, but a lot of them died that very winter, and here I am today."

And well we knew it. I used to study the faces of many of the puffy, gelatinous souls, so long confined to their comfortable offices, restaurants and homes that two hours on horseback all but wore them out, and wonder how this appealed to them. I think that in the main they took it as an illustration of either one of two things: insanity, or giant and therefore not-to-be-imitated strength.

But in regard to them Culhane was by no means so tolerant. One day, as I recall, there arrived at the sanitarium a stout and mushy-looking Hebrew, with a semi-bald pate, protruding paunch and fat arms and legs, who applied to Culhane for admission. And, as much to irritate his other guests, I think, as to torture this particular specimen into some semblance of vitality, he admitted him. And thereafter, from the hour he entered until he left about the time I did, Culhane seemed to follow him with a wolfish and savage idea. He gave him a most damnable and savage horse, one that kicked and bit, and at mounting time would place Mr. Itzky (I think his name was) up near the front of the procession where he could watch him. Always at mount-time, when we were permitted to ride, there was inside the great stable a kind of preliminary military inspection of all our accouterments, seeing that we had to saddle and bridle and bring forth our own steeds. This particular person could not saddle a horse very well nor put on his bit and bridle. The animal was inclined to rear and plunge when he came near, to fix him with an evil eye and bite at him.

And above all things Culhane seemed to value strain of this kind. If he could just make his guests feel the pressure of necessity in connection with their work he was happy. To this end he would employ the most contemptuous and grilling comment. Thus to Mr. Itzky he was most unkind. He would look over all most cynically, examining the saddles and bridles, and then say, "Oh, I see you haven't learned how to tighten a belly-band yet," or "I do believe you have your saddle hind-side to. You would if you could, that's one thing sure. How do you expect a horse to be sensible or quiet when he knows that he isn't saddled right? Any horse knows that much, and whether he has an ass for a rider. I'd kick and bite too if I were some of these horses, having a lot of damned fools and wasters to pack all over the country. Loosen that belt and fasten it right" (there might be nothing wrong with it) "and move your saddle up. Do you want to sit over the horse's rump?"

Then would come the fateful moment of mounting. There was of course the accepted and perfect way—his way: left foot in stirrup, an easy balanced spring and light descent into the seat. One should be able to slip the right foot into the right stirrup with the same motion of mounting. But imagine fifty, sixty, seventy men, all sizes, weights and differing conditions of health and mood. A number of these people had never ridden a horse before coming here and were as nervous and frightened as children. Such mounts! Such fumbling around, once they were in their saddles, for the right stirrup! And all the while Culhane would be sitting out front like an army captain on the only decent steed in the place, eyeing us with a look of infinite and weary contempt that served to increase our troubles a thousandfold.

"Well, you're all on, are you? You all do it so gracefully I like to sit here and admire you. Hulbert there throws his leg over his horse's back so artistically that he almost kicks his teeth out. And Effingham does his best to fall off on the other side. And where's Itzky? I don't even see him. Oh, yes, there he is. Well" (this to Itzky, frantically endeavoring to get one fat foot in a stirrup and pull himself up), "what about you? Can't you get your leg that high? Here's a man who for twenty-five years has been running a cloak-and-suit business and employing five hundred people, but he can't get on a horse! Imagine! Five hundred people dependent on that for their living!" (At this point, say, Itzky succeeds in mounting.) "Well, he's actually on! Now see if you can stick while we ride a block or two. You'll find the right stirrup, Itzky, just a little forward of your horse's belly on the right side—see? A fine bunch this is to lead out through a gentleman's country! Hell, no wonder I've got a bad reputation throughout this section! Well, forward, and see if you can keep from falling off."

Then we were out through the stable-door and the privet gate at a smart trot, only to burst into a headlong gallop a little farther on down the road. To the seasoned riders it was all well enough, but to beginners, those nervous about horses, fearful about themselves! The first day, not having ridden in years and being uncertain as to my skill, I could scarcely stay on. Several days later, I by then having become a reasonably seasoned rider, it was Mr. Itzky who appeared on the scene, and after him various others. On this particular trip I am thinking of, Mr. Itzky fell or rolled off and could not again mount. He was miles from the repair shop and Culhane, discovering his plight, was by no means sympathetic. We had a short ride back to where he sat lamely by the roadside viewing disconsolately the cavalcade and the country in general.

"Well, what's the matter with you now?" It was Culhane, eyeing him most severely.

"I hef hurt my foot. I kent stay on."

"You mean you'd rather walk, do you, and lead your horse?"

"Vell, I kent ride."

"All right, then, you lead your horse back to the stable if you want any lunch, and hereafter you run with the baby-class on the short block until you think you can ride without falling off. What's the good of my keeping a stable of first-class horses at the service of a lot of mush-heads who don't even know how to use 'em? All they do is ruin 'em. In a week or two, after a good horse is put in the stable, he's not fit for a gentleman to ride. They pull and haul and kick and beat, when as a matter of fact the horse has a damned sight more sense than they have."

We rode off, leaving Itzky alone. The men on either side of me—we were riding three abreast—scoffed under their breath at the statement that we were furnished decent horses. "The nerve! This nag!" "This bag of bones!" "To think a thing like this should be called a horse!" But there were no outward murmurs and no particular sympathy for Mr. Itzky. He was a fat stuff, a sweat-shop manufacturer, they would bet; let him walk and sweat.

So much for sympathy in this gay realm where all were seeking to restore their own little bodies, whatever happened.

So many of these men varied so greatly in their looks, capacities and troubles that they were always amusing. Thus I recall one lean iron manufacturer, the millionaire president of a great "frog and switch" company, who had come on from Kansas City, troubled with anæmia, neurasthenia, "nervous derangement of the heart" and various other things. He was over fifty, very much concerned about himself, his family, his business, his friends; anxious to obtain the benefits of this celebrated course of which he had heard so much. Walking or running near me on his first day, he took occasion to make inquiries in regard to Culhane, the life here, and later on confidences as to his own condition. It appeared that his chief trouble was his heart, a kind of phantom disturbance which made him fear that he was about to drop dead and which came and went, leaving him uncertain as to whether he had it or not. On entering he had confided to Culhane the mysteries of his case, and the latter had examined him, pronouncing him ("Rather roughly," as he explained to me), quite fit to do "all the silly work he would have to do here."

Nevertheless while we were out on the short block his heart was hurting him. At the same time it had been made rather clear to him that if he wished to stay here he would have to fulfill all the obligations imposed. After a mile or two or three of quick walking and jogging he was saying to me, "You know, I'm not really sure that I can do this. It's very severe, more so than I thought. My heart is not doing very well. It feels very fluttery."

"But," I said, "if he told you you could stand it, you can, I'm sure. It's not very likely he'd say you could if you couldn't. He examined you, didn't he? I don't believe he'd deliberately put a strain on any one who couldn't stand it."

"Yes," he admitted doubtfully, "that's true perhaps."

Still he continued to complain and complain and to grow more and more worried, until finally he slowed up and was lost in the background.

Reaching the gymnasium at the proper time I bathed and dressed myself quickly and waited on the balcony over the bathroom to see what would happen in this case. As a rule Culhane stood in or near the door at this time, having just returned from some route or "block" himself, to see how the others were faring. And he was there when the iron manufacturer came limping up, fifteen minutes late, one hand over his heart, the other to his mouth, and exclaiming as he drew near, "I do believe, Mr. Culhane, that I can't stand this. I'm afraid there is something the matter with my heart. It's fluttering so."

"To hell with your heart! Didn't I tell you there was nothing the matter with it? Get into the bath!"

The troubled manufacturer, overawed or reassured as the case might be, entered the bath and ten minutes later might have been seen entering the dining-room, as comfortable apparently as any one. Afterwards he confessed to me on one of our jogs that there was something about Culhane which *gave him confidence* and made him believe that there wasn't anything wrong with his heart—which there wasn't, I presume.

The intensely interesting thing about Culhane was this different, very original and forthright if at times brutal point of view. It was a blazing material world of which he was the center, the sun, and yet always I had the sense of very great life. With no knowledge of or interest in the superior mental sciences or arts or philosophies, still he seemed to suggest and even live them. He was in his way an exemplification of that ancient Greek regimen and stark thought which brought back the ten thousand from Cunaxa. He seemed even to suggest in his rough way historical perspective and balance. He knew men, and apparently he sensed how at best and at bottom life was to be lived, with not too much emotional or appetitive swaying in any one direction, and not too little either.

Yet in "trapseing" about this particular realm each day with ministers, lawyers, doctors, actors, manufacturers, papa's or mamma's young hopefuls and petted heirs, young scapegraces and so-called "society men" of the extreme "upper crust," stuffed and plethoric with money and as innocent of sound knowledge or necessary energy in some instances as any one might well be, one could not help speculating as to how it was that such a man, as indifferent and all but discourteous as this one, could attract them (and so many) to him. They came from all parts of America—the Pacific, the Gulf, the Atlantic and Canada—and yet, although they did not relish, him or his treatment of them, once here they stayed. Walking or running or idling about with them one could always hear from one or another that Culhane was too harsh, a "bounder," an "upstart," a "cheap pugilist" or "wrestler" at best (I myself thought so at times when I was angry), yet here they were, and here I was, and staying. He was low, vulgar—yet here we were. And yet, meditating on him, I began to think that he was really one of the most remarkable men I had ever known, for these people he dealt with were of all the most difficult to deal with. In the main they were of that order or condition of mind which springs from (1), too much wealth too easily acquired or inherited; or (2), from a blazing material success, the cause of which was their own savage self-interested viewpoint. Hence a colder and in some respects a more critical group of men I have never known. Most of them had already seen so much of life in a libertine way that there was little left to enjoy. They sniffed at almost everything, Culhane included, and yet they were obviously drawn to him. I tried to explain this to myself on the ground that there is some iron power in some people which literally compels this, whether one will or no; or that they were in the main so tired of life and so truly selfish and egotistic that it required some such different iron or caviar mood plus such a threatening regimen to make them really take an interest. Sick as they were, he was about the only thing left on which they could sharpen their teeth with any result.

As I have said, a part of Culhane's general scheme was to arrange the starting time for the walks and jogs about the long and short blocks so that if one moved along briskly he reached the sanitarium at twelve-thirty and had a few minutes in which to bathe and cool off and change his clothes before entering the dining-room, where, if not at the bathroom door beforehand, Culhane would be waiting, seated at his little table, ready to keep watch on the time and condition of all those due. Thus one day, a group of us having done the long block in less time than we should have devoted to it, came in panting and rejoicing that we had cut the record by seven minutes. We did not know that he was around. But in the dining-room as we entered he scoffed at our achievement.

"You think you're smart, don't you?" he said sourly and without any preliminary statement as to how he knew we had done it in less time. "You come out here and pay me one hundred a week and then you want to be cute and play tricks with your own money and health. I want you to remember just one thing: my reputation is just as much involved with the results here as your money. I don't need anybody's money, and I do need my orders obeyed. Now you all have watches. You just time yourselves and do that block in the time required. If you can't do it, that's one thing; I can forgive a man too weak or sick to do it. But I haven't any use for a mere smart aleck, and I don't want any more of it, see?"

That luncheon was very sad.

Another thing in connection with these luncheons and dinners, which were sharply timed to the minute, were these crisp table speeches, often made *in re* some particular offender or his offense, at other times mere sarcastic comments on life in general and the innate cussedness of human nature, which amused at the same time that they were certain to irritate some. For who is it that is not interested in hearing the peccadilloes of his neighbor aired?

Thus while I was there, there was a New York society man by the name of Blake, who unfortunately was given to severe periods of alcoholism, the results of which were, after a time, nervous disorders which sent him here. In many ways he was as amiable and courteous and considerate a soul as one could meet anywhere. He had that smooth, gracious something about him— good nature, for one thing, a kind of understanding and sympathy for various forms of life—which left him highly noncensorious, if genially examining at times. But his love of drink, or rather his mild attempts here to arrange some method by which in this droughty world he could obtain a little, aroused in Culhane not so much opposition as an amused contempt, for at bottom I think he really liked the man. Blake was so orderly, so sincere in his attempts to fulfill conditions, only about once every week or so he would suggest that he be allowed to go to White Plains or Rye, or even New York, on some errand or other—most of which requests were promptly and nearly always publicly refused. For although Culhane had his private suite at one end of the great building, where one might suppose one might go to make a private plea, still one could never find him there. He refused to receive complaints or requests or visits of any kind there. If you wanted to speak to him you had to do it when he was with the group in its entirety—a commonsense enough policy. But just the same there were those who had reasonable requests or complaints, and these, by a fine intuition as to who was who in this institution and what might be expected of each one, he managed to hear very softly, withdrawing slowly as they talked or inviting them into the office. In the main however the requests were very much like those of Blake—men who wanted to get off somewhere for a day or two, feeling, as they did after a week or two or three, especially fit and beginning to think no doubt of the various comforts and pleasures which the city offered.

But to all these he was more or less adamant. By hook or by crook, by special arrangements with friends or agents in nearby towns and the principal showy resorts of New York, he managed to know, providing they did leave the grounds, either with or without his consent, about where they were and what they had done, and in case any of his rules or their agreements were broken their privileges were thereafter cut off or they were promptly ejected, their trunks being set out on the roadway in front of the estate and they being left to make their way to shelter elsewhere as best they might.

On one occasion, however, Blake had been allowed to go to New York over Saturday and Sunday to attend to some urgent business, as he said, he on his honor having promised to avoid the white lights. Nevertheless he did not manage so to do but instead, in some comfortable section of that region, was seen drinking enough to last him until perhaps he should have another opportunity to return to the city.

On his return to the "shop" on Monday morning or late Sunday night, Culhane pretended not to see him until noonday lunch, when, his jog over the long block done with and his bath taken, he came dapperly into the dining-room, wishing to look as innocent and fit as possible. But Culhane was there before him at his little table in the center of the room, and patting the head of one of the two pure-blooded collies that always followed him about on the grounds or in the house, began as follows:

"A dog," he said very distinctly and in his most cynical tone and apparently apropos of nothing, which usually augured that the lightning of his criticism was about to strike somewhere, "is so much better than the average man that it's an insult to the dog to compare them. The dog's really decent. He has no sloppy vices. You set a plate of food before a regularly-fed, blooded dog, and he won't think of gorging himself sick or silly. He eats what he needs, and then stops. So does a cat" (which is of course by no means true, but still—). "A dog doesn't get a red nose from drinking too much." By now all eyes were turning in the direction of Blake, whose nose was faintly tinged. "He doesn't get gonorrhea or syphilis." The united glances veered in the direction of three or four young scapegraces of wealth, all of whom were suspected of these diseases. "He doesn't hang around hotel bars and swill and get his tongue thick and talk about how rich he is or how old his family is." (This augured that Blake did such things, which I doubt, but once more all eyes were shifted to him.) "He doesn't break his word. Within the limits of his poor little brain he's faithful. He does what he thinks he's called upon to do.

"But you take a man—more especially a gentleman—one of these fellows who is always very pointed in emphasizing that he is a gentleman" (which Blake never did). "Let him inherit eight or ten millions, give him a college education, let him be socially well connected, and what does he do? Not a damned thing if he can help it except contract vices—run from one saloon to another, one gambling house to another, one girl to another, one meal to another. He doesn't need to know anything necessarily. He may be the lowest dog physically and in every other way, and still he's a gentleman—because he has money, wears spats and a high hat. Why I've seen fifty poor boob prize fighters in my time who could put it all over most of the so-called gentlemen I have ever seen. They kept their word. They tried to be physically fit. They tried to stand up in the world and earn their own living and be somebody." (He was probably thinking of himself.) "But a gentleman wants to boast of his past and his family, to tell you that he must go to the city on business— his lawyers or some directors want to see him. Then he swills around at hotel bars, stays with some of his lady whores, and then comes back here and expects me to pull him into shape again, to make his nose a little less red. He thinks he can use my place to fall back on when he can't go any longer, to fix him up to do some more swilling later on.

"Well, I want to serve notice on all so-called gentlemen here, and *one gentleman* in particular" (and he heavily and sardonically emphasized the words), "that it won't do. This isn't a hospital attached to a whorehouse or a saloon. And as for the trashy little six hundred paid here, I don't need it. I've turned away more men who have been here once or twice and have shown me that they were just using this place and me as something to help them go on with their lousy drinking and carousing, than would fill this building. Sensible men know it. They don't try to use me. It's only the wastrels, or their mothers or fathers who bring their boys and husbands and cry, who try to use me, and I take 'em once or twice, but not oftener. When a man goes out of here cured, I know he is cured. I never want to see him again. I want him to go out in the world and stand up. I don't want him to come back here in six months sniveling to be put in shape again. He disgusts me. He makes me sick. I feel like ordering him off the place, and I do, and that's the end of him. Let him go and bamboozle somebody else. I've shown him all I know. There's no mystery. He can do as much for himself, once he's been here, as I can. If he won't, well and good. And I'm saying one thing more: There's one man here to whom this particularly applies today. This is his last call. He's been here twice. When he goes out this time he can't come back. Now see if some of you can remember some of the things I've been telling you."

He subsided and opened his little pint of wine.

Another day while I was there he began as follows:

"If there's one class of men that needs to be improved in this country, it's lawyers. I don't know why it is, but there's something in the very nature of the work of a lawyer which appears to make him cynical and to want to wear a know-it-all look. Most lawyers are little more than sharper crooks than the crooks they have to deal with. They're always trying to get in on some case or other where they have to outwit the law, save some one from getting what he justly deserves, and then they are supposed to be honest and high-minded! Think of it! To judge by some of the specimens I get up here," and then some lawyer in the place would turn a shrewd inquiring glance in his direction or steadfastly gaze at his plate or out the window, while the others stared at him, "you would think they were the salt of the earth or that they were following a really noble profession or that they were above or better than other men in their abilities. Well, if being conniving and tricky are fine traits, I suppose they are, but personally I can't see it. Generally speaking, they're physically the poorest fish I get here. They're slow and meditative and sallow, mostly because they get too little exercise, I presume. And they're never direct and enthusiastic in an argument. A lawyer always wants to stick in an 'if' or a 'but,' to get around you in some way. He's never willing to answer you quickly or directly. I've watched 'em now for nearly fifteen years, and they're all more or less alike. They think they're very individual and different, but they're not. Most of them don't know nearly as much about life as a good, all-around business or society man," this in the absence of any desire to discuss these two breeds for the time being. "For the life of me I could never see why a really attractive woman would ever want to marry a lawyer"—and so he would talk on, revealing one little unsatisfactory trait after another in connection with the tribe, sand-papering their raw places as it were, until you would about conclude, supposing you had never heard him talk concerning any other profession, that lawyers were the most ignoble, the pettiest, the most inefficient physically and mentally, of all the men he had ever encountered; and in his noble savage state there would not be one to disagree with him, for he had such an animal, tiger-like mien that you had the feeling that instead of an argument you would get a physical rip which would leave you bleeding for days.

The next day, or a day or two or four or six later—according to his mood—it would be doctors or merchants or society men or politicians he would discourse about—and, kind heaven, what a drubbing they would get! He seemed always to be meditating on the vulnerable points of his victims, anxious (and yet presumably not) to show them what poor, fallible, shabby, petty and all but drooling creatures they were. Thus in regard to merchants:

"The average man who has a little business of some kind, a factory or a wholesale or brokerage house or a hotel or a restaurant, usually has a distinctly middle-class mind." At this all the merchants and manufacturers were likely to give a very sharp ear. "As a rule, you'll find that they know just the one little line with which they're connected, and nothing more. One man knows all about cloaks and suits" (this may have been a slap at poor Itzky) "or he knows a little something about leather goods or shoes or lamps or furniture, and that's all he knows. If he's an American he'll buckle down to that little business and work night and day, sweat blood and make every one else connected with him sweat it, underpay his employees, swindle his friends, half-starve himself and his family, in order to get a few thousand dollars and seem as good as some one else who has a few thousand. And yet he doesn't want to be different from—he wants to be just like—the other fellow. If some one in his line has a house up on the Hudson or on Riverside Drive, when he gets his money he wants to go there and live. If the fellow in his line, or some other that he knows something about, belongs to a certain club, he has to belong to it even if the club doesn't want him or he wouldn't look well in it. He wants to have the same tailor, the same grocer, smoke the same brand of cigars and go to the same summer resort as the other fellow. They even want to look alike. God! And then when they're just like every one else, they think they're somebody. They haven't a single idea outside their line, and yet because they've made money they want to tell other people how to live and think. Imagine a rich butcher or cloak-maker, or any one else, presuming to tell me how to think or live!"

He stared about him as though he saw many exemplifications of his picture present. And it was always interesting to see how those whom his description really did fit look as though he could not possibly be referring to them.

Of all types or professions that came here, I think he disliked doctors most. The reason was of course that the work they did or were about to do in the world bordered on that which he was trying to accomplish, and the chances were that they sniffed at or at least critically examined what he was doing with an eye to finding its weak spots. In many cases no doubt he fancied that they were there to study and copy his methods and ideas, without having the decency later on to attribute their knowledge to him. It was short shrift for any one of them with ideas or "notions" unfriendly to him advanced in his presence. For a little while during my stay there was a smooth-faced, rather solid physically and decidedly self-opinionated mentally, doctor who ate at the same small table as I and who was never tired of airing his views, medical and otherwise. He confided to me rather loftily that there was, to be sure, something to Culhane's views and methods but that they were "over-emphasized here, over-emphasized." Still, one could over-emphasize the value of drugs too. As for himself he had decided to achieve a happy medium if possible, and for this reason (for one) he had come here to study Culhane.

As for Culhane, in spite of the young doctor's condescension and understanding, or perhaps better yet because of it, he thoroughly disliked, barely tolerated, him, and was never tired of commenting on little dancing medics with their "pill cases" and easily acquired book knowledge, boasting of their supposed learning "which somebody else had paid for," as he once said—their fathers, of course. And when they were sick, some of them at least, they had to come out here to him, or they came to steal his theory and start a shabby grafting sanitarium of their own. He knew them.

One noon we were at lunch. Occasionally before seating himself at his small central table he would walk or glance about and, having good eyes, would spy some little defect or delinquency somewhere and of course immediately act upon it. One of the rules of the repair shop was that you were to eat what was put before you, especially when it differed from what your table companion received. Thus a fat man at a table with a lean one might receive a small portion of lean meat, no potatoes and no bread or one little roll, whereas his lean acquaintance opposite would be receiving a large portion of fat meat, a baked or boiled potato, plenty of bread and butter, and possibly a side dish of some kind. Now it might well be, as indeed was often the case, that each would be dissatisfied with his apportionment and would attempt to change plates.

But this was the one thing that Culhane would not endure. So upon one occasion, passing near the table at which sat myself and the above-mentioned doctor, table-mates for the time being, he noticed that he was not eating his carrots, a dish which had been especially prepared for him, I imagine—for if one unconsciously ignored certain things the first day or two of his stay, those very things would be all but rammed down his throat during the remainder of his stay; a thing concerning which one guest and another occasionally cautioned newcomers. However this may have been in this particular case, he noticed the uneaten carrots and, pausing a moment, observed:

"What's the matter? Aren't you eating your carrots?" We had almost finished eating.

"Who, me?" replied the medic, looking up. "Oh, no, I never eat carrots, you know. I don't like them."

"Oh, don't you?" said Culhane sweetly. "You don't like them, and so you don't eat them! Well, suppose you eat them here. They may do you a little good just as a change."

"But I never eat carrots," retorted the medic tersely and with a slight show of resentment or opposition, scenting perhaps a new order.

"No, not outside perhaps, but here you do. You eat carrots here, see?"

"Yes, but why should I eat them if I don't like them? They don't agree with me. Must I eat something that doesn't agree with me just because it's a rule or to please you?"

"To please me, or the carrots, or any damned thing you please—but eat 'em."

The doctor subsided. For a day or two he went about commenting on what a farce the whole thing was, how ridiculous to make any one eat what was not suited to him, but just the same while he was there he ate them.

As for myself, I was very fond of large boiled potatoes and substantial orders of fat and lean meat, and in consequence, having been so foolish as to show this preference, I received but the weakest, most contemptible and puling little spuds and pale orders of meat—with, it is true, plenty of other "side dishes"; whereas a later table-mate of mine, a distressed and neurasthenic society man, was receiving—I soon learned he especially abhorred them— potatoes as big as my two fists.

"Now look at that! Now look at that!" he often said peevishly and with a kind of sickly whine in his voice when he saw one being put before him. "He knows I don't like potatoes, and see what I get! And look at the little bit of a thing he gives you! It's a shame, the way he nags people, especially over this food question. I don't think there's a thing to it. I don't think eating a big potato does me a bit of good, or you the little one, and yet I have to eat the blank-blank things or get out. And I need to get on my feet just now."

"Well, cheer up," I said sympathetically and with an eye on the large potato perhaps. "He isn't always looking, and we can fix it. You mash up your big potato and put butter and salt on it, and I'll do the same with my little one. Then when he's not looking we'll shift."

"Oh, that's all right," he commented, "but we'd better look out. If he sees us he'll be as sore as the devil."

This system worked well enough for a time, and for days I was getting all the potato I wanted and congratulating myself on my skill, when one day as I was slyly forking potatoes out of his dish, moved helpfully in my direction, I saw Culhane approaching and feared that our trick had been discovered. It had. Perhaps some snaky waitress has told on us, or he had seen us, even from his table.

"Now I know what's going on here at this table," he growled savagely, "and I want you two to cut it out. This big boob here" (he was referring to my esteemed self) "who hasn't strength of will or character enough to keep himself in good health and has to be brought up here by his brother, hasn't brains enough to see that when I plan a thing for his benefit it is for his benefit, and not mine. Like most of the other damned fools that come up here and waste their money and my time, he thinks I'm playing some cute game with him—tag or something that will let him show how much cuter he is than I am. And he's supposed to be a writer and have a little horse-sense! His brother claims it, anyhow. And as for this other simp here," and now he was addressing the assembled diners while nodding toward my friend, "it hasn't been three weeks since he was begging to know what I could do for him. And now look at him—entering into a petty little game of potato-cheating!

"I swear," he went on savagely, talking to the room in general, "sometimes I don't know what to do with such damned fools. The right thing would be to set these two, and about fifty others in this place, out on the main road with their trunks and let them go to hell. They don't deserve the attention of a conscientious man. I prohibit gambling—what happens? A lot of nincompoops and mental lightweights with more money than brains sneak off into a field of an afternoon on the excuse that they are going for a walk, and then sit down and lose or win a bucket of money just to show off what hells of fellows they are, what sports, what big 'I ams.' I prohibit cigarette-smoking, not because I think it's literally going to kill anybody but because I think it looks bad here, sets a bad example to a lot of young wasters who come here and who ought to be broken of the vice, and besides, because I don't like cigarette-smoking here—don't want it and won't have it. What happens? A lot of sissies and mamma's boys and pet heirs, whose fathers haven't got enough brains to cut 'em off and make 'em get out and work, come up here, sneak in cigarettes or get the servants to, and then hide out behind the barn or a tree down in the lot and sneak and smoke like a lot of cheap schoolboys. God, it makes me sick! What's the use of a man working out a fact during a lifetime and letting other people have the benefit of it—not because he needs their money, but that they need his help—if all the time he is going to have such cattle to deal with? Not one out of twenty or forty men that come here really wants me to help him or to help himself. What he wants is to have some one drive him in the way he ought to go, kick him into it, instead of his buckling down and helping himself. What's the good of bothering with such damned fools? A man ought to take the whole pack and run 'em off the place with a dog-whip." He waved his hand in the air. "It's sickening. It's impossible.

"As for you two," he added, turning to us, but suddenly stopped. "Hell, what's the use! Why should I bother with you? Do as you damned well please, and stay sick or die!"

He turned on his heel and walked out of the dining-room, leaving us to sit there. I was so dumbfounded by the harangue our pseudo-cleverness had released that I could scarcely speak. My appetite was gone and I felt wretched. To think of having been the cause of this unnecessary tongue-lashing to the others! And I felt that we were, and justly, the target for their rather censorious eyes.

"My God!" moaned my companion most dolefully. "That's always the way with me. Nothing that I ever do comes out right. All my life I've been unlucky. My mother died when I was seven, and my father's never had any use for me. I started in three or four businesses four or five years ago, but none of them ever came out right. My yacht burned last summer, and I've had neurasthenia for two years." He catalogued a list of ills that would have done honor to Job himself, and he was worth nine millions, so I heard!

Two or three additional and amusing incidents, and I am done.

One of the most outré things in connection with our rides about the countryside was Culhane's attitude toward life and the natives and passing strangers as representing life. Thus one day, as I recall very well, we were riding along a backwoods country road, very shadowy and branch-covered, a great company of us four abreast, when suddenly and after his very military fashion there came a "Halt! Right by fours! Right dress! Face!" and presently we were all lined up in a row facing a greensward which had suddenly been revealed to the left and on which, and before a small plumber's stove standing outside some gentleman's stable, was stretched a plumber and his helper. The former, a man of perhaps thirty-five, the latter a lad of, say, fourteen or fifteen, were both very grimy and dirty, but taking their ease in the morning sun, a little pot of lead on the stove being waited for, I presume, that it might boil.

Culhane, leaving his place at the head of the column, returned to the center nearest the plumber and his helper and pointing at them and addressing us in a very clear voice, said:

"There you have it. There's American labor for you, at its best—union labor, the poor, downtrodden workingman. Look at him." We all looked. "This poor hard-working plumber here," and at that the latter stirred and sat up, scarcely even now grasping what it was all about, so suddenly had we descended upon him, "earns or demands sixty cents an hour, and this poor sweating little helper here has to have forty. They're working now. They're waiting for that little bit of lead to boil, at a dollar an hour between them. They can't do a thing, either of 'em, until it does, and lead has to be well done, you know, before it can be used.

"Well, now, these two here," he continued, suddenly shifting his tone from one of light sarcasm to a kind of savage contempt, "imagine they are getting along, making life a lot better for themselves, when they lie about this way and swindle another man out of his honest due in connection with the work he is paying for. He can't help himself. He can't know everything. If he did he'd probably find what's wrong in there and fix it himself in three minutes. But if he did that and the union heard of it they'd boycott him. They'd come around and blackmail him, blow up his barn, or make him pay for the work he did himself. I know 'em. I have to deal with 'em. They fix my pipes in the same way that these two are fixing his—lying on the grass at a dollar an hour. And they want five dollars a pound for every bit of lead they use. If they forget anything and have to go back to town for it, you pay for it, at a dollar an hour. They get on the job at nine and quit at four, in the country. If you say anything, they quit altogether—they're *union* laborers—and they won't let any one else do it, either. Once they're on the job they have to rest every few minutes, like these two. Something has to boil, or they have to wait for something. Isn't it wonderful! Isn't it beautiful! And all of us of course are made free and equal! They're just as good as we are! If you work and make money and have any plumbing to do you have to support 'em—Right by fours! Guide right! Forward!" and off we trotted, breaking into a headlong gallop a little farther on as if he wished to outrun the mood which was holding him at the moment.

The plumber and his assistant, fully awake now to the import of what had occurred, stared after us. The journeyman plumber, who was short and fat, sat and blinked. At last he recovered his wits sufficiently to cry, "Aw, go to hell, you ——————!" but by that time we were well along the road and I am not sure that Culhane even heard.

Another day as we were riding along a road which led into a nearby city of, say, twenty thousand, we encountered a beer truck of great size and on its seat so large and ruddy and obese a German as one might go a long way and still not see. It was very hot. The German was drowsy and taking his time in the matter of driving. As we drew near, Culhane suddenly called a halt and, lining us up as was his rule, called to the horses of the brewery wagon, who also obeyed his lusty "Whoa!" The driver, from his high perch above, stared down on us with mingled curiosity and wonder.

"Now, here's an illustration of what I mean," Culhane began, apropos of nothing at all, "when I say that the word man ought to be modified or changed in some way so that when we use it we would mean something more definite than we mean now. That thing you see sitting up on that wagon-seat there—call that a man? And then call me one? Or a man like Charles A. Dana? Or a man like General Grant? Hell! Look at him! Look at his shape! Look at that stomach! You think a thing like that—call it a man if you want to—has any brains or that he's really any better than a pig in a sty? If you turn a horse out to shift for himself he'll eat just enough to keep in condition; same way with a dog, a cat or a bird. But let one of these things, that some people call a *man*, come along, give him a job and enough money or a chance to stuff himself, and see what happens. A thing like that connects himself with one end of a beer hose and then he thinks he's all right. He gets enough guts to start a sausage factory, and then he blows up, I suppose, or rots. Think of it! And we call him a man—or some do!"

During this amazing and wholly unexpected harangue (I never saw him stop any one before), the heavy driver, who did not understand English very well, first gazed and then strained with his eyebrows, not being able quite to make out what it was all about. From the chuckling and laughter that finally set up in one place and another he began dimly to comprehend that he was being made fun of, used as an unsatisfactory jest of some kind. Finally his face clouded for a storm and his eyes blazed, the while his fat red cheeks grew redder. "*Donnervetter!*" he began gutturally to roar. "*Schweine hunde! Hunds knoche! Nach der polizei soll man reufen!*"

I for one pulled my horse cautiously back, as he cracked a great whip, and, charging savagely through us, drove on. Culhane, having made his unkind comments, gave orders for our orderly formation once more and calmly led us away.

Perhaps the most amusing phase of him was his opposition to and contempt for inefficiency of any kind. If he asked you to do anything, no matter what, and you didn't at once leap to the task ready and willing and able so to do, he scarcely had words enough with which to express himself. On one occasion, as I recall all too well, he took us for a drive in his tally-ho—one or two or three that he possessed—a great lumbering, highly lacquered, yellow-wheeled vehicle, to which he attached seven or eight or nine horses, I forget which. This tally-ho ride was a regular Sunday morning or afternoon affair unless it was raining, a call suddenly sounding from about the grounds somewhere at eleven or at two in the afternoon, "Tally-ho at eleven-thirty" (or two-thirty, as the case might be). "All aboard!" Gathering all the reins in his hands and perching himself in the high seat above, with perhaps one of his guests beside him, all the rest crowded willy-nilly on the seats within and on top, he would carry us off, careening about the countryside most madly, several of his hostlers acting as liveried footmen or outriders and one of them perched up behind on the little seat, the technical name of which I have forgotten, waving and blowing the long silver trumpet, the regulation blasts on which had to be exactly as made and provided for such occasions. Often, having been given no warning as to just when it was to be, there would be a mad scramble to get into our *de rigueur* Sunday clothes, for Culhane would not endure any flaws in our appearance, and if we were not ready and waiting

- 121 -

when one of his stablemen swung the vehicle up to the door at the appointed time he was absolutely furious.

On the particular occasion I have in mind we all clambered on in good time, all spick and span and in our very best, shaved, powdered, hands appropriately gloved, our whiskers curled and parted, our shoes shined, our hats brushed; and up in front was Culhane, gentleman de luxe for the occasion, his long-tailed whip looped exactly as it should be, no doubt, ready to be flicked out over the farthest horse's head, and up behind was the trumpeter—high hat, yellow-topped boots, a uniform of some grand color, I forget which.

But, as it turned out on this occasion, there had been a hitch at the last minute. The regular hostler or stableman who acted as footman extraordinary and trumpeter plenipotentiary, the one who could truly and ably blow this magnificent horn, was sick or his mother was dead. At any rate, there he wasn't. And in order not to irritate Culhane, a second hostler had been dressed and given his seat and horn—only he couldn't blow it. As we began to clamber in I heard him asking, "Can any of you gentleman blow the trumpet? Do any of you gentleman know the regular trumpet call?"

No one responded, although there was much discussion in a low key. Some could, or thought they could, but hesitated to assume so frightful a risk. At the same time Culhane, hearing the fuss and knowing perhaps that his substitute could not trumpet, turned grimly around and said, "Say, do you mean to say there isn't any one back there who knows how to blow that thing? What's the matter with you, Caswell?" he called to one, and getting only mumbled explanations from that quarter, called to another, "How about you, Drewberry? Or you, Crashaw?"

All three apologized briskly. They were terrified by the mere thought of trying. Indeed no one seemed eager to assume the responsibility, until finally he became so threatening and assured us so volubly that unless some immediate and cheerful response were made he would never again waste one blank minute on a lot of blank-blank this and thats, that one youth, a rash young society somebody from Rochester, volunteered more or less feebly that he "thought" that "maybe he could manage it." He took a seat directly under the pompously placed trumpeter, and we were off.

"Heigh-ho!" Out the gate and down the road and up a nearby slope at a smart clip, all of us gazing cheerfully and possibly vainly about, for it was a bright day and a gay country. Now the trumpeter, as is provided for on all such occasions, lifted the trumpet to his lips and began on the grandiose "ta-ra-ta-ta," but to our grief and pain, although he got through fairly successfully on his first attempt, there was one place where there was a slight hitch, a "false crack," as some one rowdyishly remarked. Culhane, although tucking up his lines and stiffening his back irritably at this flaw, said nothing. For after all a poor trumpeter was better than none at all. A little later, however, the trumpeter having hesitated to begin again, he called back, "Well, what about the horn? What about the horn? Can't you do something with it? Have you quit for the day?"

Up went the horn once more, and a most noble and encouraging "Ta-ra-ta-ta" was begun, but just at the critical point, and when we were all most prayerfully hoping against hope, as it were, that this time he would round the dangerous curves of it gracefully and come to a grand finish, there was a most disconcerting and disheartening squeak. It was pathetic, ghastly. As one man we wilted. What would Culhane say to that? We were not long in doubt. "Great Christ!" he shouted, looking back and showing a countenance so black that it was positively terrifying. "Who did that? Throw him off! What do you think—that I want the whole country to know I'm airing a lot of lunatics? Somebody who can blow that thing, take it and blow it, for God's sake! I'm not going to drive around here without a trumpeter!"

For a few moments there was more or less painful gabbling in all the rows, pathetic whisperings and "go ons" or eager urgings of one and another to sacrifice himself upon the altar of necessity, insistences by the ex-trumpeter that he had blown trumpets in his day as good as any one—what the deuce had got into him anyhow? It must be the horn!

"Well," shouted Culhane finally, as a stop-gap to all this, "isn't any one going to blow that thing? Do you mean to tell me that I'm hauling all of you around, with not a man among you able to blow a dinky little horn? What's the use of my keeping a lot of fancy vehicles in my barn when all I have to deal with is a lot of shoe salesmen and floorwalkers? Hell! Any child can blow it. It's as easy as a fish-horn. If I hadn't these horses to attend to I'd blow it myself. Come on—come on! Kerrigan, what's the matter with you blowing it?"

"The truth is, Mr. Culhane," explained Mr. Kerrigan, the very dapper and polite heir of a Philadelphia starch millionaire, "I haven't had any chance to practice with one of those for several years. I'll try it if you want me to, but I can't guarantee—"

"Try!" insisted Culhane violently. "You can't do any worse than that other mutt, if you blow for a million years. Blow it! Blow it!"

Mr. Kerrigan turned back and being very cheerfully tendered the horn by the last failure, wetted and adjusted his lips, lifted it upward and backward—and—

It was pathetic. It was positively dreadful, the wheezing, grinding sounds that were emitted.

"God!" shouted Culhane, pulling up the coach to a dead stop. "Stop that! Whoa! Whoa!!! Do you mean to say that that's the best you can do? Well, this finishes me! Whoa! What kind of a bunch of cattle have I got up here, anyhow? Whoa! And out in this country too where I'm known and where they know all about such things! God! Whoa! Here I spend thousands of dollars to get together an equipment that will make a pleasant afternoon for a crowd of gentlemen, and this is what I draw—hams! A lot of barflies who never saw a tally-ho! Well, I'm done! I'm through! I'll split the damned thing up for firewood before I ever take it out again! Get down! Get out, all of you! I'll not haul one of you back a step! Walk back or anywhere you please—to hell, for all I care! I'm through! Get out! I'm going to turn around and get back to the barn as quick as I can—up some alley if I can find one. To think of having such a bunch of hacks to deal with!"

Humbly and wearily we climbed down and, while he drove savagely on to some turning-place, stood about first in small groups, then by twos and threes began making our way—rather gingerly, I must confess, in our fine clothes—along the winding road back to the place on the hill. But such swearing! Such un-Sabbath-like comments! The number of times his sturdy Irish soul was wished into innermost and almost sacrosanct portions of Sheol! He was cursed from more angles and in more artistically and architecturally nobly constructed phrases and even paragraphs than any human being that I have ever heard of before or since, phrases so livid and glistening that they smoked.

Talk about the carved ivories of speech! The mosaics of verbal precious stones!

You should have heard us on our way back!

And still we stayed.

Some two years later I was passing this place in company with some friends, when I asked my host, who also knew of the place, to turn in. During my stay it had been the privilege and custom among those who knew much of this institution to drive through the grounds and past the very doors of the "repair shop," even to stop if Culhane chanced to be visible and talking to or at least greeting him, in some cases. A custom of Culhane's was, in the summer time, to have erected on the lawn a large green-and-white striped marquee tent, a very handsome thing indeed, in which was placed a field-officer's table and several camp chairs, and some books and papers. Here of a hot day, when he was not busy with us, he would sit and read. And when he was in here or somewhere about, a little pennant was run up, possibly as guide to visiting guests or friends. At any rate, it was the presence of this pennant which caused me to know that he was about and to wish that I might have a look at him once more, great lion that he was. As "guests," none of us were ever allowed to come within more than ten feet of it, let alone in it. As passing visitors, however, we might, and many did, stop, remind him that we had once been his humble slaves, and ask leave to congratulate him on his health and sturdy years. At such times, if the visitors looked interesting enough, or he remembered them well, he would deign to come to the tent-fly and, standing there à la Napoleon at Lodi or Grant in the Wilderness, be for the first time in his relations with them a bit civil.

Anyway, on this occasion, urged on by curiosity to see my liege once more and also to learn whether he would remember me at all, I had my present host roll his car up to the tent door, where Culhane was reading. Feeling that by this venturesome deed I had "let myself in for it" and had to "make a showing," I climbed briskly out and, approaching, recalled myself to him. With a semi-wry expression, half smile, half contemptuous curl of the corners of his mouth, he recalled me and took my extended hand; then seeing that possibly my friends if not myself looked interesting, he arose and came to the door. I introduced them—one a naval officer of distinction, the other the owner of a great estate some miles farther on. For the first time in my relations with him I had an opportunity to note how grandly gracious he could be. He accepted my friends' congratulations as to the view with a princely nod and suggested that on other days it was even better. He was soon to be busy now or he would have some one show my friends through the shop. Some Saturday afternoon, if they would telephone or stop in passing, he would oblige.

I noted at once that he had not aged in the least. He was sixty-two or-three now and as vigorous and trim as ever. And now he treated me as courteously and formally as though he had never browbeaten me in the least. "Good heavens," I said, "how much better to be a visitor than a guest!" After a moment or two we offered many thanks and sped on, but not without many a backward glance on my part, for the place fascinated me. That simply furnished institution! That severe regimen! This latter-day Stoic and Spartan in his tent! And, above all things, and the most astounding to me, so little could one know him, the book he had been reading and which he had laid upon his little table as I entered—I could not help noting the title for he laid it back up, open face down—was Lecky's "History of European Morals"!

Now!

Well!

IN RETROSPECT

Two years after this visit, in a serious attempt to set down what I really did think of him, I arranged the following thoughts with which I closed my sketch then and which I now append for what they may be worth. They represented my best thought concerning him then:

"Thomas Culhane belongs to that class of society which the preachers and the world's army of conventional merchants, lawyers, judges and reputable citizens generally are presumably, if one may judge by the moral and religious literature of the day, trying to reach and reform. Yet here at his sanitarium are gathered representatives of those same orders, the so-called better element. And here we see them suddenly dominated, mind and soul, by this being whom they, theoretically at least, look upon as a brand to be snatched from the burning.

"As the Church and society view Culhane, so they view all life outside their own immediate circles. Culhane is in fact a conspicuous figure among the semi-taboo. He has been referred to in many an argument and platform and pulpit and in the press as a type of man whose influence is supposed to be vitiating. Now a minister enters the sanitarium, broken down by his habits of life, and this same Culhane is able to penetrate him, to see that his dogmatic and dictatorial mental habits are the cause of his ailment, and he has the moral courage to shock him, to drag him by apparently brutal processes out of his rut. He reads the man accurately, he knows him better than he knows himself, and he effects a cure.

"This astonishing condition is certainly a new light for those seeking to labor among men. Those who are successful gamblers, pugilists, pickpockets, saloon-keepers, book-makers, jockeys and the like are so by reason of their intelligence, their innate mental acumen and perception. It is a fact that in the sporting world and among the unconventional men-about-town you will often find as good if not better judges of human nature than elsewhere. Contact with a rough and ready and all-too-revealing world teaches them much. The world's customary pretensions and delusions are in the main ripped away. They are bruised by rough facts. Often the men gathered in some such café and whom preachers and moralists are most ready to condemn have a clearer perception of preachers, church organizations and reformers and their relative importance in the multitudinous life of the world than the preachers, church congregations and reformers have of those in the café or the world outside to which they belong.

"This is why, in my humble judgment, the Church and those associated with its aims make no more progress than they do. While they are consciously eager to better the world, they are so wrapped up in themselves and their theories, so hampered by their arbitrary and limited conceptions of good and evil, that the great majority of men move about them unseen, except in a far-away and superficial manner. Men are not influenced at arm's length. It would be interesting to know if some day a preacher or judge, who, offended by Mr. Culhane's profanity and brutality, will be able to reach the gladiator and convert him to his views as readily as the gladiator is able to rid him of his ailment."

In justice to the preachers, moralists, et cetera, I should now like to add that it is probably not any of the virtues or perfections represented by a man like Culhane with which they are quarreling, but the vices of many who are in no wise like him and do not stand for the things he stands for. At the same time, the so-called "sports" might well reply that it is not with any of the really admirable qualities of the "unco guid" that they quarrel, but their too narrow interpretations of virtue and duty and their groundless generalization as to types and classes.

Be it so.

Here is meat for a thousand controversies.

A True Patriarch

In the streets of a certain moderate-sized county seat in Missouri not many years ago might have been seen a true patriarch. Tall, white-haired, stout in body and mind, he roamed among his neighbors, dispensing sympathy and a curiously genial human interest through the leisure of his day. One might have taken him to be Walt Whitman, of whom he was the living counterpart; or, in the clear eye, high forehead and thick, appealing white hair, have seen a marked similarity to Bryant as he appeared in his later years. Already at this time he had seen man's allotted term on earth, and yet he was still strong in the councils of his people and rich in the accumulated interests of a lifetime.

At the particular time in question he was most interesting for the eccentricities which years of stalwart independence had developed, but these were lovable peculiarities and only severed from remarkable actions by the compelling power of time and his increasing infirmities. The loud, though pleasant, voice, and strong, often fiery, declamatory manner, were remnants of the days when his fellow-citizens were wholly swayed by the magnificence of his orations. Charmingly simple in manner, he still represented with it that old courtesy which made every stranger his guest. When moved by righteous indignation, there cropped out the daring and domineering insistence of one who had always followed what he considered to be the right, and who knew its power.

Even then, old as he was, if there were any topic worthy of discussion, and his fellow-citizens were in danger of going wrong, he became an haranguing prophet, as it were, a local Isaiah or Jeremiah. Every gate heard him, for he stopped on his rounds in front of each, and calling out the inhabitant poured forth such a volume of fact and argument as tended to remove all doubt of what he, at least, considered right. All of this he invariably accompanied by a magnificence of gesture worthy of a great orator.

At such times his mind, apparently, was almost wholly engrossed with these matters, and I have it from one of his daughters, who, besides being his daughter, was a sincere admirer of his, that often he might have been seen coming down his private lawn, and even the public streets when there was no one near to hear him, shaking his head, gesticulating, sometimes sweeping upward with his arms, as if addressing his fellow-citizens in assemblage.

"He used to push his big hat well back upon his forehead," she said on one occasion, "and often in winter, forgetful of the bitter cold, would take off his overcoat and carry it on his arm. Occasionally he would stop quite still, as if he were addressing a companion, and with sweeping gestures illustrate some idea or other, although, of course, there was no one present. Then, planting his big cane forcibly with each step, as though still emphasizing his recently stated ideas, he would come forward and enter the house."

The same suggestion of mental concentration might have been seen in everything that he did, and I personally have seen him leading a pet Jersey cow home for milking with the same dignity of bearing and forcefulness of manner that characterized him when he stood before his fellow-citizens at a public meeting addressing them on some important topic. He never appeared to have a sense of difference from or superiority over his fellowmen, but only the keenest sympathy with all things human. Every man was his brother, every human being honest. A cow or a horse was as much to be treated with sympathy and charity as a man or a woman. If a purse was lost, forty-nine out of every fifty men would return it without thought of reward, if you were to believe him.

In the little town where he had lived so many years, and where he finally died, he knew every living creature from cattle upwards, and could call each by name. The sick, the poor, the widows, the orphans, the insane, and dependents of all kinds, were his especial care. Every Sunday afternoon for years, it was his custom to go the rounds of the indigent, frequently carrying a basket of his good wife's dinner. This he distributed, along with consolation and advice. Occasionally he would return home of a winter's day very much engrossed with the discovery of some condition of distress hitherto unseen.

"Mother," he would say to his wife in that same oratorical manner previously noted, as he entered the house, "I've found such a poor family. They have moved into the old saloon below Solmson's. You know how open that is." This was delivered in the most dramatic style after he had indicated something important by throwing his overcoat on the bed and standing his cane in the corner. "There's a man and several children there. The mother is dead. They were on their way to Kansas, but it got so cold they've had to stop here until the winter is broken. They're without food; almost no clothing. Can't we find something for them?"

"On these occasions," said his daughter to me once, "he would, as he nearly always did, talk to himself on the way, as if he were discussing politics. But you could never tell what he was coming for."

Then with his own labor he would help his wife seek out the odds and ends that could be spared, and so armed, would return, arguing by the way as if an errand of mercy were the last thing he contemplated. Nearly always the subject of these orations was some public wrong or error which should receive, although in all likelihood it did not, immediate attention.

Always of a reverent, although not exactly religious, turn of mind, he took considerable interest in religious ministration, though he steadily and persistently refused, in his later years, to go to church. He had St. James's formula to quote in self-defense, which insists that "Pure religion and undefiled before our God and Father is this, To visit the fatherless and widows in their affliction, and to keep himself unspotted from the world." Often, when pressed too close, he would deliver this with kindly violence. One of the most touching anecdotes representative of this was related to me by his daughter, who said:

"Mr. Kent, a poor man of our town, was sick for months previous to his death, and my father used to go often, sometimes daily, to visit him. He would spend perhaps a few minutes, perhaps an hour, with him, singing, praying, and ministering to his spiritual wants. The pastor of the church living so far away and coming only once a month, this duty devolved upon some one, and my father did his share, and always felt more than repaid for the time spent by the gratitude shown by the many poor people he aided in this way.

"Mr. Kent's favorite song, for instance, was 'On Jordan's Stormy Banks I Stand.' This he would have my father sing, and his clear voice could often be heard in the latter's small house, and seemed to impart strength to the sick man.

"Upon one occasion, I remember, Mr. Kent expressed a desire to hear a certain song. My father was not very familiar with it but, anxious to grant his request, came home and asked me if I would get a friend of mine and go and sing the song for him.

"We entered the sick-room, he leading us by the hand, for we were children at the time. Mr. Kent's face at once brightened, and father said to him:

"'Mr. Kent, I told you this morning that I couldn't sing the song you asked for, but these girls know it, and have come to sing it for you.'

"Then, waving his hand gently toward us, he said:

"'Sing, children.'

"We did so, and when we had finished he knelt and offered a prayer, not for the poor man's recovery but that he might put his trust in the Lord and meet death without fear. I have never been more deeply impressed nor felt more confident in the presence of death, for the man died soon after, soothed into perfect peace."

On another occasion he was sitting with some friends in front of the courthouse in his town, talking and sunning himself, when a neighbor came running up in great excitement, calling:

"Mr. White, Mr. White, come, right quick. Mrs. Sadler wants you."

He explained that the woman in question was dying, and, being afraid she would strangle in her last moments, had asked the bystanders to run for him, her old acquaintance, in the efficacy of whose prayers she had great faith. The old patriarch was without a coat at the time, but, unmindful of that, hastened after.

"Mr. White," exclaimed the sick woman excitedly upon seeing him, "I want you to pray that I won't strangle. I'm not afraid to die, but I don't want to die that way. I want you to offer a prayer for me that I may be saved from that. I'm so afraid."

Seeing by the woman's manner that she was very much overwrought, he used all his art to soothe her.

"Have no fear, Mrs. Sadler, now," he exclaimed solemnly. "You won't strangle. I will ask the Lord for you, and this evil will not come upon you. You need not have any fear."

"Kneel down, you," he commanded, turning upon the assembled neighbors and relatives who had followed or had been there before him, while he pushed back his white hair from his forehead. "Let us now pray that this good woman here be allowed to pass away in peace." And even with the rustle of kneeling that accompanied his words he lifted up his coatless arms and began to pray.

Through his magnificent phraseology, no doubt, as well as his profound faith, he succeeded in inducing a feeling of peace and quiet in all his hearers, the sick woman included, who, listening, sank into a restful stupor, from which all agony of mind had apparently disappeared. Then when the physical atmosphere of the room had been thus reorganized, he ceased and retired to the yard in front of the house, where on a bench under a shade tree he seated himself to wipe his moist brow and recover his composure. In a few moments a slight commotion in the sick-room denoted that the end had come. Several neighbors came out, and one said, "Well, it is all over, Mr. White. She is dead."

"Yes," he replied with great assurance. "She didn't strangle, did she?"

"No," said the other, "the Lord granted her request."

"I knew He would," he replied in his customary loud and confident tone. "Prayer is always answered."

Then, after viewing the dead woman and making additional comments, he was off, as placid as though nothing had occurred.

I happened to hear of this some time after, and one day, while sitting with him on his front porch, said, "Mr. White, do you really believe that the Lord directly answered your prayer in that instance?"

"Answered!" he almost shouted defiantly and yet with a kind of human tenderness that one could never mistake. "Of course He answered! Why wouldn't He—a faithful old servant like that? To be sure, He answered."

"Might it not have been merely the change of atmosphere which your voice and strength introduced? The quality of your own thoughts goes for something in such matters. Mind acts on mind."

"Certainly," he said, in a manner as agreeable as if it had always been a doctrine with him. "I know that. But, after all, what is *that*—my mind, your mind, the sound of voices? It's all the Lord anyhow, whatever you think."

How could one gainsay such a religionist as that?

The poor, the blind, the insane, and sufferers of all sorts, as I have said before, were always objects of his keenest sympathies. Evidence of it flashed out at the most unexpected moments—loud, rough exclamations, which, however, always contained a note so tender and suggestive as to defy translation. Thus, while we were sitting on his front porch one day and hotly discussing politics to while away a dull afternoon, there came down the street, past his home, a queer, ragged, half-demented individual, who gazed about in an aimless sort of way, peering queerly over fences, looking idly down the road, staring strangely overhead into the blue. It was apparent, in a moment, that the man was crazy, some demented creature, harmless enough, however, to be allowed abroad and so save the county the expense of caring for him. The old man broke a sentence short in order to point and shake his head emotionally.

"Look at that," he said to me, with a pathetic sweep of the arm, "now just look at that! There's a poor, demented soul, with no one to look after him. His brother is a hard-working saddler. His sister is dead. No money to speak of, any of them." He paused a moment, and then added, "I don't know what we're to do in such cases. The state and the county don't always do their duty. Most people here are too poor to help, there are so many to be taken care of. It seems almost at times as if you can't do anything but leave them to the mercy of God, and yet you can't do that either, quite," and he once more shook his head sadly.

I was for denouncing the county, but he explained very charitably that it was already very heavily taxed by such cases. He did not seem to know exactly what should be done at the time, but he was very sorry, very, and for the time being the warm argument in which he had been indulging was completely forgotten. Now he lapsed into silence and all communication was suspended, while he rocked silently in his great chair and thought.

One day in passing the local poor-farm (and this is of my own knowledge), he came upon a man beating a poor idiot with a whip. The latter was incapable of reasoning and therefore of understanding why it was that he was being beaten. The two were beside a wood-pile and the demented one was crying. In a moment the old patriarch had jumped out of his conveyance, leaped over the fence, and confronted the amazed attendant with an uplifted arm.

"Not another lick!" he fairly shouted. "What do you mean by striking an idiot?"

"Why," explained the attendant, "I want him to carry in the wood, and he won't do it."

"It is not his place to bring in the wood. He isn't put here for that, and in the next place he can't understand what you mean. He's put here to be taken care of. Don't you dare strike him again. I'll see about this, and you."

Knowing his interrupter well, his position and power in the community, the man endeavored to explain that some work must be done by the inmates, and that this one was refractory. The only way he had of making him understand was by whipping him.

"Not another word," the old man blustered, overawing the county hireling. "You've done a wrong, and you know it. I'll see to this," and off he bustled to the county courthouse, leaving the transgressor so badly frightened that whips thereafter were carefully concealed, in this institution at least. The court, which was held in his home town, was not in session at the time, and only the clerk was present when he came tramping down the aisle and stood before the latter with his right hand uplifted in the position of one about to make oath.

"Swear me," he called solemnly, and without further explanation, as the latter stared at him. "I want you to take this testimony under oath."

The clerk knew well enough the remarkable characteristics of his guest, whose actions were only too often inexplicable from the ground point of policy and convention. Without ado, after swearing him, he got out ink and paper, and the patriarch began.

"I saw," he said, "in the yard of the county farm of this county, not over an hour ago, a poor helpless idiot, too weak-minded to understand what was required of him, and put in that institution by the people of this county to be cared for, being beaten with a cowhide by Mark Sheffels, who is an attendant there, because the idiot did not understand enough to carry in wood, which the people have hired Mark Sheffels to carry in. Think of it," he added, quite forgetting the nature of his testimony and that he was now speaking for dictation and not for an audience to hear, and going off into a most scorching and brilliant arraignment of the entire system in which such brutality could occur, "a poor helpless idiot, unable to frame in his own disordered mind a single clear sentence, being beaten by a sensible, healthy brute too lazy and trifling to perform the duties for which he was hired and which he personally is supposed to perform."

There was more to the effect, for instance, that the American people and the people of this county should be ashamed to think that such crimes should be permitted and go unpunished, and that this was a fair sample. The clerk, realizing the importance of Mr. White in the community, and the likelihood of his following up his charges very vigorously, quietly followed his address in a very deferential way, jotting down such salient features as he had time to write. When he was through, however, he ventured to lift his voice in protest.

"You know, Mr. White," he said, "Sheffels is a member of our party, and was appointed by us. Of course, now, it's too bad that this thing should have happened, and he ought to be dropped, but if you are going to make a public matter of it in this way it may hurt us in the election next month."

The old patriarch threw back his head and gazed at him in the most blazing way, almost without comprehension, apparently, of so petty a view.

"What!" he exclaimed. "What's that got to do with it? Do you want the Democratic Party to starve the poor and beat the insane?"

The opposition was rather flattened by the reply, and left the old gentleman to storm out. For once, at least, in this particular instance, anyhow, he had purified the political atmosphere, as if by lightning, and within the month following the offending attendant was dropped.

Politics, however, had long known his influence in a similar way. There was a time when he was the chief political figure in the county, and possessed the gift of oratory, apparently, beyond that of any of his fellow-citizens. Men came miles to hear him, and he took occasion to voice his views on every important issue. It was his custom in those days, for instance, when he had anything of special importance to say, to have printed at his own expense a few placards announcing his coming, which he would then carry to the town selected for his address and personally nail up. When the hour came, a crowd, as I am told, was never wanting. Citizens and farmers of both parties for miles about usually came to hear him.

Personally I never knew how towering his figure had been in the past, or how truly he had been admired, until one day I drifted in upon a lone bachelor who occupied a hut some fifteen miles from the patriarch's home and who was rather noted in the community at the time that I was there for his love of seclusion and indifference to current events. He had not visited the nearest neighboring village in something like five years, and had not been to the moderate-sized county seat in ten. Naturally he treasured memories of his younger days and more varied activity.

"I don't know," he said to me one day, in discussing modern statesmen and political fame in general, "but getting up in politics is a queer game. I can't understand it. Men that you'd think ought to get up don't seem to. It doesn't seem to be real greatness that helps 'em along."

"What makes you say that?" I asked.

"Well, there used to be a man over here at Danville that I always thought would get up, and yet he didn't. He was the finest orator I ever heard."

"Who was he?" I asked.

"Arch White," he said quietly. "He was really a great man. He was a good man. Why, many's the time I've driven fifteen miles to hear him. I used to like to go into Danville just for that reason. He used to be around there, and sometimes he'd talk a little. He could stir a fellow up."

"Oratory alone won't make a statesman," I ventured, more to draw him out than to object.

"Oh, I know," he answered, "but White was a good man. The plainest-spoken fellow I ever heard. He seemed to be able to tell us just what was the matter with us, or at least I thought so. He always seemed a wonderful speaker to me. I've seen as many as two thousand people up at High Hill hollerin' over what he was saying until you could hear them for miles."

"Why didn't he get up, then, do you suppose?" I now asked on my part.

"I dunno," he answered. "Guess he was too honest, maybe. It's sometimes that way in politics, you know. He was a mighty determined man, and one that would talk out in convention, whatever happened. Whenever they got to twisting things too much and doing what wasn't just honest, I suppose he'd kick out. Anyhow, he didn't get up, and I've always wondered at it."

In Danville one might hear other stories wholly bearing out this latter opinion, and always interesting—delightful, really. Thus, a long, enduring political quarrel was once generated by an incident of no great importance, save that it revealed an odd streak in the old patriarch's character and his interpretation of charity and duty.

A certain young man, well known to the people of this county and to the patriarch, came to Danville one day and either drank up or gambled away a certain sum of money intrusted to him by his aunt for disposition in an entirely different manner. When the day was all over, however, he was not too drunk to realize that he was in a rather serious predicament, and so, riding out of town, traveled a little way and then tearing his clothes and marking his skin, returned, complaining that he had been set upon by the wayside, beaten, and finally robbed. His clothes were in a fine state of dilapidation after his efforts, and even his body bore marks which amply seconded his protestation. In the slush and rain of the dark village street he was finally picked up by the county treasurer seemingly in a wretched state, and the latter, knowing the generosity of White and the fact that his door was always open to those in distress, took the young man by the arm and led him to the patriarch's door, where he personally applied for him. The old patriarch, holding a lamp over his head, finally appeared and peered outward into the darkness.

"Yes," he exclaimed, as he always did, eyeing the victim; "what is it you want of me?"

"Mr. White," said the treasurer, "it's me. I've got young Squiers here, who needs your sympathy and aid tonight. He's been beaten and robbed out here on the road while he was on his way to his mother's home."

"Who?" inquired the patriarch, stepping out on the porch and eyeing the newcomer, the while he held the lamp down so as to get a good look. "Billy Squiers!" he exclaimed when he saw who it was. "Mr. Morton, I'll not take this man into my house. I know him. He's a drunkard and a liar. No man has robbed him. This is all a pretense, and I want you to take him away from here. Put him in the hotel. I'll pay his expenses for the night, but he can't come into my home," and he retired, closing the door after him.

The treasurer fell back amazed at this onslaught, but recovered sufficiently to knock at the door once more and declare to his friend that he deemed him no Christian in taking such a stand and that true religion commanded otherwise, even though he suspected the worst. The man was injured and penniless. He even went so far as to quote the parable of the good Samaritan who passed down by way of Jericho and rescued him who had fallen among thieves. The argument had long continued into the night and rain before the old patriarch finally waved them both away.

"Don't you quote Scripture to me," he finally shouted defiantly, still holding the light and flourishing it in an oratorical sweep. "I know my Bible. There's nothing in it requiring me to shield liars and drunkards, not a bit of it," and once more he went in and closed the door.

Nevertheless the youth was housed and fed at his expense and no charge of any kind made against him, although many believed, as did Mr. White, that he was guilty of theft, whereas others of the opposing political camp believed not. However, considerable opposition, based on old Mr. White's lack of humanity in this instance, was generated by this argument, and for years he was taunted with it although he always maintained that he was justified and that the Lord did not require any such service of him.

The crowning quality of nearly all of his mercies, as one may easily see, was their humor. Even he was not unaware, in retrospect, of the figure he made at times, and would smilingly tell, under provocation, of his peculiar attitude on one occasion or another. Partially from himself, from those who saw it, and the judge presiding in the case, was the following characteristic anecdote gathered.

In the same community with him at one time lived a certain man by the name of Moore, who in his day had been an expert tobacco picker, but who later had come by an injury to his hand and so turned cobbler, and a rather helpless, although not hopeless, one at that. Mr. White had known this man from boyhood up, and had been a witness at various times to the many changes in his fortunes, from the time, for instance, when he had earned as much as several dollars a day—good pay in that region—to the hour when he took a cobbler's kit upon his back and began to eke out a bare livelihood for his old age by traveling about the countryside mending shoes. At the time under consideration, this ex-tobacco picker had degenerated into so humble a thing as Uncle Bobby Moore, a poor, half-remembered cobbler, whose earlier state but few knew, and who at this time had only a few charitably inclined friends, with some of whom he spent the more pleasant portion of the year from spring to fall. Thus, it was his custom to begin his annual pilgrimage with a visit of ten days to Mr. White, where he would sit and cobble shoes for all the members of the household. From here he would go to another acquaintance some ten miles farther on, where he could enjoy the early fruit which was then ripening in delicious quantity. Then he would visit a friendly farmer whose home was upon the Missouri River still farther away, where he did his annual fishing, and so on by slow degrees, until at last he would reach a neighborhood rich in cider presses, where he would wind up the fall, and so end his travel for the winter, beginning his peculiar round once more the following spring at the home of Mr. White. Naturally the old patriarch knew him and liked him passing well.

As he grew older, however, Uncle Bobby reached the place where even by this method and his best efforts he could scarcely make enough to sustain him in comfort during the winter season, which was one of nearly six months, free as his food and lodging occasionally were. He was too feeble. Not desiring to put himself upon any friend for more than a short visit, he finally applied to the patriarch.

"I come to you, Mr. White," he said, "because I don't think I can do for myself any longer in the winter season. My hand hurts a good deal and I get tired so easily. I want to know if you'd won't help me to get into the county farm during the winter months, anyhow. In summer I can still look out for myself, I think."

In short, he made it clear that in summer he preferred to be out so that he might visit his friends and still enjoy his declining years.

The old patriarch was visibly moved by this appeal, and seizing him by the arm and leading off toward the courthouse where the judge governing such cases was then sitting he exclaimed, "Come right down here, Uncle Bobby. I'll see what can be done about this. Your old age shouldn't be troubled in this fashion—not after all the efforts you have made to maintain yourself," and bursting in on the court a few moments later, where a trial was holding at the time, he deliberately led his charge down the aisle, disturbing the court proceedings by so doing, and calling as he came:

"Your Honor, I want you to hear this case especially. It's a very important and a very sad case, indeed."

Agape, the spectators paused to listen. The judge, an old and appreciative friend of his, turned a solemn eye upon this latest evidence of eccentricity.

"What is it, Mr. White?" he inquired.

"Your Honor," returned the latter in his most earnest and oratorical manner, "this man here, as you may or may not know, is an old and honorable citizen of this county. He has been here nearly all the days of his life, and every day of that time he has earned an honest living. These people here," he said, gazing about upon the interested spectators, "can witness whether or not he was one of the best tobacco pickers this county ever saw. Mayhew," he interrupted himself to call to a spectator on one of the benches, "you know whether Uncle Bobby always earned an honest living. Speak up. Tell the Court, did he?"

"Yes, Mr. White," said Mayhew quickly, "he did."

"Morrison," he called, turning in another direction, where an aged farmer sat, "what do you know of this man?"

Mr. Morrison was about to reply, when the Court interfered.

"The Court knows, Mr. White, that he is an honest man. Now what would you have it do?"

"Well, your Honor," resumed the speaker, indifferently following his own oratorical bent, the while the company surveyed him, amused and smiling, "this man has always earned an honest living until he injured his hand here in some way a number of years ago, and since then it has been difficult for him to make his way and he has been cobbling for a living. However, he is getting so old now that he can't even earn much at that, except in the spring and summer, and so I brought him here to have him assigned a place in the county infirmary. I want you to make out an order admitting him to that institution, so that I can take it and go with him and see that he is comfortably placed."

"All right, Mr. White," replied the judge, surveying the two figures in mid-aisle, "I so order."

"But, your Honor," he went on, "there's an exception I want made in this case. Mr. Moore has a few friends that he likes to visit in the summer, and who like to have him visit them. I want him to have the privilege of coming out in the summer to see these people and to see me."

"All right, Mr. White," said the judge, "he shall have that privilege. Now, what else?"

Satisfied in these particulars, the aged citizen led his charge away, and then went with him to the infirmary, where he presented the order of the Court and then left him.

Things went very well with his humble client for a certain time, and Uncle Bobby was thought to be well disposed of, when one day he came to his friend again. It appeared that only recently he had been changed about in his quarters at the infirmary and put into a room with a slightly demented individual, whose nocturnal wanderings greatly disturbed his very necessary sleep.

"I want to know if you won't have them put me by myself, Mr. White," he concluded. "I need my sleep. But they say they can't do it without an order."

Once more the old patriarch led his charge before the Court, then sitting, as it happened, and breaking in upon the general proceedings as before, began:

"Your Honor, this man here, Mr. Moore, whom I brought before you some time ago, has been comfortably housed by your order, and he's deeply grateful for it, as he will tell you, and as I can, but he's an old man, your Honor, and, above all things, needs his rest. Now, of late they've been quartering him with a poor, demented sufferer down there who walks a good deal in his sleep, and it wears upon him. I've come here with him to ask you to allow him to have a room by himself, where he will be alone and rest undisturbed."

"Very well, Mr. White," said the Court, "it shall be as you request."

Without replying, the old gentleman turned and led the supplicant away.

Everything went peacefully now for a number of years, until finally Uncle Bobby, having grown so feeble with age that he feared he was soon to die, came to his friend and asked him to promise him one thing.

"What is it?" asked the latter.

By way of replying, the supplicant described an old oak tree which grew in the yard of the Baptist Church some miles from Danville, and said:

"I want you to promise that when I am dead, wherever I happen to be at the time, that you will see that I am buried under that tree." He gave no particular reason save that he had always liked the tree and the view it commanded, but made his request a very secret matter and begged to be assured that Mr. White would come and get his body and carry it to the old oak.

The latter, always a respecter of the peculiarities and crotchets of his friends, promised. After a few years went by, suddenly one day he learned that Uncle Bobby was not only dead but buried, a thing which astonished him greatly. No one locally being supposed to know that he was to have had any special form of burial, the old patriarch at once recalled his promise.

"Where is his body?" he asked.

"Why, they buried it under the old white oak over at Mt. Horeb Church," was the answer.

"What!" he exclaimed, too astonished to think of anything save his lost privilege of mercy, "who told them to bury him there?"

"Why, *he* did," said the friend. "It was his last wish, I believe."

"The confounded villain," he shouted, amusingly enough. "He led me to believe that I was the only one he told. I alone was to have looked after his burial, and now look at him—going and having himself buried without a word. The scoundrel! Would you believe that an old friend like Uncle Bobby would do anything like that? However," he added after a time, "I think I know how it was. He got so old and feeble here of late that he must have lost his mind—otherwise he would never have done anything like that to me."

And with this he was satisfied to rest and let bygones be bygones.

De Maupassant, Junior

He dawned on me in the spring of 1906, a stocky, sturdy, penetrative temperament of not more than twenty-four or-five years of age, steady of eye, rather aloof and yet pervasive and bristling; a devouring type. Without saying much, and seeming to take anything I had to say with a grain of salt, he managed to impress himself on me at once. Frankly, I liked him very much, although I could see at a glance that he was not so very much impressed with me. I was an older man than he by, say, ten years, an editor of an unimportant magazine, newly brought in (which he did not know) to turn it into something better. In order to earn a few dollars he had undertaken to prepare for the previous editor a most ridiculous article, some silly thing about newspaper writing as a career for women. It had been ordered or encouraged, and I felt that it was but just that it should be paid for.

"Why do you waste your time on a thing like that?" I inquired, smiling and trying to criticize and yet encourage him at one and the same time, for I had been annoyed by many similar assignments given out by the old management which could not now be used. "You look to me to have too much force and sense for that. Why not undertake something worth your time?"

"My time, hell!" he bristled, like a fighting sledge-dog, of which by the way he reminded me. "You show me a magazine in this town that would buy anything that I thought worthy of my time! You're like all the rest of them: you talk big, but you really don't want anything very important. You want little things probably, written to a theory or down to 'our policy.' I know. Give me the stuff. You don't have to take it. It was ordered, but I'll throw it in the waste basket."

"Not so fast! Not so fast!" I replied, admiring his courage and moved by his contempt of the editorial and book publishing conditions in America. He was so young and raw and savage in his way, quite animal, and yet how interesting! There was something as fresh and clean about him as a newly plowed field or the virgin prairies. He typified for me all the young unsophisticated strength of my country, but with more "punch" than it usually manifests, in matters intellectual at least. "Now, don't get excited, and don't snarl," I cooed. "I know what you say is true. They don't really want much of what you have to offer. I don't. Working for some one else, as most of us do, for the dear circulation department, it's not possible for us to get very far above crowd needs and tastes. I've been in your position exactly. I am now. Where do you come from?"

He told me—Missouri—and some very few years before from its state university.

"And what is it you want to do?"

"What's that to you?" he replied irritatingly, with an ingrowing and obvious self-conviction of superiority and withdrawing as though he highly resented my question as condescending and intrusive. "You probably wouldn't understand if I told you. Just now I want to write enough magazine stuff to make a living, that's all."

"Dear, dear!" I said, laughing at the slap. "What a bravo we are! Really, you're interesting. But suppose now you and I get down to brass tacks. You want to do something interesting, if you can, and get paid for it. I rather like you, and anyhow you look to me as though you might do the things I want, or some of them. Now, you want to do the least silly thing you can—something better than this. I want the least silly stuff I can get away with in this magazine—genuine color out of the life of New York, if such a thing can be published in an ordinary magazine. Roughly, here's the kind of thing I want," and I outlined to him the probable policy of the magazine under my direction. I had taken an anæmic "white-light" monthly known as *The Broadway* (!) and was attempting to recast it into a national or international metropolitan picture. He thawed slightly.

"Well, maybe with that sort of idea behind it, it might come to something. I don't know. It's *possible* that you may be the one to do it." He emphasized the "possible." "At any rate, it's worth trying. Judging by the snide editors and publications in this town, no one in America wants anything decent." His lip curled. "I have ambitions of my own, but I don't expect to work them out through the magazines of this town; maybe not of this country. I didn't know that any change was under way here."

"Well, it is," I said. "Still, you can't expect much from this either, remember. After all, it seeks to be a popular magazine. We'll see how far we can go with really interesting material. And now if you know of any others like yourself, bring them in here. I need them. I'll pay you for that article, only I'll include it in a better price I'll give you for something else later, see?"

I smiled and he smiled. His was a warmth which was infectious when he chose to yield, but it was always a repressed warmth, cynical, a bit hard; heat chained to a purpose, I thought. He went away and I saw him no more until about a week later when he brought me his first attempt to give me what I wanted.

In the meantime I was busy organizing a staff which should if possible, I decided after seeing him, include him. I could probably use him as a salaried "special" writer, provided he could be trained to write "specials." He looked so intelligent and ambitious that he promised much. Besides, the little article which he had left when he came again, while not well organized or arranged as to its ideas or best points, was exceedingly well written from the point of mere expression.

And the next thing I had given him to attempt was even better. It was, if I recall correctly, a stirring picture of the East Side, intended to appeal to readers elsewhere than in the city, but while in the matter of color and definiteness of expression as well as choice of words it was exceptional, it was lacking in, quite as the first one had been, the arrangement of its best points. This I explained to him, and also made it clear to him that I could show him how if he would let me. He seemed willing enough, quite anxious, although always with an air of reserve, as if he were accommodating himself to me in this much but no more. He grasped the idea of order swiftly, and in a little while, having worked at a table in an outer room, brought me the rearranged material, almost if not quite satisfactory. During a number of weeks and months thereafter, working on one "special" and another in this way with me, he seemed finally to grasp the theory I had, or at least to develop a method of his own which was quite as satisfactory to me, and I was very much pleased. A little later I employed him at a regular salary.

It was pathetic, as I look at it now, the things we were trying to do and the conditions under which we were trying to do them—the raw commercial force and theory which underlay the whole thing, the necessity of explaining and fighting for so much that one should not, as I saw it then, have to argue over at all. We were in new rooms, in a new building, filled with lumber not yet placed and awaiting the completion of partitions which, as some one remarked, "would divide us up." Our publisher and owner was a small, energetic, vibrant and colorful soul, all egotism and middle-class conviction as to the need of "push," ambition, "closeness to life," "punch," and what not else, American to the core, and descending on us, or me rather, hourly as it were, demanding the "hows" and the "whyfors" of the dream which the little group I was swiftly gathering about me was seeking to make real.

It was essential to me, therefore, that something different should be done, some new fresh note concerning metropolitan life and action be struck; the old, slow and somewhat grandiose methods of reporting and describing things dispensed with, at least in this instance, and here was a youth who seemed able to help me do it. He was so vigorous, so avid of life, so anxious to picture the very atmosphere which this magazine was now seeking to portray. I felt stronger, better for having him around. The growth of the city, the character and atmosphere of a given neighborhood, the facts concerning some great social fortune, event, condition, crime interested him intensely; on the other hand he was so very easy to teach, quick to sense what was wanted and the order in which it must be presented. A few brief technical explanations from me, and he had the art of writing a "special" at his fingertips, and thereafter gave me no real difficulty.

But what was more interesting to me than his success in grasping my theory of "special" writing was his own character, as it was revealed to me from day to day in intimate working contact with him under these conditions. Here, as I soon learned, and was glad to learn, was no namby-pamby scribbler of the old happy-ending, pretty-nothing school of literary composition. On the contrary he sounded, for the first time in my dealings with literary aspirants of every kind, that sure, sane, penetrating, non-sentimental note so common to the best writers of the Continent, a note entirely free from mush, bravado and cant. He had a style as clear as water, as simple as rain; color, romance, humor; and if a little too much of vanity and self-importance, still one could forgive him for they were rather well-based. Already used to dealing with literary and artistic aspirants of different kinds in connection with the publications of which I had been a part, this one appealed to me as being the best of them all and a very refreshing change.

One day, only a few weeks after I had met him, seeing that I was alert for fiction, poetry and short essays or prose phantasies, all illustrative of the spirit of New York, he brought me a little poem entitled "Neuvain," which interested me greatly. It was so brief and forceful and yet so delicate, a double triolet of the old French order, but with the modernity and flavor of the streets outside, the conduit cars, hand-organs and dancing children of the pavements. The title seemed affected, seeing that the English word "Spring" would have done as well, but it was typical of his mood at the time, his literary adorations. He was in leash to the French school of which de Maupassant was the outstanding luminary, only I did not know it at the time.

"Charming," I exclaimed quite enthusiastically. "I like this. Let me see anything else you have. Do you write short stories?"

For answer he merely stared at me for a little while in the most examining and arrogant and contemptuous way, as much as to say, "Let me see if you are really worth my time and trouble in this matter," or "This sad specimen of alleged mentality is just beginning to suspect that I might write a short story." Seeing that I merely smiled most genially in return, he finally deigned to say, "Sure, I write short stories. What do you think I'm in the writing game for?"

"But you might be interested in novels only or plays, or poetry."

"No," he returned after a pause and with that same air of unrelieved condescension, "the short story is what I want to specialize in."

"Well," I said to myself, "here is a young cub who certainly has talent, is crowded with it, and yet owing to the kind of thing he is starting out to do and the fact that life will give him slaps and to spare before he is many years older, he needs to be encouraged. I was like that myself not so long ago. And besides, if I do not encourage this type of work financially (which is the best way of all), who will?"

About a week later I was given another and still more gratifying surprise, for one day, in his usual condescending manner, he brought to me two short pieces of fiction and laid them most gingerly on my desk with scarcely a word—"Here was something I might read if I chose," I believe. The reading of these two stories gave me as much of a start as though I had discovered a fully developed genius. They were so truly new or different in their point of view, so very clear, incisive, brief, with so much point in them (*The Second Motive*; *The Right Man*). For by then having been struggling with the short-story problem in other magazine offices before this, I had become not a little pessimistic as to the trend of American short fiction, as well as long—the impossibility of finding any, even supposing it publishable once we had it. My own experience with "Sister Carrie" as well as the fierce opposition or chilling indifference which, as I saw, overtook all those who attempted anything even partially serious in America, was enough to make me believe that the world took anything even slightly approximating the truth as one of the rankest and most criminal offenses possible. One dared not "talk out loud," one dared not report life as it was, as one lived it. And one of the primary warnings I had received from the president of this very organization—a most eager and ambitious and distressing example of that American pseudo-morality which combines a pirate-like acquisitiveness with an inward and absolute conviction of righteousness—was that while he wanted something new in fiction, something more virile and life-like than that "mush," as he characterized it, to be found in the current magazines, still (1), it must have a strong appeal for the general reader (!); and (2), be very compelling in fact and *clean*, as the dear general reader would of course understand that word—a solid little pair of millstones which would unquestionably end in macerating everything vital out of any good story.

Still I did not despair; something might be done. And though I sighed, I hoped to be able to make my superior stretch a point in favor of the exceptional thing, or, as the slang phrase went, "slip a few over on him," but that of course meant nothing or something, as you choose. My dream was really to find one or many like this youth, or a pungent kind of realism that would be true and yet within such limits as would make it usable. Imagine, then, my satisfaction in finding these two things, tales that I could not only admire genuinely but that I could publish, things that ought to have an interest for all who knew even a little about life. True, they were ironic, cruel, but still with humor and color, so deftly and cleanly told that they were smile-provoking. I called him and said as much, or nearly so—a mistake, as I sometimes think now, for art should be long—and bought them forthwith, hoping, almost against hope, to find many more such like them.

By this time, by the way, and as I should have said before, I had still further enlarged my staff by one art director of the most flamboyant and erratic character, a genius of sorts, volatile, restless, emotional, colorful, a veritable Verlaine-Baudelaire-Rops soul, who, not content to arrange and decorate the magazine each month, must needs wish to write, paint, compose verse and music and stage plays, as well as move in an upper social world, *entrée* to which was his by birth. Again, there was by now an Irish-Catholic makeup editor, a graduate of some distinguished sectarian school, who was more interested in St. Jerome and his *Vulgate*, as an embodiment of classic Latin, than he was in getting out the magazine. Still he had the advantage of being interesting—"and I learned about Horace from him." Again, there was a most interesting and youthful and pretty, if severe, example of the Wellesley-Mt. Holyoke-Bryn Mawr school of literary art and criticism, a most engagingly interesting intellectual maiden, who functioned as assistant editor and reader in an adjoining room, along with the art-director, the makeup editor and an office boy. This very valuable and in some respects remarkable young woman, who while holding me in proper contempt, I fear, for my rather loose and unliterary ways, was still, as I had suspected before employing her, as keen for something new and vital in fiction and every other phase of the scriptic art as any one well could be. She was ever for culling, sorting, eliminating—repression carried to the N-th power. At first L——cordially hated her, calling her a "simp," a "bluff," a "la-de-da," and what not. In addition to these there was a constantly swelling band of writers, artists, poets, critics, dreamers of reforms social, and I know not what else, who, holding the hope of achieving their ends or aims through some really forceful magazine, were by now beginning to make our place a center. It fairly swarmed for a time with aspirants; an amusing, vivid, strident world.

As for L——, all this being new to him, he was as interested, fascinated even, as any one well might be. He responded to it almost gayly at times, wondering whether something wonderful, international, enduring might not be made to come of it. He rapidly developed into one of the most pertinacious and even disconcerting youths I have ever met. At times he seemed to have a positive genius for saying and doing irritable and disagreeable things, not only to me but to others. Never having heard of me before he met me here, he was convinced, I think, that I was a mere nothing, with some slight possibilities as an editor maybe, certainly with none as a writer or as one who could even suggest anything to writers. I had helped him, but that was as it should be. As for my art-director, he was at first a fool, later a genius; ditto my makeup man.

As for Miss E——, the Wellesley-Bryn Mawr-Mt. Holyoke assistant, who from the first had agreed with me that here indeed was a writer of promise, a genius really, he, as I have said, at first despised her. Later, by dint of exulting in his force, sincerity of purpose, his keen insight and all but braggart strength, she managed, probably on account of her looks and physical graces, to install herself in his confidence and to convince him that she was not only an honest admirer of his skill but one who had taste and judgment of no mean caliber. Thereafter he was about as agreeable as a semi-caged wild animal would be about any office.

But above all he was affronted by M——, the publisher of the paper, concerning whom he could find no words equal to his contemptuous thoughts of him. The publisher, as L——made quite bold to say to me, was little more than a "dodging, rat-like financial ferret," a "financial stool-pigeon for some trust or other," a "shrewd, material little shopkeeper." This because M—— was accustomed to enter and force a conversation here and there, anxious of course to gather the full import of all these various energies and enthusiasms. One of the things which L—— most resented in him at the time was his air of supreme material well-being, his obvious attempt and wish not to convey it, his carefully-cut clothes, his car, his numerous assistants and secretaries following him here and there from various other organizations with which he was connected.

M——'s idea, as he always said, was to spend and to live, only it wasn't. He merely induced others so to do. One of his customs (and it must have impressed L—— very much, innocent newcomer that he was) was to have one or another of his hirelings announce his passing from one "important" meeting to another, within or without his own building, telephone messages being "thrown in" on his line or barred out, wherever he happened to be at the moment and when, presumably, he was deep in one of those literary conferences or confidences with one employee or another or with a group, for which he rapidly developed a passion. Another of his vanities was to have his automobile announced and he be almost forced into it by impetuous secretaries, who, because of orders previously given, insisted that he must be made to keep certain important engagements. Or he would send for one of his hirelings, wherever he chanced to be—club, restaurant, his home— midnight if necessary, to confer with him on some subject of great moment, and the hireling was supposed to call a taxi and come post haste in order that he might not be kept waiting.

"God!" L—— once remarked in my presence. "To think that a thinking being has to be beholden to a thing like that for his weekly income! Somebody ought to tap him with a feather-duster and kill him!"

But the manner in which L—— developed in this atmosphere! It was interesting. At first, before the magazine became so significant or well-organized, it was a great pleasure for me to associate with him outside office hours, and a curious and vivid companion he made. He was so intensely avid of life, so intolerant of the old, of anything different to that which he personally desired or saw, that at times it was most difficult to say anything at all for fear of meeting a rebuff or at least a caustic objection. As I was very pleased to note, he had a passion for seeing, as all youth should have when it first comes to the great city—the great bridges, the new tunnels just then being completed or dug, the harbor and bay, Coney Island, the two new and great railway terminals, then under construction. Most, though, he reveled in different and even depressing neighborhoods—Eighth Avenue, for instance, about which he later wrote a story, and a very good one ("A Quiet Duet"); Hell's Kitchen, that neighborhood that lies (or did), on the West Side of Manhattan, between Eighth and Tenth Avenues, Thirty-sixth and Forty-first Streets; Little Italy, the region below Delancey and north of Worth Street on the East Side; Chinatown; Washington Street (Syria in America); the Greeks in Twenty-seventh and -eighth Streets, West Side. All these and many more phases of New York's multiplex life took his full and restless attention. Once he said to me quite excitedly, walking up Eighth Avenue at two in the morning—I was showing him some rear tenement slums in the summertime—"God, how I hate to go to bed in this town! I'm afraid something will happen while I'm asleep and I won't see it!" That was exactly how he felt all the time, I am sure.

And in those days he was most simple, a very Spartan of a boy. He hadn't the least taste for drink, lived in a small hall-bedroom somewhere—Eighth Avenue, I believe—and took his meals in those shabby little quick-lunch rooms where the characters were more important to him than the food. (My hat—my hat is in my hand!) Intellectually he was so stern and ambitious that I all but stood in awe of and reverence before him. Here, I said to myself, is one who will really do; let him be as savage as he pleases. In America he probably needs to be.

And during this short time, what scraps of his early life he revealed! By degrees I picked up bits of his early deprivations and difficulties, if such they might be called. He had been a newspaper reporter, or had tried to be, in Kansas City, had worked in the college restaurant and laundry of the middle-West State university from which he had graduated, to help pay his way. Afterward he had assisted the janitor of some great skyscraper somewhere—Kansas City, I believe—and, what was most pleasing to me, he in nowise emphasized these as youthful difficulties or made any comment as to their being "hard." Neither did he try to boastingly minimize them as nothing at all—another wretched pose. From him I learned that throughout his youth he had been carried here and there by the iron woman who was his mother and whom he seemed to adore in some grim contentious way, smothering his comments as though he disliked to say anything at all, and yet describing her at times as coarse and vulgar, but a mother to him "all right," someone who had made marked sacrifices for him.

She had once "run" a restaurant in a Western mining camp, had then or later carried him as a puling baby under her shawl or cloak across the Mojave Desert, on foot a part of the way. Apparently he did not know who his father was, and he was not very much concerned to know whether she did or not. His father had died, he said, when he was a baby. Later his mother, then a cook in some railroad hotel in Texas, had sent him to school there. Later still she had been a "bawler out," if you know what that means, an employee of a loan shark and used by him to compel delinquent, albeit petty and pathetic, creditors to pay their dues or then and there, before all their fellow-workers, be screamed at for their delinquency about the shop in which they worked! Later she became a private detective! an insurance agent—God knows what—a kind of rough man-woman, as she turned out to be, but all the while clinging to this boy, her pet, no doubt her dream of perfection. She had by turns sent him to common and high school and to college, remitting him such sums of money as she might to pay his way. Later still (at that very time in fact) she was seeking to come to New York to keep house for him, only he would not have that, perhaps sensing the need of greater freedom. But he wrote her regularly, as he confessed to me, and in later years I believe sent her a part of his earnings, which were to be saved by her for him against a rainy day. Among his posthumous writings later I found a very lovely story ("His Mother"), describing her and himself in unsparing and yet loving terms, a compound of the tender and the brutal in his own soul.

The thing that always made me hope for the best was that at that time he was not at all concerned with the petty little *moralic* and economic definitions and distinctions which were floating about his American world in one form and another. Indeed he seemed to be entirely free of and even alien to them. What he had heard about the indwelling and abiding perfections of the human soul had gone, and rightly so, in one ear and out the other. He respected the virtues, but he knew of and reckoned with die antipathetic vices which gave them their reason for being. To him the thief was almost as important as the saint, the reason for the saint's being. And, better still, he had not the least interest in American politics or society—a wonderful sign. The American dream of "getting ahead" financially and socially was not part of him—another mark royal. All life was fascinating, acceptable, to be interpreted if one had the skill; it was a great distinction to have the skill— worth endless pains to acquire it.

But how unwilling would the average American of his day have been, stuffed as he was and still is with book and picture drivel about artists and art, to accept L—— as anything more than a raw, callow yokel, presuming to assail the outer portals of the temple with his muddy feet! A romping, stamping, irritable soul, with more the air of a young railroad brakeman or "hand," than an artist, and with so much coarse language at times and such brutality of thought as to bar him completely, one might say, from having anything to do with great fiction, great artistic conceptions, or the temple of art. What, sit with the mighty!—that coarse youth, with darkish-brown hair parted at one side and combed over one ear, in the manner of a grandiose barber; with those thick-soled and none too shapely brown shoes, that none too well-made store suit of clothes, that little round brown hat, more often a cap, pulled rather savagely and vulgarly, even insultingly, over one eye; that coarse frieze overcoat, still worn on cold spring days, its "corners" back and front turned up by the damp and from being indifferently sat on; that brash corn-cob pipe and bag of cheap tobacco, extracted and lit at odd moments; what, that youth with the aggressive, irritating vibrant manner—almost the young tough with a chip on his shoulder looking for one to even so much as indicate that he is not all he should be! Positively, there was something brutal and yet cosmic (not comic) about him, his intellectual and art pretensions considered. At times his waspishness and bravado palled even on me. He was too aggressive, too forceful, too intolerant, I said. He should be softer. At other times I felt that he needed to be all that and more to "get by," as he would have said. I wanted to modify him a little—and yet I didn't—and I remained drawn to him in spite of many irritating little circumstances, all but infuriating at times, and actually calculated, it seemed, with a kind of savage skill to reduce what he conceived to be my lofty superiority. At times I thought he ought to be killed—like a father meditating on an unruly son—but the mood soon passed and his literary ability made amends for everything.

In so far as the magazine was concerned, once it began to grow and attract attention he was for me its most important asset; not that he did so much directly as that he provided a definite standard toward which we all had to work. Not incuriously, he was swiftly recognized for what he was by all who came in touch with the magazine. In the first place, interested in his progress, I had seen to it that he was properly introduced wherever that was possible and of benefit to him, and later on, by sheer force of his mental capacity and integrity, his dreams and his critical skill, he managed to center about him an entire band of seeking young writers, artists, poets, playwrights, aspiring musicians; an amusing and as interesting a group as I have ever seen. Their points of rendezvous appeared to be those same shabby quick-lunches in back streets or even on the principal thoroughfares about Times Square, or they met in each other's rooms or my office at night after I had gone, giving me as an excuse that they had work to do. And during all this time the air fairly hummed with rumors of new singers, dancers, plays, stories being begun or under way, articles and essays contemplated; avid, if none too well financed frolics or bohemian midnight suppers here and there. Money was by no means plentiful, and in consequence there was endless borrowing and "paying up" among them. Among the most enthusiastic members of this circle, as I had begun to note, and finally rather nervously, were my art-director, a valiant knight in Bohemia if ever there was one, and she of Bryn Mawr-Wellesley standards. My makeup editor, as well as various contributors who had since become more or less closely identified with the magazine, were also following him up all the time.

If not directly profitable it was enlivening, and I was fairly well convinced by now that from the point of view of being "aware," "in touch with," "in sympathy with" many of the principal tendencies and undercurrents which make for a magazine's success and precedence, this group was as valuable to me as any might well be. It constituted a "kitchen cabinet" of sorts and brought hundreds of interesting ideas to the surface, and from all directions. Now it would be a new and hitherto unheard-of tenor who was to be brought from abroad and introduced with great noise to repute-loving Americans; a new sculptor or painter who had never been heard of in America; a great actor, perhaps, or poet or writer. I listened to any quantity of gossip in regard to new movements that were ready to burst upon the world, in sculpture, painting, the scriptic art. About the whole group there was much that was exceedingly warm, youthful, full of dreams. They were intensely informative and full of hope, and I used to look at them and wonder which one, if any, was destined to have his dreams realized.

Of L—— however I never had the least doubt. He began, it is true, to adopt rather more liberal tendencies, to wish always to be part and parcel of this gayety, this rushing here and there; and he drank at times—due principally, as I thought, to my wildling art-director, who had no sense or reserve in matters material or artistic and who was all for a bacchanalian career, cost what it might. On more than one occasion I heard L—— declaring roundly, apropos of some group scheme of pilgrimage, "No, no! I will not. I am going *home* now!" He had a story he wanted to work on, an article to finish. At the same time he would often agree that if by a certain time, when he was through, they were still at a certain place, or a second or third, he would look them up. Never, apparently, did his work suffer in the least.

And it was about this time that I began to gather the true source and import of his literary predisposition. He was literally obsessed, as I now discovered, with Continental and more especially the French conception of art in writing. He had studied the works as well as the temperaments and experiences (more especially the latter, I fear) of such writers as de Maupassant, Flaubert, Baudelaire, Balzac, de Musset, Sand, Daudet, Dumas junior, and Zola, as well as a number of the more recent writers: Hervieu, Bourget, Louys and their contemporaries. Most of all, though, he was impressed, and deeply, by the life and art of de Maupassant, his method of approach, his unbiased outlook on life, his freedom from moral and religious and even sentimental predisposition. In the beginning of his literary career I really believe he slaved to imitate him exactly, although he could not very well escape the American temperament and rearing by which he was hopelessly conditioned. A certain Western critic and editor, to whom he had first addressed his hopes and scribblings before coming to me, writing me after L——'s death in reference to a period antedating that in which I had known him, observed, "He was crazy about the *fin de siècle* stuff that then held the boards and from which (I hope the recording angel will put it to my credit) I steered him clear." I think so; but he was still very much interested in it. He admired Aubrey Beardsley, the poster artists of France, Verlaine, Baudelaire, Rops, the Yellow Book, even Oscar Wilde, although his was a far more substantial and plebeian and even radical point of view.

Unfortunately for L——, I have always thought, there now thrust himself forward the publisher and owner of the magazine, who from previously having been content to see that the mercantile affairs of the magazine were in good order, had decided that since it was attracting attention he should be allowed to share in its literary and artistic prestige, should indeed be closely identified with it and recognized as its true source and inspiration—a thing which in no fashion had been contemplated by me when I went there. From having agreed very distinctly with me that no such interference would at any time be indulged in, he now came forward with a plan for an advisory council which was to consist of himself and the very members of the staff which I had created.

I could not object and it did not disturb me so much personally. For some time I had been sensing that the thing was for me no end in itself, but an incident. This same I felt to be true for L——, who had been taking more and more interest in the magazine's technical composition. At the same time I saw no immediate way of arranging my affairs and departing, which left me, for a very little while, more or less of a spectator. During this time I had the dissatisfaction of noting the growth of an influence with L—— which could, as I saw, prove only harmful. M—— was no suitable guide for him. He was a brilliant but superficial and very material type who was convinced that in the having and holding of many things material—houses, lands, corporation stocks, a place in the clubs and circles of those who were materially prosperous—was really to achieve all that was significant in the now or the hereafter. Knowing comparatively nothing of either art or letters, or that subtle thing which makes for personality and atmosphere in a magazine or in writing (and especially the latter), that grateful something which attracts and detains one, he was nevertheless convinced that he did. And what was more, he was determined not only to make friends with and hold all those whom I might have attracted, providing they could prove useful to him, but also a number of a much more successful group in these fields, those who had already achieved repute in a more commonplace and popular way and were therefore presumably possessed of a following and with the power to exact a high return for their product, and for the magazine, regardless of intrinsic merit. His constant talk was of money, its power to attract and buy, the significance of all things material. He now wanted the magazine to be representative of this glowing element, and at the same time, paradoxical as it might seem, the best that might be in literary and artistic thought.

Naturally the thing was impossible, but he had a facile and specious method of arguing, a most gay and in some respects magnetic personality, far from stodgy or gross, which for a time attracted many to him. Very briskly then indeed he proceeded to make friends with all those with whom I had surrounded myself, to enter into long and even private discussions with them as to the proper conduct of the magazine, to hint quite broadly at a glorious future in which all, each one particularly to whom he talked, was to share. Curiously, this new and (as I would have thought) inimical personality of M—— seemed to appeal to L—— very much.

I do not claim that the result was fatal. It may even, or at least might, have had value, combined with an older or slightly more balanced temperament. But it seemed to me that it offered too quickly what should have come, if at all, as the result of much effort. For in regard to the very things L—— should have most guarded against—show and the shallow pleasures of social and night and material life in New York—M—— was most specious. I never knew a more intriguing and fascinating man in this respect nor one who cared less for those he used to obtain his unimportant ends. He had positive genius for making the gaudy and the unworthy seem worthy and even perfect. During his earlier days there, L—— had more than once "cursed him out" (in his absence, of course), to use his own expressive phrase, for his middle-West trade views, as he described them, his shabby social and material ideals, and yet, as I could plainly see, even at that time the virus of his theories was working. For it must be remembered that L—— was very new to New York, very young, and never having had much of anything he was no doubt slightly envious of the man's material facility, the sense of all-sufficiency, exclusiveness and even a kind of petty trade grandeur with which he tried to surround himself.

Well, that might not have proved fatal either, only L——needed some one to keep him true to himself, his individual capabilities, to constantly caution and if possible sober him to his very severe taste, and as it was he was all but surrounded by acolytes and servitors.

A little later, having left M——'s and assumed another editorial position, and being compelled to follow the various current magazines more or less professionally, I was disturbed to note that there began to appear in various publications—especially M——'s, which was flourishing greatly for the moment—stories which while exhibiting much of the deftness and repression as well as an avidity for the true color of things, still showed what I had at first feared they might: a decided compromise. That curse of all American fiction, the necessarily happy ending, had been impressed on him—by whom? To my sincere dissatisfaction, he began writing stories, some at least, which concerned (1), a young woman who successfully abandoned art dreams for advertising; (2), a middle-aged charmer, female, who attempted *libertinage* and was defeated, American style; (3), a Christmas picture with sweetness and light reigning on every hand (Dickens at his sentimentalest could have done no worse); (4), a Broadway press agent who, attempting to bring patronage to a great hotel via chic vice, accidentally and unintentionally mates an all-too-good young society man turned hotel manager to a grand heiress. And so on and so on, not ad infinitum but for a period at least—the ten years in which he managed to live and work.

And, what was more, during this new period I heard and occasionally saw discouraging things in connection with him from time to time. True to his great promise, for I sincerely think M—— had a genuine fondness for his young protégé, as much of a fondness as he could well have for anything, he guaranteed him perhaps as much as three thousand a year; sent him to Stockholm at the age of twenty-four or-five to meet and greet the famous false pole discoverer, Doctor Cook; allowed him to go to Paris in connection with various articles; to Rome; sent him into the middle and far West; to Broadway for dramatic and social studies. Well and good, only he wanted always in what was done for him the "uplift" note, the happy ending—or at least one not vulgar or low—whereas my idea in connection with L——, gifted as he was, was that he should confine himself to fiction as an art and without any regard to theories or types of ending, believing, as I did, that he would definitely establish himself in that way in the long run. I had no objection of course to experiences of various kinds, his taking up with any line of work which might seem at the moment far removed from realistic writing, providing always that the star of his ideal was in sight. Whenever he wrote, be it early or late, it must be in the clear, incisive, uncompromising vein of these first stories and with that passion for revelation which characterized him at first, that same unbiased and unfettered non-moral viewpoint.

But after meeting with and working for M—— under this new arrangement and being apparently fascinated for the moment by his personality, he seemed to me to gradually lose sight of his ideal, to be actually taken in by the plausible arguments which the latter could spin with the ease that a spider spins gossamer. In that respect I insist that M—— was a bad influence. Under his tutelage L—— gradually became, for instance, an habitué of a well-known and pseudo-bohemian chop-house, a most mawkish and naïvely imitative affair, intended frankly to be a copy or even the original, forsooth, of an old English inn, done, in so far as its woodwork was concerned, in smoked or dark-stained oak to represent an old English interior, its walls covered with long-stemmed pipes and pictures of English hunting and drinking scenes, its black-stained but unvarnished tables littered with riding, driving and country-life society papers, to give it that air of *sans ceremonie* with an upper world of which its habitués probably possessed no least inkling but most eagerly craved. Here, along with a goodly group of his latter-day friends, far different from those by whom he had first been surrounded—a pretentious society poet of no great merit but considerable self-emphasis, a Wall Street broker, posing as a club man, *raconteur*, "first-nighter" and what not, and several young and ambitious playwrights, all seeking the heaven of a Broadway success—he began to pose as one of the intimates of the great city, its bosom child as it were, the cynosure and favorite of its most glittering precincts—a most M——— like proceeding. His clothes by now, for I saw him on occasion, had taken on a more lustrous if less convincing aspect than those he had worn when I first knew him. The small round hat or rakish cap, typical of his Western dreams, had now given way to a most pretentious square-topped derby, beloved, I believe, of undertakers and a certain severe type of banker as well as some clergymen, only it was a light brown. His suit and waistcoat were of a bright English tweed, reddish-brown or herring-bone gray by turns, his shoes box-toed perfections of the button type. He carried a heavy cane, often a bright leather manuscript case, and seemed intensely absorbed in the great and dramatic business of living and writing. "One must," so I read him at this time, "take the pleasures as well as the labors of this world with the utmost severity." Here, with a grand manner, he patronized the manager and the waiters, sent word to his friend the cook, who probably did not know him at all, that his chop or steak was to be done just so. These friends of his, or at least one of them (the poet) he met every day at five for an all-essential game of chess, after which an evening paper was read and the chop ordered. Ale—not beer—in a pewter mug was *comme il faut*, the only thing for a gentleman of letters, worthy of the name, to drink.

I am sorry to write so, for after all youth must have its fling. Still, I had expected better of L———, and I was a little disappointed to see that earlier dream of simplicity and privation giving way to an absolutely worthless show. Besides, twenty or thirty such stories as "The Right Man," "Sweet Dreams," "The Man With the Broken Fingers," "The Second Motive," would outweigh a thousand of the things he was getting published and the profits of which permitted him these airs.

Again, during the early days of his success with M———, he had married—a young nurse who had previously been a clerk in a store, a serious, earnest and from one point of view helpful person, seeing that she could keep his domestic affairs in order and bear him children, which she did, but she had no understanding of, or flair for, the type of thing he was called upon to do. She had no instinct for literature or the arts, and aside from her domestic capacities little skill or taste for "socializing." And, naturally, he was neglecting her. His head was probably surging with great ideas of art and hence a social supremacy which might well carry him anywhere. He had bought a farm some distance from New York, where in a community supposedly inhabited by successful and superior men of letters he posed as a farmer at times, mowing and cocking hay as became a Western plow-boy; and also, as the mood moved him, and as became a great and secluded writer, working in a den entirely surrounded by books in fine leather bindings (!) and being visited by those odd satellites of the scriptic art who see in genius of this type the *summum bonum* of life. It was the thing to do at that time, for a writer to own a farm and work it. Horace had. One individual in particular, a man of genuine literary and critical ability and great taste in the matter of all the arts but with no least interest in or tolerance for the simplicities of effort, came here occasionally, as I heard, to help him pile hay, and this in a silk shirt and a monocle; a second—and a most fascinating intellectual *flaneur*, who, however, had no vision or the gift of dreams—came to eat, drink, talk of many things to be done, to steal a few ideas, borrow a little money perhaps or consume a little morphine, and depart; a third came to spout of his success in connection with plays, or his proposed successes; a fourth to paint a picture, urged on by L——; a fifth to compose rural verse; a sixth, a broker or race-track tout or city bar-tender (for color, this last), to marvel that one of L——'s sense, or any one indeed, should live in the country at all. There were drinking bouts, absolute drunkenness, in which, according to the Johnsonian tradition and that of Messieurs Rabelais and Molière, the weary intellect and one's guiding genius were immersed in a comforting Lethe of rye.

Such things cost money, however. In addition, my young friend, due to a desire no doubt to share in the material splendors of his age (a doctrine M—— was ever fond of spouting—and as a duty, if you please), had saddled himself, for a time at least, with an apartment in an exclusive square on the East Side, the rent of which was a severe drain. Before this there had been, and after it were still, others, obligations too much for him to bear financially, all in the main taken for show, that he might be considered a literary success. Now and again (so I was told by several of his intimates), confronted by a sudden exhaustion of his bank balance, he would leave some excellent apartment house or neighborhood, where for a few months he had been living in grand style, extracting his furniture as best he might, or leaving it and various debts beside, and would take refuge in some shabby tenement, or rear rooms even, and where, touched by remorse or encouraged by the great literary and art traditions (Balzac, Baudelaire, Johnson, Goldsmith, Verlaine) he would toil unendingly at definite money-yielding manuscripts, the results of which carried to some well-paying *successful magazine* would yield him sufficient to return to the white lights—often even to take a better apartment than that which last had been his. By now, however, one of the two children he eventually left behind him had been born. His domestic cares were multiplying, the marriage idea dull. Still he did not hesitate to continue those dinners given to his friends, the above-mentioned group or its spiritual kin, either in his apartment or in a bohemian restaurant of great show in New York. In short, he was a fairly successful short-story writer and critic in whom still persisted a feeling that he would yet triumph in the adjacent if somewhat more difficult field of popular fiction.

It was during this period, if I may interpolate an incident, that I was waiting one night in a Broadway theater lobby for a friend to appear, when who should arrive on the scene but L——, most outlandishly dressed in what I took to be a *reductio ad absurdum* of his first pose, as I now half-feared it to be: that of the uncouth and rugged young American, disclaiming style in dress at least, and content to be a clod in looks so long as he was a Shelley in brains. His suit was of that coarse ill-fitting character described as Store, and shelf-worn; his shoes all but dusty brogans, his headgear a long-visored yellowish-and-brown cross-barred cap. He had on a short, badly-cut frieze overcoat, his hands stuck defiantly in his trousers pockets, forcing its lapels wide open. And he appeared to be partially if not entirely drunk, and very insolent. I had the idea that the drunkenness and the dress were a pose, or else that he had been in some neighborhood in search of copy which required such an outfit. Charitably let us accept the last. He was accompanied by two satellic souls who were doing their best to restrain him.

"Come, now! Don't make a scene. We'll see the show all right!"

"Sure we'll see the show!" he returned contentiously. "Where's the manager?"

A smug mannikin whose uniform was a dress suit, the business manager himself, eyed him in no friendly spirit from a nearby corner.

"This is Mr. L——," one of the satellites now approached and explained to the manager. "He's connected with M——'s Magazine. He does short stories and dramatics occasionally."

The manager bowed. After all, M——'s Magazine had come to have some significance on Broadway. It was as well to be civil. Courtesy was extended for three, and they went in.

As for myself, I resented the mood and the change. It was in no way my affair—his life was his own—and still I resented it. I did not believe that he was as bad as he seemed. He had too much genuine sense. It was just boyish swagger and show, and still it was time that he was getting over that and settling down. I really hoped that time would modify all this.

One thing that made me hope for the best was that very shortly after this M——'s Magazine blew completely up, leaving him without that semi-financial protection which I felt was doing him so much harm. The next favorable sign that I observed was that a small volume of short stories, some sixteen in number, and containing the cream of his work up to that time, was brought to a publishing house with which I was financially identified at the time, and although no word was said to me (I really think he took great care not to see me), still it was left and on my advice eventually published (it sold, I believe, a little under five hundred copies). But the thing that cheered me was that it contained not one story which could be looked upon as a compromise with his first views. And better, it had been brought to the concern with which I was connected—intentionally, I am sure. I was glad to have had a hand in its publication. "At least," I said, "he has not lost sight of his first ideal. He may go on now."

And thereafter, in one magazine and another, excellent enough to have but a small circulation, I saw something of his which had genuine merit. A Western critical journal began to publish a series of essays by him, for which I am sure he received nothing at all. Again, three or four years later, a second volume of stories, almost if not quite as good as his first, was issued by this same Western paper. He was trying to do serious work; but he still sought and apparently craved those grand scenes on the farm or in some New York restaurant or an expensive apartment, and when he could no longer afford it. He still wrote happy-ending, or compromise, stories for any such magazine as would receive him, and was apparently building up a reasonably secure market for them. In the meantime the moving-picture scenario market had developed, and he wrote for it. His eyes were also turning toward the stage, as one completed manuscript and several "starts" turned over to me after his death proved. One day some one who knew him and me quite well assured me that L——, having sent out many excellent stories only to have them returned, had one day cried and then raged, cursing America for its attitude toward serious letters—an excellent sign, I thought, good medicine for one who must eventually forsake his hope of material grandeur and find himself. "In time, in time," I said, "he will eat through the husks of these other things, the 'M—— complex,' and do something splendid. He can't help it. But this fantastic dream of grandeur, of being a popular success, will have to be lived down."

For a time now I heard but little more save once that he was connected with a moving-picture concern, suggesting plots and making some money. Then I saw a second series of essays in the same Western critical paper—that of the editor who had published his book—and some of them were excellent, very searching and sincere. I felt that he was moving along the right line, although they earned him nothing. Then one week, very much to my surprise, there was a very glowing and extended commentary on myself, concerning which for the time being I decided to make no comment; and a little later, perhaps three weeks, a telephone call. Did I recall him? (!) Could he come and see me? (!) I invited him to dinner, and he came, carrying, of all things— and for him, the ex-railroad boy—a great armful of red roses. This touched me.

"What's the idea?" I inquired jovially, laughing at him.

He blushed like a girl, a little irritably too, I thought, for he found me (as perhaps he had hoped not to) examining and critical, and he may have felt that I was laughing at him, which I wasn't. "I wished to give them to you, and I brought 'em. Why shouldn't I?"

"You know you should bring them if you want me to have them, and I'm only too glad to get them, anyway. Don't think I'm criticizing."

He smiled and began at once on the "old days," as he now called them, a sad commentary on our drifting days. Indeed he seemed able to talk of little else or fast enough or with too much enthusiasm. He went over many things and people—M——; K——, the wonderful art-director, now insane and a wreck; the group of which he and I had once been a part; his youthful and unsophisticated viewpoint at the time. "You know," he confessed quite frankly finally, "my mother always told me then and afterwards that I made a mistake in leaving you. You were the better influence for me. She was right. I know it now. Still, a life's a life, and we have to work through it and ourselves somehow."

I agreed heartily.

He told me of his wife, children, farm, his health and his difficulties. It appeared that he was making a bare living at times, at others doing very well. His great bane was the popular magazine, the difficulty of selling a good thing. It was true, I said, and at midnight he left, promising to come again, inviting me to come to his place in the country at my convenience. I promised.

But one thing and another interfered. I went South. One day six months later, after I had returned, he called up once more, saying he wished to see me. Of course I asked him down and he came and spoke of his health. Some doctor, an old college pal of his, was assuring him that he had Bright's disease and that he might die at any time. He wanted to know, in case anything happened to him, would I look after his many mss., most of which, the most serious efforts at least, had never been published. I agreed. Then he went away and I never saw him again. A year later I was one day informed that he had died three days before of kidney trouble. He had been West to see a moving-picture director; on his way East he had been taken ill and had stopped off with friends somewhere to be treated, or operated upon. A few weeks later he had returned to New York, but refusing to rest and believing that he could not die, so soon, had kept out of doors and in the city, until suddenly he did collapse. Or, rather, he met his favorite doctor, an intellectual savage like himself, who with some weird desire to appear forceful, definite, unsentimental perhaps—a mental condition L——most fancied—had told him to go home and to bed, for he would be dead in forty-eight hours!—a fine bit of assurance which perhaps as much as anything else assisted L—— to die. At any rate and in spite of the ministrations of his wife, who wished to defy the doctor and who in her hope for herself and her children as well as him strove to contend against this gloom, he did so go to bed and did die. On the last day, realizing no doubt how utterly indifferent his life had been, how his main aspirations or great dreams had been in the main nullified by passions, necessities, crass chance (how well he was fitted to understand that!) he broke down and cried for hours. Then he died.

A friend who had known much of this last period, said to me rather satirically, "He was dealing with death in the shape of a medic. Have you ever seen him?" The doctor, he meant. "He looks like an advertisement for an undertaker. I do believe he was trying to discover whether he could kill somebody by the power of suggestion, and he met L—— in the nick of time. You know how really sensitive he was. Well, that medic killed him, the same as you would kill a bird with a bullet. He said 'You're already dead,' and he was."

And—oh yes—M——, his former patron. At the time of L——'s sickness and death he was still owing him $1100 for services rendered during the last days of that unfortunate magazine. He had never been called upon to pay his debts, for he had sunk through one easy trapdoor of bankruptcy only to rise out of another, smiling and with the means to continue. Yes, he was rich again, rated A No. 1, the president of a great corporation, and with L——'s $1100 still unpaid and now not legally "collectible." His bank balance, established by a friend at the time, was exactly one hundred thousand.

But Mrs. L——, anxious to find some way out of her difficulty since her husband was lying cold, and knowing of no one else to whom to turn, had written to him. There was no food in the house, no medicine, no way to feed the children at the moment. That matter of $1100 now—could he spare a little? L—— had thought——

A letter in answer was not long in arriving, and a most moving M——y document it was. M—— had been stunned by the dreadful news, stunned. Could it really be? Could it? His young brilliant friend? Impossible! At the dread, pathetic news he had cried—yes he had—cried—and cried—and cried—and then he had even cried some more. Life was so sad, so grim. As for him, his own affairs were never in so wretched a condition. It was unfortunate. Debts there were on every hand. They haunted him, robbed him of his sleep. He himself scarcely knew which way to turn. They stood in serried ranks, his debts. A slight push on the part of any one, and he would be crushed—crushed—go down in ruin. And so, as much as he was torn, and as much as he cried, even now, he could do nothing, nothing, nothing. He was agonized, beaten to earth, but still——. Then, having signed it, there was a P.S. or an N.B. This stated that in looking over his affairs he had just discovered that by stinting himself in another direction he *could* manage to scrape together twenty-five dollars, and this he was enclosing. Would that God had designed that he should be better placed at this sad hour!

However that may be, I at once sent for the mss. and they came, a jumbled mass in two suitcases and a portfolio; and a third suitcase, so I was informed, containing all of a hundred mss., mostly stories, had been lost somewhere! There had been much financial trouble of late and more than one enforced move. Mrs. L—— had been compelled—but I will not tell all. Suffice it to say that he had such an end as his own realistic pen might have satirically craved.

The mss., finally sorted, tabulated and read, yielded two small volumes of excellent tales, all unpublished, the published material being all but uniformly worthless. There was also the attempt at a popular comedy, previously mentioned, a sad affair, and a volume of essays, as well as a very, very slender but charming volume of verse, in case a publisher could ever be found for them—a most agreeable little group, showing a pleasing sense of form and color and emotion. I arranged them as best I could and finally——

But they are still unpublished.

P.S. As for the sum total of the work left by L——, its very best, it might be said that although he was not a great psychologist, still, owing to a certain pretentiousness of assertion at times, one might unthinkingly suppose he was. Neither had he, as yet, any fixed theories of art or definite style of his own, imitating as he was now de Maupassant, now O. Henry, now Poe; but also it must be said that slowly and surely he was approximating one, original and forceful and water-clear in expression and naturalness. At times he veered to a rather showy technique, at others to a cold and even harsh simplicity. Yet always in the main he had color, beauty, emotion, poignance when necessary. Like his idol, de Maupassant, he had no moral or strong social prejudices, no really great or disturbing imagination, no wealth of perplexing ideas. He saw America and life as something to be painted as all masters see life and paint it. Gifted with a true vein of satire, he had not, at the time of his death, quite mastered its possibilities. He still retained prejudice of one type or another, which he permitted to interfere with the very smooth arrangement of his colors. At the same time, had he not been disturbed by so many of the things which in America, as elsewhere, ordinarily assail an ambitious and earnest writer—the prejudice against naturalness and sincerity in matters of the intellect and the facts of life, and the consequent difficulty of any one so gifted in obtaining funds at any time—he might have done much better sooner. He was certain to come into his own eventually had he lived. His very accurate and sensitive powers of observation, his literary taste, his energy and pride in his work, were destined to carry him there. It could not have been otherwise. Ten years more, judging by the rate at which he worked, his annual product and that which he did leave, one might say that in the pantheon of American letters it is certain that he would have proved a durable if not one of its great figures, and he might well have been that. As it stands, it is not impossible that he will be so recognized, if for no more than the sure promise of his genius.

The Village Feudists

In a certain Connecticut fishing-town sometime since, where, besides lobstering, a shipyard and some sail-boat-building there existed the several shops and stores which catered to the wants of those who labored in those lines, there dwelt a groceryman by the name of Elihu Burridge, whose life and methods strongly point the moral and social successes and failures of the rural man.

Sixty years of age, with the vanities and desires of the average man's life behind rather than before him, he was at the time not unlike the conventional drawings of Parson Thirdly, which graced the humorous papers of that day. Two moon-shaped eyes, a long upper lip, a mouth like the sickle moon turned downward, prominent ears, a rather long face and a mutton-chop-shaped whisker on either cheek, served to give him that clerical appearance which the humorous artists so religiously seek to depict. Add to this that he was middle-sized, clerically spare in form, reserved and quiet in demeanor, and one can see how he might very readily give the impression of being a minister. His clothes, however, were old, his trousers torn but neatly mended, his little blue gingham jumper which he wore about the store greasy and aged. Everything about him and his store was so still and dark that one might have been inclined on first sight to consider him crusty and morose.

Even more remarkable than himself, however, was his store. I have seen many in my time that were striking because of their neatness; I never saw one before that struck me as more remarkable for its disorder. In the first place it was filled neck-deep with barrels and boxes in the utmost confusion. Dark, greasy, provision-lined alleys led off into dingy sections which the eye could not penetrate. Old signs hung about, advertising things which had long since ceased to sell and were forgotten by the public. There were pictures in once gilt but now time-blackened frames, wherein queerly depicted children and pompous-looking grocers offered one commodity and another, all now almost obliterated by fly-specks. Shelves were marked on the walls by signs now nearly illegible. Cobwebs hung thickly from corners and pillars. There were oil, lard, and a dust-laden scum of some sort on three of the numerous scales with which he occasionally weighed things and on many exteriors of once salable articles. Pork, lard, molasses, and nails were packed in different corners of the place in barrels. Lying about were household utensils, ship-rigging, furniture and a hundred other things which had nothing to do with the grocery business.

As I entered the store the first afternoon I noticed a Bible open at Judges and a number of slips of paper on which questions had been written. On my second visit for oil and vinegar, two strangers from off a vagrant yacht which had entered the little harbor nudged one another and demanded to know whether either had ever seen anything like it. On the third, my companion protested that it was not clean, and seeing that there were other stores we decided to buy our things elsewhere. This was not so easily accomplished.

"Where can I get a flatiron?" I inquired at the Postoffice when I first entered the village.

"Most likely at Burridge's," was the reply.

"Do you know where I can get a pair of row-locks?" I asked of a boy who was lounging about the town dock.

"At Burridge's," he replied.

When we wanted oars, pickles of a certain variety, golden syrup, and a dozen other things which were essential at times, we were compelled to go to Burridge's, so that at last he obtained a very fair portion of our trade despite the condition of his store.

During all these earlier dealings there cropped up something curt and dry in his conversation. One day we lost a fruit jar which he had loaned, and I took one very much like it back in its place. When I began to apologize he interrupted me with, "A jar's a jar, isn't it?"

Another time, when I remarked in a conciliatory tone that he owed me eight cents for a can of potted ham which had proved stale, he exclaimed, "Well, I won't owe you long," and forthwith pulled the money out of the loose jacket of his jumper and paid me.

I inquired one day if a certain thing were good. "If it isn't," he replied, with a peculiar elevation of the eyebrows, "your money is. You can have that back."

"That's the way you do business, is it?"

"Yes, sir," he replied, and his long upper lip thinned out along the line of the lower one like a vise.

I was in search of a rocking-chair one day and was directed to Burridge's as the only place likely to have any!

"Do you keep furniture?" I inquired.

"Some," he said.

"Have you a rocking-chair?"

"No, sir."

A day or two later I was in search of a table and on going to Burridge's found that he had gone to a neighboring city.

"Have you got a table?" I inquired of the clerk.

"I don't know," he replied. "There's some furniture in the back room, but I don't know as I dare to sell any of it while he's away."

"Why?"

"Well, he don't like me to sell any of it. He's kind of queer that way. I dunno what he intends to do with it. Gar!" he added in a strangely electric way, "he's a queer man! He's got a lot of things back there—chairs and tables and everything. He's got a lot more in a loft up the street here. He never seems to want to sell any of 'em. Heard him tell people he didn't have any."

I shook my head in puzzled desperation.

"Come on, let's go back and look anyway. There's no harm in seeing if he has one."

We went back and there amid pork and molasses barrels, old papers, boxes and signs, was furniture in considerable quantity—tables, rocking-chairs, washstands, bureaus—all cornered and tumbled about.

"Why, here are rocking-chairs, lots of them," I exclaimed. "Just the kind I want! He said he didn't have any."

"Gar! I dunno," replied the clerk. "Here's a table, but I wouldn't dare sell it to you."

"Why should he say he didn't have a rocking-chair?"

"Gar! I dunno. He's goin' out of the furniture business. He don't want to sell any. I don't know what he intends to do with it."

"Well," I said in despair, "what about the table? You can sell that, can't you?"

"I couldn't—not till he comes back. I don't know what he'd want to do about it."

"What's the price of it?"

"I dunno. He could tell you."

I went out of the thick-aired stuffy backroom with its unwashed windows, and when I got opposite the Bible near the door I said:

"What's the matter with him anyhow? Why doesn't he straighten things out here?"

Again the clerk awoke. "Huh!" he exclaimed. "Straighten it out! Gar! I'd like to see anybody try it."

"It could be," I said encouragingly.

"Gar!" he chuckled. "One man did try to straighten it out once when Mr. Burridge was away. Got about a third of it cleaned up when he come back. Gar! You oughta seen him! Gar!"

"What did he do?"

"What did he do! What didn't he do! Gar! Just took things an' threw them about again. Said he couldn't find anything."

"You don't say!"

"Gar! I should say so! Man come in an' asked for a hammer. Said he couldn't find any hammer, things was so mixed up. Did it with screws, water-buckets an' everything just the same. Took 'em right off the shelves, where they was all in groups, an' scattered 'em all over the room. Gar! 'Now I guess I can find something when I want it,' he said." The clerk paused to squint and add, "There ain't anybody tried any straightenin' out around here since then, you bet. Gar!"

"How long ago has that been?"

"About fourteen years now."

Surprised by this sharp variation from the ordinary standards of trade, I began thinking of possible conditions which had produced it, when one evening I happened in on the local barber. He was a lean, inquisitive individual with a shock of sandy hair and a conspicuous desire to appear a well-rounded social factor.

"What sort of person is this Burridge over here? He keeps such a peculiar store."

"Elihu is a bit peculiar," he replied, his smile betraying a desire to appear conservative. "The fault with Elihu, if he has one, is that he's terribly strong on religion. Can't seem to agree with anybody around here."

"What's the trouble?" I asked.

"It's more'n I could ever make out, what is the matter with him. They're all a little bit cracked on the subject around here. Nothing but revivals and meetin's, year in and year out. They're stronger on it winters than they are in summer."

"How do you mean?"

"Well, they'll be more against yachtin' and Sunday pleasures when they can't go than when they can."

"What about Elihu?" I asked.

"Well, he can't seem to get along, somehow. He used to belong to the Baptist Church, but he got out o' that. Then he went to a church up in Graylock, but he had a fallin' out up there. Then he went to Northfield and Eustis. He's been all around, even over on Long Island. He goes to church up at Amherst now, I believe."

"What seems to be the trouble?"

"Oh, he's just strong-headed, I guess." He paused, and ideas lagged until finally I observed:

"It's a very interesting store he keeps."

"It's just as Billy Drumgold told him once: 'Burridge,' he says, 'you've got everything in this store that belongs to a full-rigged ship 'cept one thing.' 'What's that?' Burridge asks. 'A second-hand pulpit.' 'Got that too,' he answered, and takes him upstairs, and there he had one sure enough."

"Well," I said, "what was he doing with it?"

"Danged if I know. He had it all right. Has it yet, so they say."

Days passed and as the summer waned the evidences of a peculiar life accumulated. Noank, apparently, was at outs with Burridge on the subject of religion, and he with it. There were instances of genuine hard feeling against him.

Writing a letter in the Postoffice one day I ventured to take up this matter with the postmaster.

"You know Mr. Burridge, don't you—the grocer?"

"Well, I should guess I did," he replied with a flare.

"Anything wrong with him?"

"Oh, about everything that's just plain cussed—the most wrangling man alive. I never saw such a man. He don't get his mail here no more because he's mad at me, I guess. Took it away because I had Mr. Palmer's help in my fight, I suppose. Wrote me that I should send all his mail up to Mystic, and he goes there three or four miles out of his way every day, just to spite me. It's against the law. I hadn't ought to be doing it, re-addressing his envelopes three or four times a day, but I do do it. He's a strong-headed man, that's the trouble with Elihu."

I had no time to follow this up then, but a little later, sitting in the shop of the principal sailboat maker, which was situated in the quiet little lane which follows the line of the village, I was one day surprised by the sudden warm feeling which the name of Elihu generated. Something had brought up the subject of religion, and I said that Burridge seemed rather religious.

"Yes," said the sailboat maker quickly, "he's religious, all right, only he reads the Bible for others, not for himself."

"What do you mean by that?"

"Why, he wants to run things, that's what. As long as you agree with Elihu, why, everything's all right. When you don't, the Bible's against you. That's the way he is."

"Did he ever disagree with you?" I asked, suspecting some personal animus in the matter.

"Me and Elihu was always good friends as long as I agreed with him," he went on bitterly. "We've been raised together, man and boy, for pretty near sixty years. We never had a word of any kind but what was friendly, as long as I agreed with him, but just as soon as I didn't he took a set against me, and we ain't never spoke a word since."

"What was the trouble?" I inquired sweetly, anxious to come at the kernel of this queer situation.

"Well," he said, dropping his work and looking up to impress me, "I'm a man that'll sometimes say what I don't believe; that is, I'll agree with what I hadn't ought to, just to be friendly like. I did that way a lot o' times with Elihu till one day he came to me with something about particular salvation. I'm a little more liberal myself. I believe in universal redemption by faith alone. Well, Elihu came to me and began telling me what he believed. Finally he asked me something about particular salvation and wanted to know whether I didn't agree with him. I didn't, and told him so. From that day on he took a set against me, and he ain't never spoke a word to me since."

I was unaware that there was anything besides a religious disagreement in this local situation until one day I happened to come into a second friendly contact with the postmaster. We were speaking of the characteristics of certain individuals, and I mentioned Burridge.

"He's all right when you take him the way he wants to be taken. When you don't you'll find him quite a different man."

"He seems to be straightforward and honest," I said.

"There ain't anything you can tell me about Elihu Burridge that I don't know," he replied feelingly. "Not a thing. I've lived with him, as you might say, all my life. Been raised right here in town with him, and we went to school together. Man and boy, there ain't ever been a thing that Elihu has agreed with, without he could have the running of it. You can't tell me anything about him that I don't know."

I could not help smiling at the warmth of feeling, although something about the man's manner bespoke a touch of heart-ache, as if he were privately grieving.

"What was the trouble between you two?" I asked.

"It's more'n I could ever find out," he replied in a voice that was really mournful, so difficult and non-understandable was the subject to him. "Before I started to work for this office there wasn't a day that I didn't meet and speak friendly with Elihu. He used to have a good many deeds and papers to sign, and he never failed to call me in when I was passing. When I started to work for this office I noticed he took on a cold manner toward me, and I tried to think of something I might have done, but I couldn't. Finally I wrote and asked him if there was anything between us if he wouldn't set a time and place so's we might talk it over and come to an understanding." He paused and then added, "I wish you could see the letter he wrote me. Comin' from a Christian man—from him to me—I wish you could see it."

"Why don't you show it to me?" I asked inquisitively.

He went back into the office and returned with an ancient-looking document, four years old it proved to be, which he had been treasuring. He handed me the thumbed and already yellowed page, and I read:

"MATTHEW HOLCOMB, ESQUIRE,

> "DEAR SIR:—In reply to your letter asking me to set a time
> and place in which we might talk over the trouble between
> us, would say that the time be Eternity and the place where
> God shall call us to judgment.

"Very truly,"ELIHU BURRIDGE."

His eyes rested on me while I read, and the moment I finished he began with:

"I never said one word against that man, not one word. I never did a thing he could take offense at, not one thing. I don't know how a man can justify himself writing like that."

"Perhaps it's political," I said. "You don't belong to the same party, do you?"

"Yes, we do," he said. "Sometimes I've thought that maybe it was because I had the support of the shipyard when I first tried to get this office, but then that wasn't anything between him and me," and he looked away as if the mystery were inexplicable.

This shipyard was conducted by a most forceful man but one as narrow and religionistic as this region in which it had had its rise. Old Mr. Palmer, the aged founder of it, had long been a notable figure in the streets and private chambers of the village. The principal grocery store, coal-yard, sail-loft, hotel and other institutions were conducted in its interests. His opinion was always foremost in the decision of the local authorities. He was still, reticent, unobtrusive. Once I saw him most considerately helping a cripple up the lane to the local Baptist Church.

"What's the trouble between Burridge and Palmer?" I asked of the sail-maker finally, coming to think that here, if anywhere, lay the solution of the difficulty.

"Two big fish in too small a basket," he responded laconically.

"Can't agree, eh?"

"They both want to lead, or did," he said. "Elihu's a beaten man, though, now." He paused and then added, "I'm sorry for Elihu. He's a good man at heart, one of the kindest men you ever saw, when you let him follow his natural way. He's good to the poor, and he's carried more slow-pay people than any man in this country, I do believe. He won't collect an old debt by law. Don't believe in it. No, sir. Just a kind-hearted man, but he loves to rule."

"How about Palmer?" I inquired.

"Just the same way exactly. He loves to rule, too. Got a good heart, too, but he's got a lot more money than Elihu and so people pay more attention to him, that's all. When Elihu was getting the attention he was just the finest man you ever saw, kind, generous, good-natured. People love to be petted, at least some people do—you know they do. When you don't pet 'em they get kind o' sour and crabbed like. Now that's all that's the matter with Elihu, every bit of it. He's sour, now, and a little lonely, I expect. He's drove away every one from him, or nearly all, 'cept his wife and some of his kin. Anybody can do a good grocery business here, with the strangers off the boats"—the harbor was a lively one—"all you have to do is carry a good stock. That's why he gets along so well. But he's drove nearly all the local folks away from him."

I listened to this comfortable sail-loft sage, and going back to the grocery store one afternoon took another look at the long, grim-faced silent figure. He was sitting in the shadow of one of his moldy corners, and if there had ever been any light of merriment in his face it was not there now. He looked as fixed and solemn as an ancient puritan, and yet there was something so melancholy in the man's eye, so sad and disappointed, that it seemed anything but hard. Two or three little children were playing about the door and when he came forward to wait on me one of them sidled forward and put her chubby hand in his.

"Your children?" I asked, by way of reaching some friendly understanding.

"No," he replied, looking fondly down, "she belongs to a French lady up the street here. She often comes down to see me, don't you?" and he reached over and took the fat little cheek between his thumb and forefinger.

The little one rubbed her face against his worn baggy trousers' leg and put her arm about his knee. Quietly he stood there in a simple way until she loosened her hold upon him, when he went about his labor.

I was sitting one day in the loft of the comfortable sail-maker, who, by the way, was brother-in-law to Burridge, when I said to him:

"I wish you'd tell me the details about Elihu. How did he come to be what he is? You ought to know; you've lived here all your life."

"So I do know," he replied genially. "What do you want me to tell you?"

"The whole story of the trouble between him and Palmer; how he comes to be at outs with all these people."

"Well," he began, and here followed with many interruptions and side elucidations, which for want of space have been eliminated, the following details:

Twenty-five years before Elihu had been the leading citizen of Noank. From operating a small grocery at the close of the Civil War he branched out until he sold everything from ship-rigging to hardware. Noank was then in the height of its career as a fishing town and as a port from which expeditions of all sorts were wont to sail. Whaling was still in force, and vessels for whaling expeditions were equipped here. Wealthy sea-captains frequently loaded fine three-masted schooners here for various trading expeditions to all parts of the world; the fishers for mackerel, cod and herring were making three hundred and fifty dollars a day in season, and thousands of dollars' worth of supplies were annually purchased here.

Burridge was then the only tradesman of any importance and, being of a liberal, strong-minded and yet religious turn, attracted the majority of this business to him. He had houses and lands, was a deacon in the local Baptist Church and a counselor in matters political, social and religious, whose advice was seldom rejected. Every Fourth of July during these years it was his custom to collect all the children of the town in front of his store and treat them to ice-cream. Every Christmas Eve he traveled about the streets in a wagon, which carried half a dozen barrels of candy and nuts, which he would ladle out to the merry shouting throng of pursuing youngsters, until all were satisfied. For the skating season he prepared a pond, spending several thousand dollars damming up a small stream, in order that the children might have a place to skate. He created a library where all might obtain suitable reading, particularly the young.

On New Year's morning it was his custom to visit all the poor and bereaved and lonely in Noank, taking a great dray full of presents and leaving a little something with his greetings and a pleasant handshake at every door. The lonely rich as well as the lonely poor were included, for he was certain, as he frequently declared, that the rich could be lonely too.

He once told his brother-in-law that one New Year's Day a voice called to him in church: "Elihu Burridge, how about the lonely rich and poor of Noank?" "Up I got," he concluded, "and from that day to this I have never neglected them."

When any one died who had a little estate to be looked after for the benefit of widows or orphans, Burridge was the one to take charge of it. People on their deathbeds sent for him, and he always responded, taking energetic charge of everything and refusing to take a penny for his services. After a number of years the old judge to whom he always repaired with these matters of probate, knowing his generosity in this respect, also refused to accept any fee. When he saw him coming he would exclaim:

"Well, Elihu, what is it this time? Another widow or orphan that we've got to look after?"

After Elihu had explained what it was, he would add:

"Well, Elihu, I do hope that some day some rich man will call you to straighten out his affairs. I'd like to see *you* get a little something, so that *I* might get a little something. Eh, Elihu?" Then he would jocularly poke his companion in charity in the ribs.

These general benefactions were continuous and coeval with his local prosperity and dominance, and their modification as well as the man's general decline the result of the rise of this other individual—Robert Palmer,— "operating" to take the color of power and preëminence from him.

Palmer was the owner of a small shipyard here at the time, a thing which was not much at first but which grew swiftly. He was born in Noank also, a few years before Burridge, and as a builder of vessels had been slowly forging his way to a moderate competence when Elihu was already successful. He was a keen, fine-featured, energetic individual, with excellent commercial and strong religious instincts, and by dint of hard labor and a saving disposition he obtained, soon after the Civil War, a powerful foothold. Many vessels were ordered here from other cities. Eventually he began to build barges in large numbers for a great railroad company.

Early becoming a larger employer of labor than any one else in the vicinity he soon began to branch out, possessed himself of the allied industries of ship-rigging, chandlering, and finally established a grocery store for his employees, and opened a hotel. Now the local citizens began to look upon him as their leading citizen. They were always talking of his rise, frequently in the presence of Burridge. He said nothing at first, pretending to believe that his quondam leadership was unimpaired. Again, there were those who, having followed the various branches of labor which Palmer eventually consolidated, viewed this growth with sullen and angry eyes. They still sided with Burridge, or pretended still to believe that he was the more important citizen of the two. In the course of time, however—a period of thirty years or more—some of them failed; others died; still others were driven away for want of a livelihood. Only Burridge's position and business remained, but in a sadly weakened state. He was no longer a man of any great importance.

Not unnaturally, this question of local supremacy was first tested in the one place in which local supremacy is usually tested—the church where they both worshiped. Although only one of five trustees, Burridge had been the will of the body. Always, whatever he thought, the others had almost immediately agreed to it. But now that Palmer had become a power, many of those ardent in the church and beholden to him for profit became his humble followers. They elected him trustee and did what he wished, or what they thought he wished. To Burridge this made them sycophants, slaves.

Now followed the kind of trivialities by which most human feuds are furthered. The first test of strength came when a vagrant evangelist from Alabama arrived and desired to use the church for a series of evening lectures. The question had to be decided at once. Palmer was absent at the time.

"Here is a request for the use of the church," said one of the trustees, explaining its nature.

"Well," said Burridge, "you'd better let him have it."

"Do you think we ought to do anything about it," the trustee replied, "until Mr. Palmer returns?"

Although Burridge saw no reason for waiting, the other trustees did, and upon that the board rested. Burridge was furious. By one fell stroke he was put in second place, a man who had to await the return of Palmer—and that in his own church, so to speak.

"Why," he told some one, "the rest of us are nothing. This man is a king."

From that time on differences of opinion within the church and elsewhere were common. Although no personal animosity was ever admitted, local issues almost invariably found these two men opposed to each other. There was the question of whether the village should be made into a borough—a most trivial matter; another, that of creating public works for the manufacture of gas and distribution of water; a third, that of naming a State representative. Naturally, while these things might be to the advantage of Palmer or not, they were of no great import to Burridge, but yet he managed to see in them an attempt or attempts to saddle a large public debt upon widows and orphans, those who could not afford or did not need these things, and he proceeded to so express himself at various public meetings. Slowly the breach widened. Burridge became little more than a malcontent in many people's eyes. He was a "knocker," a man who wanted to hold the community back.

Although defeated in many instances he won in others, and this did not help matters any. At this point, among other things the decay of the fishing industry helped to fix definitely the position of the two men as that of victor and vanquished. Whaling died out, then mackerel and cod were caught only at farther and farther distances from the town, and finally three-and even two-masted schooners ceased entirely to buy their outfits here, and Burridge was left dependent upon local patronage or smaller harbor trade for his support. Coextensively, he had the dissatisfaction of seeing Palmer's industries grow until eventually three hundred and fifty men were upon his payrolls and even his foremen and superintendents were considered influential townspeople. Palmer's son and two daughters grew up and married, branched out and became owners of industries which had formerly belonged to men who had traded with Burridge. He saw his grocery trade dwindle and sink, while with age his religiosity grew, and he began to be little more than a petty disputant, one constantly arguing as to whether the interpretation of the Bible as handed down from the pulpit of what he now considered *his* recalcitrant church was sound or not. When those who years before had followed him obediently now pricked him with theological pins and ventured to disagree with him, he was quick and sometimes foolish in his replies. Thus, once a former friend and fellow-church-member who had gone over to the opposition came into his store one morning and said:

"Elihu, for a man that's as strong on religion as you are, I see you do one thing that can't quite be justified by the Book."

"What's that?" inquired Burridge, looking up.

"I see you sell tobacco."

"I see you chew it," returned the host grimly.

"I know I do," returned his visitor, "but I'll tell you what I'll do, Elihu. If you'll quit selling, I'll quit chewing it," and he looked as if he had set a fancy trap for his straw-balancing brother, as he held him to be.

"It's a bargain," said Burridge on the instant. "It's a bargain!"

And from that day on tobacco was not offered for sale in that store, although there was a large local demand for it.

Again, in the pride of his original leadership, he had accepted the conduct of the local cemetery, a thing which was more a burden than a source of profit. With his customary liberality in all things reflecting credit upon himself he had spent his own money in improving it, much more than ever the wardens of the church would have thought of returning to him. In one instance, when a new receiving vault was desired, he had added seven hundred dollars of his own to three hundred gathered by the church trustees for the purpose, and the vault was immediately constructed. Frequently also, in his pride of place, he had been given to asserting he was tired of conducting the cemetery and wished he could resign.

In these later evil days, therefore, the trustees, following the star of the newer power, saw fit to intimate that perhaps some one else would be glad to look after it if he was tired of it. Instantly the fact that he could no longer boast as formerly came home to him. He was not essential any longer in anything. The church did not want him to have a hand in any of its affairs! The thought of this so weighed on him that eventually he resigned from this particular task, but thereafter also every man who had concurred in accepting his resignation was his bitter enemy. He spoke acidly of the seven hundred he had spent, and jibed at the decisions of the trustees in other matters. Soon he became a disturbing element in the church, taking a solemn vow never to enter the graveyard again, and not long after resigned all his other official duties—passing the plate, et cetera—although he still attended services there.

Decoration Day rolled around, the G.A.R. Post of which he was an ardent member prepared for the annual memorial services over the graves of its dead comrades. Early on the morning of the thirtieth of May they gathered before their lodge hall, Burridge among them, and after arranging the details marched conspicuously to the cemetery where the placing of the wreaths and the firing of the salute were to take place. No one thought of Burridge until the gate was reached, when, gun over shoulder and uniform in perfect trim, he fell conspicuously out of line and marched away home alone. It was the cemetery he had vowed not to enter, his old pet and protégé.

Men now looked askance at him. He was becoming queer, no doubt of it, not really sensible—or was he? Up in Northfield, a nearby town, dwelt a colonel of the Civil War who had led the very regiment of which Burridge was a member but who during the war had come into serious difficulty through a tangle of orders, and had been dishonorably discharged. Although wounded in one of the engagements in which the regiment had distinguished itself, he had been allowed to languish almost forgotten for years and finally, failing to get a pension, had died in poverty. On his deathbed he had sent for Burridge, and reminding him of the battle in which he had led him asked that after he was gone, for the sake of his family, he would take up the matter of a pension and if possible have his record purged of the stigma and the pension awarded.

Burridge agreed most enthusiastically. Going to the local congressman, he at once began a campaign, but because of the feeling against him two years passed without anything being done. Later he took up the matter in his own G.A.R. Post, but there also failing to find the measure of his own enthusiasm, he went finally direct to one of the senators of the State and laying the matter before him had the records examined by Congress and the dead colonel honorably discharged.

One day thereafter in the local G.A.R. he commented unfavorably upon the indifference which he deemed had been shown.

"There wouldn't have been half so much delay if the man hadn't been a deserter," said one of his enemies—one who was a foreman in Palmer's shipyard.

Instantly Burridge was upon his feet, his eyes aflame with feeling. Always an orator, with a strangely declamatory style he launched into a detailed account of the late colonel's life and services, his wounds, his long sufferings and final death in poverty, winding up with a vivid word picture of a battle (Antietam), in which the colonel had gallantly captured a rebel flag and come by his injury.

When he was through there was great excitement in the Post and much feeling in his favor, but he rather weakened the effect by at once demanding that the traitorous words be withdrawn, and failing to compel this, preferred charges against the man who had uttered them and attempted to have him court-martialed.

So great was the bitterness engendered by this that the Post was now practically divided, and being unable to compel what he considered justice he finally resigned. Subsequently he took issue with his former fellow-soldiers in various ways, commenting satirically on their church regularity and professed Christianity, as opposed to their indifference to the late colonel, and denouncing in various public conversations the double-mindedness and sharp dealings of the "little gods," as he termed those who ran the G.A.R. Post, the church, and the shipyards.

Not long after his religious affairs reached a climax when the minister, once a good friend of his, following the lead of the dominant star, Mr. Palmer, publicly denounced him from the pulpit one Sunday as an enemy of the church and of true Christianity!

"There is a man in this congregation," he exclaimed in a burst of impassioned oratory, "who poses as a Christian and a Baptist, who is in his heart's depth the church's worst enemy. Hell and all its devils could have no worse feelings of evil against the faith than he, and he doesn't sell tobacco, either!"

The last reference at once fixed the identity of the person, and caused Burridge to get up and leave the church. He pondered over this for a time, severed his connections with the body, and having visited Graylock one Sunday drove there every Sabbath thereafter, each time going to a different church. After enduring this for six months he generated a longing for a more convenient meeting-place, and finally allied himself with the Baptist Church of Eustis. Here his anchor might possibly have remained fast had it not been that subtle broodings over his wrongs, a calm faith in the righteousness of his own attitude, and disgust with those whom he saw calmly expatiating upon the doctrines and dogmas of religion in his own town finally caused him to suspect a universal misreading of the Bible. This doubt, together with his own desire for justification according to the Word, finally put the idea in his mind to make a study of the Bible himself. He would read it, he said. He would study Hebrew and Greek, and refer all questionable readings of words and passages back to the original tongue in which it had been written.

With this end in view he began a study of these languages, the importance of the subject so growing upon him that he neglected his business. Day after day he labored, putting a Bible and a Concordance upon a pile of soap-boxes near the door of his store and poring over them between customers, the store meantime taking care of itself. He finally mastered Greek and Hebrew after a fashion, and finding the word "repent" frequently used, and that God had made man in the image of Himself, with a full knowledge of right and wrong, he gravitated toward the belief that therefore his traducers in Noank knew what they were doing, and that before he needed to forgive them—though his love might cover all—they must repent.

He read the Bible from beginning to end with this one feeling subconsciously dominant, and all its loving commands about loving one another, forgiving your brother seventy times seven, loving those that hate you, returning good for evil, selling all that you have and giving it to the poor, were made to wait upon the duty of others to repent. He began to give this interpretation at Eustis, where he was allowed to have a Sunday-school, until the minister came and told him once, "to his face," as the local report ran: "We don't want you here."

Meekly he went forth and, joining a church across the Sound on Long Island, sailed over every Sunday and there advanced the same views until he was personally snubbed by the minister and attacked by the local papers. Leaving there he went to Amherst, always announcing now that he held distinctive views about some things in the Bible and asking the privilege of explaining. In this congregation he was still comfortably at rest when I knew him.

"All sensitiveness," the sail-maker had concluded after his long account. "There ain't anything the matter with Elihu, except that he's piqued and grieved. He wanted to be the big man, and he wasn't."

I was thinking of this and of his tender relationship with children as I had noticed it, and of his service to the late colonel when one day being in the store, I said:

"Do you stand on the Bible completely, Mr. Burridge?"

"Yes, sir," he replied, "I do."

"Believe every word of it to be true?"

"Yes, sir."

"If your brother has offended you, how many times must you forgive him?"

"Seventy times seven."

"Do you forgive your brothers?"

"Yes, sir—if they repent."

"If they repent?"

"Yes, sir, if they repent. That's the interpretation. In Matthew you will find, 'If he repent, forgive him.'"

"But if you don't forgive them, even before they repent," I said, "aren't you harboring enmity?"

"No, sir, I'm not treasuring up enmity. I only refuse to forgive them."

I looked at the man, a little astonished, but he looked so sincere and earnest that I could not help smiling.

"How do you reconcile that with the command, 'Love one another?' You surely can't love and refuse to forgive them at the same time?"

"I don't refuse to forgive them," he repeated. "If John there," indicating an old man in a sun-tanned coat who happened to be passing through the store at the time, "should do me a wrong—I don't care what it was, how great or how vile—if he should come to me and say, 'Burridge, I'm sorry,'" he executed a flashing oratorical move in emphasis, and throwing back his head, exclaimed: "It's gone! It's gone! There ain't any more of it! All gone!"

I stood there quite dumbfounded by his virility, as the air vibrated with his force and feeling. So manifestly was his reading of the Bible colored by the grief of his own heart that it was almost painful to tangle him with it. Goodness and mercy colored all his ideas, except in relation to his one-time followers, those who had formerly been his friends and now left him to himself.

"Do you still visit the poor and the afflicted, as you once did?" I asked him once.

"I'd rather not say anything about that," he replied sternly.

"But do you?"

"Yes, sir."

"Still make your annual New Year round?"

"Yes, sir."

"Well, you'll get your reward for that, whatever you believe."

"I've had my reward," he said slowly.

"Had it?"

"Yes, sir, had it. Every hand that's been lifted to receive the little I had to offer has been my reward."

He smiled, and then said in seemingly the most untimely way:

"I remember once going to a lonely woman here on New Year's Day and taking her a little something—basket of grapes or fruit of some kind it was. I was stopping a minute—never stay long, you know; just run in and say 'Happy New Year!' leave what I have and get out—and so said, 'Good morning, Aunt Mary!'

"'Good morning, Elihu,' says she.

"'Can't stay long, Aunt Mary,' I said. 'Just want to leave you these. Happy New Year!'

"Well, sir, you know I was just turning around and starting when she caught hold of my sleeve and says:

"'Elihu Burridge,' she says, 'give me that hand!' and do you know, before I knew what she was about she took it up to her lips and kissed it! Yes, she did—kissed my hand!

"Now," he said, drawing himself up, with eyes bright with intense feeling, "you know whether I've had my reward or not, don't you?"

"Vanity, Vanity," Saith the Preacher

Sometimes a single life will clearly and effectively illustrate a period. Hence, to me, the importance of this one.

I first met X—— at a time when American financial methods and American finances were at their apex of daring and splendor, and when the world was in a more or less tolerant mood toward their grandiose manners and achievements. It was the golden day of Mr. Morgan, Senior, Mr. Belmont, Mr. Harriman, Mr. Sage, Mr. Gates, Mr. Brady, and many, many others who were still extant and ruling distinctly and drastically, as was proved by the panic of 1907. In opposition to them and yet imitating their methods, now an old story to those who have read "Frenzied Finance," "Lawless Wealth," and other such exposures of the methods which produced our enormous American fortunes, were such younger men as Charles W. Morse (the victim of the 1907 panic), F. Augustus Heinze (another if less conspicuous victim of the same "panic"), E.R. Thomas, an ambitious young millionaire, himself born to money, David A. Sullivan, and X——. I refuse to mention his name because he is still alive although no longer conspicuous, and anxious perhaps to avoid the uncomfortable glare of publicity when all the honors and comforts which made it endurable in the first place are absent.

The person who made X—— essentially interesting to me long before I met him was one Lucien de Shay, a ne'er-do-well pianist and voice culturist, who was also a connoisseur in the matters of rugs, hangings, paintings and furniture, things in which X—— was just then most intensely interested, erecting, as he was, a great house on Long Island and but newly blossoming into the world of art or fashion or culture or show—those various things which the American multi-millionaire always wants to blossom or bloom into and which he does not always succeed in doing. De Shay was one of those odd natures so common to the metropolis—half artist and half man of fashion who attach themselves so readily to men of strength and wealth, often as advisors and counselors in all matters of taste, social form and social progress. How this particular person was rewarded I never quite knew, whether in cash or something else. He was also a semi-confidant of mine, furnishing me "tips" and material of one sort and another in connection with the various publications I was then managing. As it turned out later, X—— was not exactly a multi-millionaire as yet, merely a fledgling, although the possibilities were there and his aims and ambitions were fast nearing a practical triumph the end of which of course was to be, as in the case of nearly all American multi-millionaires of the newer and quicker order, bohemian or exotic and fleshly rather than cultural or æsthetic pleasure, although the latter were never really exactly ignored.

But even so. He was a typical multi-millionaire in the showy and even gaudy sense of the time. For if the staid and conservative and socially well-placed rich have the great houses and the ease and the luxury of paraphernalia, the bohemian rich of the X—— type have the flare, recklessness and imagination which lend to their spendings and flutterings a sparkle and a shine which the others can never hope to match.

Said this friend of mine to me one day: "Listen, I want you to meet this man X——. You will like him. He is fine. You haven't any idea what a fascinating person he really is. He looks like a Russian Grand Duke. He has the manners and the tastes of a Medici or a Borgia. He is building a great house down on Long Island that once it is done will have cost him five or six hundred thousand. It's worth seeing already. His studio here in the C—— studio building is a dream. It's thick with the loveliest kinds of things. I've helped buy them myself. And he isn't dull. He wrote a book at twenty, 'Icarus,' which is not bad either and which he says is something like himself. He has read your book ("Sister Carrie") and he sympathizes with that man Hurstwood. Says parts of it remind him of his own struggles. That's why he wants to meet you. He once worked on the newspapers too. God knows how he is making his money, but I know how he is spending it. He's decided to live, and he's doing it splendidly. It's wonderful."

I took notice, although I had never even heard of the man. There were so very, very many rich men in America. Later I heard much more concerning him from this same de Shay. Once he had been so far down in the scale that he had to shine shoes for a living. Once he had walked the streets of New York in the snow, his shoes cracked and broken, no overcoat, not even a warm suit. He had come here a penniless emigrant from Russia. Now he controlled four banks, one trust company, an insurance company, a fire insurance company, a great real estate venture somewhere, and what not. Naturally all of this interested me greatly. When are we indifferent to a rise from nothing to something?

At de Shay's invitation I journeyed up to X——'s studio one Wednesday afternoon at four, my friend having telephoned me that if I could I must come at once, that there was an especially interesting crowd already assembled in the rooms, that I would meet a long list of celebrities. Two or three opera singers of repute were already there, among them an Italian singer and sorceress of great beauty, a veritable queen of the genus adventuress, who was setting the town by the ears not only by her loveliness but her voice. Her beauty was so remarkable that the Sunday papers were giving full pages to her face and torso alone. There were to be several light opera and stage beauties there also, a basso profundo to sing, writers, artists, poets.

I went. The place and the crowd literally enthralled me. It was so gay, colorful, thrillful. The host and the guests were really interesting—to me. Not that it was so marvelous as a studio or that it was so gorgeously decorated and furnished—it was impressive enough in that way—but that it was so gracefully and interestingly representative of a kind of comfort disguised as elegance. The man had everything, or nearly so—friends, advisors, servants, followers. A somewhat savage and sybaritic nature, as I saw at once, was here disporting itself in velvets and silks. The iron hand of power, if it was power, was being most gracefully and agreeably disguised as the more or less flaccid one of pleasure and friendship.

My host was not visible at first, but I met a score of people whom I knew by reputation, and listened to clatter and chatter of the most approved metropolitan bohemian character. The Italian sorceress was there, her gorgeous chain earrings tinkling mellifluously as she nodded and gesticulated. De Shay at once whispered in my ear that she was X——'s very latest flame and an expensive one too. "You should see what he buys her!" he exclaimed in a whisper. "God!" Actresses and society women floated here and there in dreams of afternoon dresses. The automobiles outside were making a perfect uproar. The poets and writers fascinated me with their praises of the host's munificence and taste. At a glance it was plain to me that he had managed to gather about him the very element it would be most interesting to gather, supposing one desired to be idle, carefree and socially and intellectually gay. If America ever presented a smarter drawing-room I never saw it.

My friend de Shay, being the fidus Achates of the host, had the power to reveal the inner mysteries of this place to me, and on one or two occasions when there were not so many present and while the others were chattering in the various rooms—music-, dining-, ball-, library and so forth—I was being shown the kitchen, pantry, wine cellar, and also various secret doors and passages whereby mine host by pressing a flower on a wall or a spring behind a picture could cause a door to fly open or close which gave entrance to or from a room or passage in no way connected with the others save by another secret door and leading always to a private exit. I wondered at once at the character of the person who could need, desire or value this. A secret bedroom, for instance; a lounging-room! In one of these was a rather severe if handsome desk and a steel safe and two chairs—no more; a very bare room. I wondered at this silent and rather commercial sanctum in the center of this frou-frou of gayety, no trace of the sound of which seemed to penetrate here. What I also gained was a sense of an exotic, sybaritic and purely pagan mind, one which knew little of the conventions of the world and cared less.

On my first visit, as I was leaving, I was introduced to the host just within his picture gallery, hung with many fine examples of the Dutch and Spanish schools. I found him to be as described: picturesque and handsome, even though somewhat plump, phlegmatic and lethargic—yet active enough. He was above the average in height, well built, florid, with a huge, round handsome head, curly black hair, keen black eyes, heavy overhanging eyebrows, full red lips, a marked chin ornamented by a goatee. In any costume ball he would have made an excellent Bacchus or Pan. He appeared to have the free, easy and gracious manner of those who have known much of life and have achieved, in part at least, their desires. He smiled, wished to know if I had met all the guests, hoped that the sideboard had not escaped me, that I had enjoyed the singing. Would I come some evening when there was no crowd—or, better yet, dine with him and my friend de Shay, whose personality appeared to be about as agreeable to him as his own. He was sorry he could not give me more attention now.

Interestingly enough, and from the first, I was impressed with this man; not because of his wealth (I knew richer men) but because of a something about him which suggested dreams, romance, a kind of sense or love of splendor and grandeur which one does not often encounter among the really wealthy. Those cracked shoes were in my mind, I suppose. He seemed to live among great things, but in no niggardly, parsimonious or care-taking way. Here was ease, largess, a kind of lavishness which was not ostentation but which seemed rather to say, "What are the minute expenses of living and pleasuring as contrasted with the profits of skill in the world outside?" He suggested the huge and Aladdin-like adventures with which so many of the great financiers of the day, the true tigers of Wall Street, were connected.

It was not long thereafter that I was once more invited, this time to a much more lavish affair and something much more sybaritic in its tone, although I was really not conscious of what it was to be like when I went there. It began at twelve midnight, and to this day it glitters in my mind as among the few really barbaric and exotic things that I have ever witnessed. Not that the trappings or hangings or setting were so outré or amazing as that the atmosphere of the thing itself was relaxed, bubbling, pagan. There were so many daring and seeking people there. The thing sang and was talked of for months after—in whispers! The gayety! The abandon! The sheer intoxication, mental and physical! I never saw more daring costumes, so many really beautiful women (glitteringly so) in one place at one time, wonderful specimens of exotic and in the main fleshy or sensuous femininity. There was, among other things, as I recall, a large nickeled ice-tray on wheels packed with unopened bottles of champagne, and you had but to lift a hand or wink an eye to have another opened for you alone, ever over and over. And the tray was always full. One wall of the dining-room farther on was laden with delicate novelties in the way of food. A string quartette played for the dancers in the music-room. There were a dozen corners in different rooms screened with banks of flowers and concealing divans. The dancing and singing were superb, individual, often abandoned in character, as was the conversation. As the morning wore on (for it did not begin until after midnight) the moods of all were either so mellowed or inflamed as to make intentions, hopes, dreams, the most secret and sybaritic, the order of expression. One was permitted to see human nature stripped of much of its repression and daylight reserve or cant. At about four in the morning came the engaged dancers, quite the pièce de résistance—with wreaths about heads, waists and arms for clothing and well, really nothing more beyond their beautiful figures—scattering rose leaves or favors. These dancers the company itself finally joined, single file at first, pellmell afterwards—artists, writers, poets—dancing from room to room in crude Bacchic imitation of their leaders—the women too—until all were singing, parading, swaying and dancing in and out of the dozen rooms. And finally, liquor and food affecting them, I suppose, many fell flat, unable to do anything thereafter but lie upon divans or in corners until friends assisted them elsewhere—to taxis finally. But mine host, as I recall him, was always present, serene, sober, smiling, unaffected, bland and gracious and untiring in his attention. He was there to keep order where otherwise there would have been none.

I mention this merely to indicate the character of a long series of such events which covered the years 19— to 19—. During that time, for the reason that I have first given (his curious pleasure in my company), I was part and parcel of a dozen such more or less vivid affairs and pleasurings, which stamped on my mind not only X—— but life itself, the possibilities and resources of luxury where taste and appetite are involved, the dreams of grandeur and happiness which float in some men's minds and which work out to a wild fruition—dreams so outré and so splendid that only the tyrant of an obedient empire, with all the resources of an enslaved and obedient people, could indulge with safety. Thus once, I remember, that a dozen of us—writers and artists—being assembled in his studio in New York one Friday afternoon for the mere purpose of idling and drinking, he seeming to have nothing better to do for the time being, he suddenly suggested, and as though it had but now occurred to him, that we all adjourn to his country house on Long Island, which was not yet quite finished (or, rather, furnished), but which was in a sufficient state of completion to permit of appropriate entertainment providing the necessaries were carried out there with us.

As I came to think of this afterward, I decided that after all it was not perhaps so unpremeditated as it seemed and that unconsciously we served a very useful purpose. There was work to do, suggestions to be obtained, an overseer, decorator and landscape gardener with whom consultations were absolutely necessary; and nothing that X—— ever did was without its element of calculation. Why not make a gala affair of a rather dreary November task—

Hence—

At any rate the majority of us forthwith agreed, since plainly it meant an outing of the most lavish and pleasing nature. At once four automobiles were pressed into service, three from his own garage and one specially engaged elsewhere. There was some telephoning *in re* culinary supplies to a chef in charge of the famous restaurant below who was *en rapport* with our host, and soon some baskets of food were produced and subsequently the four cars made their appearance at the entryway below. At dusk of a gray, cold, smoky day we were all bundled into these—poets, playwrights, novelists, editors (he professed a great contempt for actors), and forthwith we were off, to do forty-five miles between five-thirty and seven p.m.

I often think of that ride, the atmosphere of it, and what it told of our host's point of view. He was always so grave, serene, watchful yet pleasant and decidedly agreeable, gay even, without seeming so to be. There was something so amazingly warm and exotic about him and his, and yet at the same time something so cold and calculated, as if after all he were saying to himself, "I am the master of all this, am stage-managing it for my own pleasure." I felt that he looked upon us all not so much as intimates or friends as rather fine birds or specimens of one kind and another, well qualified to help him with art and social ideas if nothing more—hence his interest in us. Also, in his estimation no doubt, we reflected some slight color or light into his life, which he craved. We had done things too. Nevertheless, in his own estimation, he was the master, the Can Grande. He could at will, "take us up or leave us out," or so he thought. We were mere toys, fine feathers, cap-and-bell artists. It was nice to, "take us around," have us with him. Smothered in a great richly braided fur coat and fur cap, he looked as much the Grand Duke as one might wish.

But I liked him, truly. And what a delicious evening and holiday, all told, he made of it for us. By leaving a trail of frightened horses, men and women, and tearing through the gloom as though streets were his private race-track— I myself as much frightened as any at the roaring speed of the cars and the possibilities of the road—we arrived at seven, and by eight were seated to a course dinner of the most gratifying character. There was no heat in the house as yet, but from somewhere great logs had been obtained and now blazed in the large fireplaces. There was no electricity as yet—a private plant was being installed—but candles and lamps blazed in lovely groups, casting a soft glow over the great rooms. One room lacked a door, but an immense rug took its place. There were rugs, hangings and paintings in profusion, many of them as yet unhung. Some of the most interesting importations of furniture and statuary were still in the cases in which they had arrived, with marks of ships and the names of foreign cities upon the cases. Scattered about the great living-room, dining-room, music-room and library were enough rugs, divans and chairs as well as musical instruments—a piano among others—to give the place an air of completeness and luxury. The walls and ceilings had already been decorated—in a most florid manner, I must say. Outside were great balconies and verandahs commanding, as the following morning proved, a very splendid view of a very bleak sea. The sand dunes! The distant floor of the sea! The ships! Upstairs were nine suites of one-and two-rooms and bath. The basement was an intricate world of kitchen, pantry, engine-room, furnace, wine cellars and what not. Outside was a tawny waste of sand held together in places in the form of hummocks and even concealing hills by sand-binding grasses.

That night, because it was windy and dull and bleak, we stayed inside, I for one going outside only long enough to discover that there were great wide verandahs of concrete about the house, fit for great entertainments in themselves, and near at hand, hummocks of sand. Inside all was warm and flaring enough. The wine cellar seemed to contain all that one might reasonably desire. Our host once out here was most gay in his mood. He was most pleasantly interested in the progress of his new home, although not intensely so. He seemed to have lived a great deal and to be making the best of everything as though it were something to go through with. With much talking on the part of us all, the evening passed swiftly enough. Some of the men could play and sing. One poet recited enchanting bits of verse. For our inspection certain pieces of furniture and statuary were unpacked and displayed—a bronze faun some three feet in height, for one thing. All the time I was sensible of being in contact with some one who was really in touch with life in a very large way, financially and otherwise. His mind seemed to be busy with all sorts of things. There were two Syrians in Paris, he said, who owned a large collection of rugs suitable for an exhibition. He had an agent who was trying to secure the best of them for his new home. De Shay had recently introduced him to a certain Italian count who had a great house in Italy but could not afford its upkeep. He was going to take over a portion of its furnishings, after due verification, of course. Did I know the paintings of Monticelli and Mancini? He had just secured excellent examples of both. Some time when his new home was further along I must come out. Then the pictures would be hung, the statuary and furniture in place. He would get up a week-end party for a select group.

The talk drifted to music and the stage. At once I saw that because of his taste, wealth and skill, women formed a large and yet rather toy-like portion of his life, holding about as much relation to his inner life as do the concubines of an Asiatic sultan. Madame of the earrings, as I learned from

De Shay, was a source of great expense to him, but at that she was elusive, not easily to be come at. The stage and Broadway were full of many beauties in various walks of life, many of whom he knew or to whom he could obtain access. Did I know thus, and so—such-and-such, and one?

"I'll tell you," he said after a time and when the wine glasses had been refilled a number of times, "we must give a party out here some time, something extraordinary, a real one. De Shay and Bielow" (naming another artist) "and myself must think it out. I know three different dancers"—and he began to enumerate their qualities. I saw plainly that even though women played a minor part in his life, they were the fringe and embroidery to his success and power. At one a.m. we went to our rooms, having touched upon most of the themes dear to metropolitan lovers of life and art.

The next morning was wonderful—glittering, if windy. The sea sparkled beyond the waste of sand. I noted anew the richness of the furnishings, the greatness of the house. Set down in so much sand and facing the great sea, it was wonderful. There was no order for breakfast; we came down as we chose. A samovar and a coffee urn were alight on the table. Rolls, chops, anything, were brought on order. Possibly because I was one of the first about, my host singled me out—he was up and dressed when I came down—and we strolled over the estate to see what we should see.

Curiously, although I had seen many country homes of pretension and even luxury, I never saw one that appealed to me more on the ground of promise and, after a fashion, of partial fulfillment. It was so unpretentiously pretentious, so really grand in a limited and yet poetic way. Exteriorly its placement, on a rise of ground commanding that vast sweep of sea and sand, its verandahs, so very wide—great smooth floors of red concrete—bordered with stone boxes for flowers and handsomely designed stone benches, its long walks and drives but newly begun, its stretch of beach, say a half mile away and possibly a mile and a half long, to be left, as he remarked, "au naturel," driftwood, stones and all, struck me most favorably. Only one long pier for visiting yachts was to be built, and a certain stretch of beach, not over three hundred feet, cleared for bath houses and a smooth beach. On one spot of land, a high hummock reaching out into the sea, had already been erected a small vantage tower, open at the bottom for shade and rest, benches turning in a circle upon a concrete floor, above it, a top looking more like a small bleak lighthouse than anything else. In this upper portion was a room reached by small spiral concrete stairs!

I could not help noting the reserve and *savoir faire* with which my host took all this. He was so healthy, assured, interested and, I am glad to say, not exactly self-satisfied; at least he did not impress me in that way—a most irritating condition. Plainly he was building a very splendid thing. His life was nearing its apex. He must not only have had millions, but great taste to have undertaken, let alone accomplished, as much as was already visible here. Pointing to a bleak waste of sand between the house and the sea—and it looked like a huge red and yellow bird perched upon a waste of sand—he observed, "When you come again in the spring, that will contain a garden of 40,000 roses. The wind is nearly always off the sea here. I want the perfume to blow over the verandahs. I can rotate the roses so that a big percentage of them will always be in bloom."

We visited the stables, the garage, an artesian well newly driven, a drive that was to skirt the sea, a sunken garden some distance from the house and away from the sea.

Next spring I came once more—several times, in fact. The rose garden was then in bloom, the drives finished, the pictures hung. Although this was not a world in which society as yet deigned to move, it was entirely conceivable that at a later period it might, and betimes it was crowded with people smart enough and more agreeable in the main than the hardy, strident members of the so-called really inner circles. There were artists, writers, playwrights, singers, actresses, and some nondescript figures of the ultra-social world— young men principally who seemed to come here in connection with beautiful young women, models and other girls whose beauty was their only recommendation to consideration.

The scene was not without brilliance. A butler and numerous flunkeys fluttered to and fro. Guests were received at the door by a footman. A housekeeper and various severe-looking maids governed in the matter of cleaning. One could play golf, tennis, bridge, motor, fish, swim, drink in a free and even disconcerting manner or read quietly in one angle or another of the grounds. There were affairs, much flirting and giggling, suspicious wanderings to and fro at night—no questions asked as to who came or whether one was married, so long as a reasonable amount of decorum was maintained. It was the same on other occasions, only the house and grounds were full to overflowing with guests and passing friends, whose machines barked in the drives. I saw as many gay and fascinating costumes and heard as much clever and at times informative talk here as anywhere I have been.

During this fall and winter I was engaged in work which kept me very much to myself. During the period I read much of X——, banks he was combining, new ventures he was undertaking. Yet all at once one winter's day, and out of a clear sky, the papers were full of an enormous financial crash of which he was the center. According to the newspapers, the first and foremost of a chain of banks of which he was the head, to say nothing of a bonding and realty company and some street-railway project on Long Island, were all involved in the crash. Curiously, although no derogatory mention had previously been made of him, the articles and editorials were now most vituperative. Their venom was especially noticeable. He was a get-rich-quick villain of the vilest stripe; he had been juggling a bank, a trust company, an insurance company and a land and street-railway speculative scheme as one would glass balls. The money wherewith he gambled was not his. He had robbed the poor, deceived them. Yet among all this and in the huge articles which appeared the very first day, I noted one paragraph which stuck in my mind, for I was naturally interested in all this and in him. It read:

> "Wall Street heard yesterday that Superintendent H——got his first information concerning the state in which X——'s affairs were from quarters where resentment may have been cherished because of his activity in the Long Island Traction field. This is one of the Street's 'clover patches' and the success which the newcomer seemed to be meeting did not provoke great pleasure."

Another item read:

> "A hitch in a deal that was to have transferred the South Shore to the New York and Queens County System, owned by the Long Island Railroad, at a profit of almost $2,000,000 to X——, was the cause of all the trouble. Very active displeasure on the part of certain powers in Wall Street blocked, it is said, the closing of the deal for the railroad. They did not want him in this field, and were powerful enough to prevent it. At the same time pressure from other directions was brought to bear on him. The clearing-house refused to clear for his banks. X—— was in need of cash, but still insisting on a high rate of remuneration for the road which he had developed to an important point. Their sinister influences entered and blocked the transfer until it was no longer possible for him to hold out."

Along with these two items was a vast mass of data, really pages, showing how, when, where he had done thus and so, "juggled accounts" between one bank and another, all of which he controlled however, and most of which he owned, drew out large sums and put in their place mortgages on, or securities in, new companies which he was organizing—tricks which were the ordinary routine of Wall Street and hence rather ridiculous as the sub-stone of so vast a hue and cry.

I was puzzled and, more than that, moved by the drama of the man's sudden end, for I understood a little of finance and its ways, also of what place and power had plainly come to mean to him. It must be dreadful. Yet how could it be, I asked myself, if he really owned fifty-one per cent or more in so many companies that he could be such a dark villain? After all, ownership is ownership, and control, control. On the face of the reports themselves his schemes did not look so black. I read everything in connection with him with care.

As the days passed various other things happened. For one thing, he tried to commit suicide by jumping out of a window of his studio in New York; for another, he tried to take poison. Now of a sudden a bachelor sister, of whom I had never heard in all the time I had known him, put in an appearance as his nearest of kin—a woman whose name was not his own but a variation of it, an "-ovitch" having suddenly been tacked onto it. She took him to a sanitarium, from which he was eventually turned out as a criminal, then to a hospital, until finally he surrendered himself to the police. The names of great lawyers and other bankers began to enter the case. Alienists of repute, those fine chameleons of the legal world, were employed who swore first that he was insane, then that he was not. His sister, who was a physician and scientist of repute, asked the transfer of all his property to her on the ground that he was incompetent and that she was his next of kin. To this she swore, giving as her reasons for believing him insane that he had "illusions of grandeur" and that he believed himself "persecuted by eminent financiers," things which smacked more of sanity than anything else to me. At the same time he and she, as time rather indicated, had arranged this in part in the hope of saving something out of the great wreck. There were other curious features: Certain eminent men in politics and finance who from revelations made by the books of the various banks were in close financial if not personal relations with X—— denied this completely. Curiously, the great cry on the part of these was that he was insane, must be, and that he was all alone in his schemes. His life on Broadway, on Long Island, in his studio in New York, were ransacked for details. Enough could not be made of his gay, shameful, spendthrift life. No one else, of course, had ever been either gay or shameful before—especially not the eminent and hounding financiers.

Then from somewhere appeared a new element. In a staggeringly low tenement region in Brooklyn was discovered somehow or other a very old man and woman, most unsatisfactory as relatives of such imposing people, who insisted that they were his parents, that years before because he and his sister were exceedingly restless and ambitious, they had left them and had only returned occasionally to borrow money, finally ceasing to come at all. In proof of this, letters, witnesses, old photos, were produced. It really did appear as if he and his sister, although they had long vigorously denied it, really were the son and daughter of the two who had been petty bakers in Brooklyn, laying up a little competence of their own. I never knew who "dug" them up, but the reason why was plain enough. The sister was laying claim to the property as the next of kin. If this could be offset, even though X—

— were insane, the property would at once be thrown into the hands of the various creditors and sold under a forced sale, of course—in other words, for a song—for their benefit. Naturally it was of interest to those who wished to have his affairs wound up to have the old people produced. But the great financier had been spreading the report all along that he was from Russia, that his parents, or pseudo-parents, were still there, but that really he was the illegitimate son of the Czar of Russia, boarded out originally with a poor family. Now, however, the old people were brought from Brooklyn and compelled to confront him. It was never really proved that he and his sister had neglected them utterly or had done anything to seriously injure them, but rather that as they had grown in place and station they had become more or less estranged and so ignored them, having changed their names and soared in a world little dreamed of by their parents. Also a perjury charge was made against the sister which effectually prevented her from controlling his estate, a lease long enough to give the financiers time for their work. Naturally there was a great hue and cry over her, the scandal, the shame, that they should thus publicly refuse to recognize their parents as they did or had when confronted by them. Horrible! There were most heavily illustrated and tearful Sunday articles, all blazoned forth with pictures of his house and studio, his banks, cars, yacht, groups of guests, while the motives of those who produced the parents were overlooked. The pictures of the parents confronting X—— and his sister portrayed very old and feeble people, and were rather moving. They insisted that they were his parents and wept brokenly in their hands. But why? And he denying it! His sister, who resented all this bitterly and who stood by him valiantly, repudiated, for his sake of course, his and her so-called parents and friends.

I never saw such a running to cover of "friends" in all my life. Of all those I had seen about his place and in his company, scores on scores of people reasonably well known in the arts, the stage, the worlds of finance and music, all eating his dinners, riding in his cars, drinking his wines, there was scarcely any one now who knew him anything more than "casually" or "slightly"— oh, so slightly! When rumors as to the midnight suppers, the Bacchic dancing, the automobile parties to his great country place and the spirited frolics which occurred there began to get abroad, there was no one whom I knew who had ever been there or knew anything about him or them. For instance, of all the people who had been close or closest and might therefore have been expected to be friendly and deeply concerned was de Shay, his fidus Achates and literally his pensioner—yet de Shay was almost the loudest in his denunciation or at least deprecation of X——, his habits and methods! Although it was he who had told me of Mme.—— and her relation to X—— —, who urged me to come here, there and the other place, especially where X—— was the host, always assuring me that it would be so wonderful and that X—— was really such a great man, so generous, so worth-while, he was now really the loudest or at least the most stand-offish in his comments, pretending never to have been very close to X——, and lifting his eyebrows in astonishment as though he had not even guessed what he had actually engineered. His "Did-you-hears," "Did-you-knows" and "Wouldn't-have-dreamed" would have done credit to a tea-party. He was so shocked, especially at X——'s robbing poor children and orphans, although in so far as my reading of the papers went I could find nothing that went to prove that he had any intention of robbing anybody—that is, directly. In the usual Wall Street high finance style he was robbing Peter to pay Paul, that is, he was using the monies of one corporation which he controlled to bolster up any of the others which he controlled, and was "washing one hand with the other," a proceeding so common in finance that to really radically and truly oppose it, or do away with it, would mean to bring down the whole fabric of finance in one grand crash.

Be that as it may. In swift succession there now followed the so-called "legal" seizure and confiscation of all his properties. In the first place, by alienists representing the District Attorney and the State banking department, he was declared sane and placed on trial for embezzlement. Secondly, his sister's plea that his property be put into her hands as trustee or administrator was thrown out of court and she herself arrested and confined for perjury on the ground that she had perjured herself in swearing that she was his next of kin when in reality his real parents, or so they swore, were alive and in America. Next, his banks, trust companies and various concerns, including his great country estate, were swiftly thrown into the hands of receivers (what an appropriate name!) and wound up "for the benefit of creditors." All the while X——was in prison, protesting that he was really not guilty, that he was solvent, or had been until he was attacked by the State bank examiner or the department back of him, and that he was the victim of a cold-blooded conspiracy which was using the State banking department and other means to drive him out of financial life, and that solely because of his desire to grow and because by chance he had been impinging upon one of the choicest and most closely guarded fields of the ultra-rich of Wall Street—the street railway area in New York and Brooklyn.

One day, so he publicly swore to the grand jury, by which he was being examined, as he was sitting in his great offices, in one of the great sky-scrapers of New York, which occupied an entire floor and commanded vast panoramas in every direction (another evidence of the man's insane "delusion of grandeur," I presume), he was called to answer the telephone. One Mr. Y——, so his assistant said, one of the eminent financiers of Wall Street and America, was on the wire. Without any preliminary and merely asking was this Mr. X——on the wire, the latter proceeded, "This is Mr. Y——. Listen closely to what I am going to say. I want you to get out of the street railway business in New York or something is going to happen to you. I am giving you a reasonable warning. Take it." Then the phone clicked most savagely and ominously and superiorly at the other end.

"I knew at the time," went on X——, addressing the grand jury, "that I was really listening to the man who was most powerful in such affairs in New York and elsewhere and that he meant what he said. At the same time I was in no position to get out without closing up the one deal which stood to net me two million dollars clear if I closed it. At the same time I wanted to enter this field and didn't see why I shouldn't. If I didn't it spelled not ruin by any means but a considerable loss, a very great loss, to me, in more ways than one. Oddly enough, just at this time I was being pressed by those with whom I was associated to wind up this particular venture and turn my attention to other things. I have often wondered, in the light of their subsequent actions, why they should have become so pressing just at this time. At the same time, perhaps I was a little vain and self-sufficient. I had once got the better of some agents of another great financier in a Western Power deal, and I felt that I could put this thing through too. Hence I refused to heed the warning. However, I found that all those who were previously interested to buy or at least develop the property were now suddenly grown cold, and a little later when, having entered on several other matters, I needed considerable cash, the State banking department descended on me and, crying fraud and insolvency, closed all my banks.

"You know how it is when they do this to you. Cry 'Fire!' and you can nearly wreck a perfectly good theater building. Depositors withdraw, securities tumble, investigation and legal expenses begin, your financial associates get frightened or ashamed and desert you. Nothing is so squeamish or so retiring and nervous as money. Time will show that I was not insolvent at the time. The books will show a few technically illegal things, but so would the books or the affairs of any great bank, especially at this time, if quickly examined. I was doing no more than all were doing, but they wanted to get me out—and they did."

Regardless of proceedings of various kinds—legal, technical and the like—X—— was finally sent to the penitentiary, and spent some time there. At the same time his confession finally wrecked about nine other eminent men, financiers all. A dispassionate examination of all the evidence eight years later caused me to conclude without hesitation that the man had been a victim of a cold-blooded conspiracy, the object of which was to oust him from opportunities and to forestall him in methods which would certainly have led to enormous wealth. He was apparently in a position and with the brains to do many of the things which the ablest and coldest financiers of his day had been and were doing, and they did not want to be bothered with, would not brook, in short, his approaching rivalry. Like the various usurpers of regal powers in ancient days, they thought it best to kill a possible claimant to the throne in his infancy.

But that youth of his! The long and devious path by which he had come! Among the papers relating to the case and to a time when he could not have been more than eighteen, and when he was beginning his career as a book agent, was a letter written to his mother (August, 1892), which read:

> "MY DEAR PARENTS: Please answer me at once if I can have anything of you, or something of you or nothing. Remember this is the first and the last time in my life that I beg of you anything. You have given to the other child not $15 but hundreds, and now when I, the very youngest, ask of you, my parents, $15, are you going to be so hard-hearted as to refuse me? Without these $15 it is left to me to be without income for two or three weeks.
>
> "For God's sake, remember what I ask of you, and send me at once so that I should cease thinking of it. Leon, as I have told you, will give me $10, $15 he has already paid for the contract, and your $15 will make $25. Out of this I need $10 for a ticket and $15 for two or three weeks' board and lodging.
>
> "Please answer at once. Don't wait for a minute, and send me the money or write me one word 'not.' Remember this only that if you refuse me I will have nothing in common with you.
>
> "Your son,"———"

There was another bit of testimony on the part of one Henry Dom, a baker, who for some strange reason came forward to identify him as some one he had known years before in Williamsburgh, which read:

> "I easily recognize them" (X——— and his sister) "from their pictures in the newspapers. I worked for X———'s father, who was a baker in Williamsburgh, and frequently addressed letters that were written by X——— Senior and his wife to Dr. Louise X——— who was then studying medicine in Philadelphia. X——— was then a boy going to school, but working in his father's bakery mornings and evenings. He did not want to do that, moaned a great deal, and his parents humored him in his attitude. He was very vain, liked to appear intellectual. They kept saying to their friends that he should have a fine future. Five years later, after I had left

them once, I met the mother and she told me that X——
was studying banking and getting along fine."

Some seven years after the failure and trial by which he had so summarily
been disposed of and after he had been released from prison, I was standing
at a certain unimportant street corner in New York waiting for a car when I
saw him. He was passing in the opposite direction, not very briskly, and, as I
saw, plainly meditatively. He was not so well dressed. The clothes he wore
while good were somehow different, lacking in that exquisite something
which had characterized him years before. His hat—well, it was a hat, not a
Romanoff shako nor a handsome panama such as he had affected in the old
days. He looked tired, a little worn and dusty, I thought.

My first impulse was of course to hail him, my second not, since he had not
seen me. It might have been embarrassing, and at any rate he might not have
even remembered me. But as he walked I thought of the great house by the
sea, the studio, the cars, the 40,000 roses, the crowds at his summer place,
the receptions in town and out, Madame of the earrings (afterward married
to a French nobleman), and then of the letter to his mother as a boy, the
broken shoes in the winter time, his denial of his parents, the telephone
message from the financial tiger. "Vanity, vanity," saith the preacher. The
shores of our social seas are strewn with pathetic wrecks, the whitening bone
of half-sand-buried ships.

At the next corner he paused, a little uncertain apparently as to which way to
go, then turned to the left and was lost. I have never seen nor heard of him
since.

The Mighty Rourke

When I first met him he was laying the foundation for a small dynamo in the engine-room of the repair shop at Spike, and he was most unusually loud in his protestations and demands. He had with him a dozen Italians, all short, swarthy fellows of from twenty-five to fifty years of age, who were busy bringing material from a car that had been pushed in on the side-track next to the building. This was loaded with crushed stone, cement, old boards, wheelbarrows, tools, and the like, all of which were to be used in the labor that he was about to undertake. He himself was standing in the doorway of the shop where the work was to be conducted, coat off, sleeves rolled up, and shouting with true Irish insistence, "Come, Matt! Come, Jimmie! Get the shovels, now! Get the picks! Bring some sand here! Bring some stone! Where's the cement, now? Where's the cement? Jasus Christ! I must have some cement! What arre ye all doin'? What do ye think ye're up here fer? Hurry, now, hurry! Bring the cement!" and then, having concluded this amazing fanfare, calmly turning to gaze about as if he were the only one in the world who had the right to stand still.

More or less oppressed with life myself at the time, I was against all bosses, and particularly against so seemingly a vicious one as this. "What a slave driver!" I thought. "What a brute!" And yet I remember thinking that he was not exactly unpleasant to look at, either—quite the contrary. He was medium in height, thick of body and neck, with short gray hair and mustache, and bright, clear, twinkling Irish gray eyes, and he carried himself with an air of unquestionable authority. It was much as if he had said, "I am the boss here"; and, indeed, he was. Is it this that sends the Irish to rule as captains of hundreds the world over?

The job he was bossing was not very intricate or important, but it was interesting. It consisted of digging a trench ten by twelve feet, and shaping it up with boards into a "form," after which concrete was to be mixed and poured in, and some iron rods set to fasten the engine to—an engine bed, no less. It was not so urgent but that it might have been conducted with far less excitement, but what are you to do when you are naturally excitable, love to make a great noise, and feel that things are going forward whether they are or not? Plainly this particular individual loved noise and a great stir. So eager was he to have done with it, no matter what it was or where, that he was constantly trotting to and fro, shouting, "Come, Matt! Come, Jimmie! Hurry, now, bring the shovels! Bring the picks!" and occasionally bursting forth with a perfect avalanche of orders. "Up with it! Down with it! Front with it! Back with it! In with it! Out with it!" all coupled with his favorite expletive, "Jasus Christ," which was as innocent of evil, I subsequently came to know, as a prayer. In short, he was simply wild Irish, and that was all there was to him—a delightful specimen, like Namgay Doola.

But, as I say, at the time he seemed positively appalling to me, a virulent specimen, and I thought, "The Irish brute! To think of human beings having to work for a brute like that! To think of his driving men like that!" However, I soon began to discover that he was not so bad as he seemed, and then I began to like him.

The thing that brought about this swift change of feeling in me was the attitude of his men toward him. Although he was so insistent with his commands, they did not seem to mind nor to strain themselves working. They were not killing themselves, by any means. He would stand over them, crying, "Up with it! Up with it! Up with it! Up with it!" or "Down with it! Down with it! Down with it!" until you would have imagined their nerves would be worn to a frazzle. As it was, however, they did not seem to care any more than you would for the ticking of a clock; rather, they appeared to take it as a matter of course, something that had to be, and that one was prepared for. Their steps were in the main as leisurely as those of idlers on Fifth Avenue or Broadway. They carried boards or stone as one would objects of great value. One could not help smiling at the incongruity of it; it was farcical. Finally gathering the full import of it all, I ventured to laugh, and he turned on me with a sharp and yet not unkindly retort.

"Ha! ha! ha!" he mocked. "If ye had to work as hard as these min, ye wouldn't laugh."

I wanted to say, "Hard work, indeed!" but instead I replied, "Is that so? Well, I don't see that they're killing themselves, or you either. You're not as fierce as you sound."

Then I explained that I was not laughing at them but at him, and he took it all in good part. Since I was only a nominal laborer here, not a real one—permitted to work for my health, for twelve cents an hour—we fell to conversing upon railroad matters, and in this way our period of friendship began.

As I learned that morning, Rourke was the foreman-mason for minor tasks for all that part of the railroad that lay between New York and fifty miles out, on three divisions. He had a dozen or so men under him and was in possession of one car, which was shunted back and forth between the places in which he happened to be working. He was a builder of concrete platforms, culverts, coal-bins, sidewalks, bridge and building piers, and, in fact, anything that could be made out of crushed stone and cement, or bricks and stone, and he was sent here and there, as necessity required. As he explained to me at the time, he sometimes rose as early as four a.m. in order to get to his place of labor by seven. The great railroad company for which he toiled was no gentle master, and did not look upon his ease, or that of his men, as important. At the same time, as he himself confessed, he did not mind hard work—liked it, in short. He had been working now for the company for all of twenty-two years, "rain or shine." Darkness or storm made no difference to him. "Shewer, I have to be there," he observed once with his quizzical, elusive Irish grin. "They're not payin' me wages fer lyin' in bed. If ye was to get up that way yerself every day fer a year, me b'y," he added, eyeing my spare and none too well articulated frame, "it'd make a man av ye."

"Yes?" I said tolerantly. "And how much do you get, Rourke?"

"Two an' a half a day."

"You don't say!" I replied, pretending admiration.

The munificence of the corporation that paid him two and a half dollars a day for ten hours' work, as well as for superintending and constructing things of such importance, struck me forcibly. Perhaps, as we say in America, he "had a right" to be happy, only I could not see it. At the same time, I could not help thinking that he was better situated than myself at the time. I had been ill, and was now earning only twelve cents an hour for ten hours' work, and the sight of the foreman for whom I was working was a torture to my soul. He was such a loud-mouthed, blustering, red-headed ignoramus, and I wanted to get out from under him. At the same time, I was not without sufficient influence so to do, providing I could find a foreman who could make use of me. The great thing was to do this, and the more I eyed this particular specimen of foreman the better I liked him. He was genial, really kindly, amazingly simple and sincere. I decided to appeal to him to take me on his staff.

"How would you like to take me, Mr. Rourke, and let me work for you?" I asked hopefully, after explaining to him why I was here.

"Shewer," he replied. "Ye'd do fine."

"Would I have to work with the Italians?" I asked, wondering how I would make out with a pick and shovel. My frame was so spare at the time that the question must have amused him, considering the type of physique required for day labor.

"There'll be plenty av work fer ye to do without ever yer layin' a hand to a pick er shovel," he replied comfortingly. "Shewer, that's no work fer white min. Let the nagurs do it. Look at their backs an' arrms, an' then look at yers."

I was ready to blush for shame. These poor Italians whom I was so ready to contemn were immeasurably my physical superiors.

"But why do you call them negroes, Rourke?" I asked after a time. "They're not black."

"Well, bedad, they're not white, that's waan thing shewer," he added. "Aany man can tell that be lookin' at thim."

I had to smile. It was so dogmatic and unreasoning.

"Very well, then, they're black," I said, and we left the matter.

Not long after I put in a plea to be transferred to him, at his request, and it was granted. The day that I joined his flock, or gang, as he called it, he was at Williamsbridge, a little station north on the Harlem, building a concrete coal-bin. It was a pretty place, surrounded by trees and a grass-plot, a vast improvement upon a dark indoor shop, and seemed to me a veritable haven of rest. Ah, the smiling morning sun, the green leaves, the gentle fresh winds of heaven!

Rourke was down in an earthen excavation under the depot platform when I arrived, measuring and calculating with his plumb-bob and level, and when I looked in on him hopefully he looked up and smiled.

"So here ye arre at last," he said with a grin.

"Yes," I laughed.

"Well, ye're jist in time; I waant ye to go down to the ahffice."

"Certainly," I replied, but before I could say more he climbed out of his hole, his white jeans odorous of the new-turned earth, and fished in the pocket of an old gray coat which lay beside him for a soiled and crumpled letter, which he finally unfolded with his thick, clumsy fingers. Then he held it up and looked at it defiantly.

"I waant ye to go to Woodlawn," he continued, "an' look after some bolts that arre up there—there's a keg av thim—an' sign the bill fer thim, an' ship thim down to me. An' thin I waant ye to go down to the ahffice an' take thim this o.k." Here again he fished around and produced another crumpled slip, this time of a yellow color (how well I came to know them!), which I soon learned was an o.k. blank, a form which had to be filled in and signed for everything received, if no more than a stick of wood or a nail or a bolt. The company demanded these of all foremen, in order to keep its records straight. Its accounting department was useless without them. At the same time, Rourke kept talking of the "nonsinse av it," and the "onraisonableness" of demanding o.k.s for everything. "Ye'd think some one was goin' to sthale thim from thim," he declared irritably and defiantly.

I saw at once that some infraction of the railroad rules had occurred and that he had been "called down," or "jacked up" about it, as the railroad men expressed it. He was in a high state of dudgeon, and as defiant and pugnacious as his royal Irish temper would allow. At the same time he was pleased to think that I or some one had arrived who would relieve him of this damnable "nonsinse," or so he hoped. He was not so inexperienced as not to imagine that I could help him with all this. In fact, as time proved, this was my sole reason for being here.

He flung a parting shot at his superior as I departed.

"Tell him that I'll sign fer thim when I get thim, an' not before," he declared.

I went on my way, knowing full well that no such message was for delivery, and that he did not intend that it should be. It was just the Irish of it. I went off to Woodlawn and secured the bolts, after which I went down to the "ahffice" and reported. There I found the chief clerk, a mere slip of a dancing master in a high collar and attractive office suit, who was also in a high state of dudgeon because Rourke, as he now explained, had failed to render an o.k. for this and other things, and did not seem to understand that he, the chief clerk, must have them to make up his reports. Sometimes o.k.s did not come in for a month or more, the goods lying around somewhere until Rourke could use them. He wanted to know what explanation Rourke had to offer, and when I suggested that the latter thought, apparently, that he could leave all consignments of goods in one station or another until such time as he needed them before he o.k.ed for them, he fairly foamed.

"Say," he almost shouted, at the same time shoving his hands distractedly through his hair, "what does he think I am? How does he think I'm going to make up my books? He'll leave them there until he needs them, will he? Well, he's a damned fool, and you go back and tell him I said so. He's been long enough on the road to know better. You go back and tell him I said that I want a signed form for everything consigned to him the moment he learns that it's waiting for him, and I want it right away, without fail, whether it's a single nut or a car of sand. I want it. He's got to come to time about this now, or something's going to drop. I'm not going to stand it any longer. How does he think I'm going to make up my books? I wish he'd let you attend to these matters while you're up there. It will save an awful lot of trouble in this office and it may save him his job. There's one thing sure: he's got to come to time from now on, or either he quits or I do."

These same o.k.s plus about twenty-five long-drawn-out reports or calculations, retroactive and prospective, covering every possible detail of his work from the acknowledgment of all material received up to and including the expenditure of even so much as one mill's worth of paper, were the bane of my good foreman's life. As I learned afterward, he had nearly his whole family, at least a boy and two girls, assisting him nights on this part of the work. In addition, while they were absolutely of no import in so far as the actual work of construction was concerned—and that was really all that interested Rourke—they were an essential part of the system which made it possible for him to do the work at all—a point which he did not seem to be able to get clear. At the same time, there was an unsatisfactory side to this office technicalia, and it was this: If a man could only sit down and reel off a graphic account of all that he was doing, accompanied by facts and figures, he was in excellent standing with his superiors, no matter what his mechanical defects might be; whereas, if his reports were not clear, or were insufficient, the efficiency of his work might well be overlooked. In a vague way, Rourke sensed this and resented it. He knew that his work was as good as could be done, and yet here were these constant reports and o.k.s to irritate and delay him. Apparently they aided actual construction no whit—but, of course, they did. Although he was a better foreman than most, still, because of his lack of skill in this matter of accounting, he was looked upon as more or less a failure, especially by the chief clerk. Naturally, I explained that I would do my best, and came away.

When I returned, however, I decided to be politic. I could not very well work with a pick and shovel, and this was about all that was left outside of that. I therefore explained as best I could the sad plight of the chief clerk, who stood in danger of losing his job unless these things came in promptly.

"You see how it is, Rourke, don't you?" I pleaded.

He seemed to see, but he was still angry.

"An o.k. blank! An o.k. blank!" he echoed contentiously, but in a somewhat more conciliatory spirit. "He wants an o.k. blank, does he? Well, I expect ye might as well give thim to him, thin. I think the man lives on thim things, the way he's aalways caallin' fer thim. Ye'd think I was a bookkeeper an' foreman at the same time; it's somethin' aaful. An o.k. blank! An o.k. blank!" and he sputtered to silence.

A little while later he humorously explained that he had "clane forgot thim, anyhow."

The ensuing month was a busy one for us. We had a platform to lay at Morrisania, a chimney to build at Tarrytown, a sidewalk to lay at White Plains, and a large cistern to dig and wall in at Tuckahoe. Besides these, there were platforms to build at Van Cortlandt and Mount Kisco, water-towers at Highbridge and Ardsley, a sidewalk and drain at Caryl, a culvert and an ash-pit at Bronx Park, and some forty concrete piers for a building at Melrose—all of which required any amount of running and figuring, to say nothing of the actual work of superintending and constructing, which Rourke alone could look after. It seemed ridiculous to me at the time that any one doing all this hard practical labor should not be provided with a clerk or an accountant to take at least some of this endless figuring off his hands. At the same time, if he had been the least bit clever, he could have provided himself with one permanently by turning one of his so-called laborers into a clerk—carrying a clerk as a laborer—but plainly it had never occurred to him. He depended on his family. The preliminary labor alone of ordering and seeing that the material was duly shipped and unloaded was one man's work; and yet Rourke was expected to do it all.

In spite of all this, however, he displayed himself a masterful worker. I have never seen a better. He preferred to superintend, of course, to get down into the pit or up on the wall, and measure and direct. At the same time, when necessary to expedite a difficult task, he would toil for hours at a stretch with his trowel and his line and his level and his plumb-bob, getting the work into shape, and you would never hear a personal complaint from him concerning the weariness of labor. On the contrary, he would whistle and sing until something went wrong, when suddenly you would hear the most terrific uproar of words: "Come out av that! Come out, now! Jasus Christ, man, have ye no sinse at aall? Put it down! Put it down! What arre ye doin'? What did I tell ye? Have ye no raison in ye, no sinse, ye h'athen nagur?"

"Great heavens!" I used to think, "what has happened now?"

You would have imagined the most terrible calamity; and yet, all told, it might be nothing of any great import—a little error of some kind, more threatening than real, and soon adjusted. It might last for a few moments, during which time the Italians would be seen hurrying excitedly to and fro; and then there would come a lull, and Rourke would be heard to raise his voice in tuneful melody, singing or humming or whistling some old-fashioned Irish "Come-all-ye."

But the thing in Rourke that would have pleased any one was his ready grasp for the actualities of life—his full-fledged knowledge that work is the thing, not argument, or reports, or plans, but the direct accomplishment of something tangible, the thing itself. Thus, while I was working with him, at least nothing that might concern the clerical end of the labor could disturb him, but, if the sky fell, and eight thousand chief clerks threatened to march upon him in a body demanding reports and o.k.s, he would imperturbably make you wait until the work was done. Once, when I interrupted him to question him concerning some of these same wretched, pestering aftermaths of labor, concerning which he alone could answer, he shut me off with: "The reports! The reports! What good arre the reports! Ye make me sick. What have the reports to do with the work? If it wasn't fer the work, where would the reports be?" And I heartily echoed "Where?"

Another thing was his charming attitude toward his men, kindly and sweet for all his storming, that innate sense of something intimate and fatherly. He had a way of saying kindly things in a joking manner which touched them. When he arrived in the morning, for instance, it was always in the cheeriest way that he began. "Come, now, b'ys, ye have a good day's work before ye today. Get the shovels, Jimmie. Bring the line, Matt!" and then he would go below himself, if below it was, and there would be joy and peace until some obstacle to progress interfered. I might say in passing that Matt and Jimmie, his faithful henchmen, were each between forty and fifty, if they were a day— poor, gnarled, dusty, storm-tossed Italians who had come from heaven knows where, had endured God knows what, and were now rounding out a work-a-day existence under the sheltering wing of this same Rourke, a great and protecting power to them.

This same Matt was a funny little Italian, soft of voice and gentle of manner, whom Rourke liked very much, but with whom he loved to quarrel. He would go down in any hole where the latter was working, and almost invariably shortly after you would hear the most amazing uproar issuing therefrom, shouts of: "Put it here, I say! Put it here! Down with it! Here! Here! Jasus Christ, have ye no sinse at aall?"—coupled, of course, with occasional guttural growls from Matt, who was by no means in awe of his master and who feared no personal blows. The latter had been with Rourke for so long that he was not in the least overawed by his yelling and could afford to take such liberties. Occasionally, not always, Rourke would come climbing out of the hole, his face and neck fairly scarlet with heat, raging and shouting, "I'll get shut av ye! I'll have no more thruck with ye, ye blitherin', crazy loon! What good arre ye? What work can ye do? Naathin'! Naathin'! I'll be shut av ye now, an' thin maybe I'll have a little p'ace." Then he would dance around and threaten and growl until something else would take his attention, when he would quiet down and be as peaceful as ever. Somehow, I always felt that in spite of all the difficulties involved, he enjoyed these rows—must fight, in short, to be happy. Sometimes he would go home without saying a word to Matt, a conclusion which at first I imagined portended the end of the latter, but soon I came to know better. For the next morning Matt would reappear as unconcernedly as though nothing had happened, and Rourke would appear not to notice or remember.

Once, anent all this, I said to him, "Rourke, how many times have you threatened to discharge Matt in the last three years?"

"Shewer," he replied, with his ingratiating grin, "a man don't mane aall he says aall the time."

The most humorous of all his collection of workingmen, however, was the aforementioned Jimmie, a dark, mild-eyed, soft-spoken Calabrian, who had the shrewdness of a Machiavelli and the pertness of a crow. He lived in the same neighborhood as Rourke, far out in one of those small towns on the

Harlem, sheltering so many Italians, for, like a hen with a brood of chicks, Rourke kept all his Italians gathered close about him. Jimmie, curiously, was the one who was always selected to run his family errands for him, a kind of valet to Rourke, as it were—selected for some merit I could never discover, certainly not one of speed. He was nevertheless constantly running here and there like an errand boy, his worn, dusty, baggy clothes making him look like a dilapidated bandit fresh from a sewer. On the job, however, no matter what it might be, Jimmie could never be induced to do real, hard work. He was always above it, or busy with something else. But as he was an expert cement-mixer and knew just how to load and unload the tool-car, two sinecures of sorts, nothing was ever said to him. If any one dared to reprove him, myself for instance (a mere interloper to Jimmie), he would reply: "Yeh! Yeh! I know-a my biz. I been now with Misha Rook fifteen year. I know-a my biz." If you made any complaint to Rourke, he would merely grin and say, "Ha! Jimmie's the sharp one," or perhaps, "I'll get ye yet, ye fox," but more than that nothing was ever done.

One day, however, Jimmie failed to comply with an extraordinary order of Rourke's, which, while it resulted in no real damage, produced a most laughable and yet characteristic scene. A strict rule of the company was that no opening of any kind into which a person might possibly step or fall should be left uncovered at any station during the approach, stay, or departure of any train scheduled to stop at that station. Rourke was well aware of this rule. He had a copy of it on file in his collection of circulars. In addition, he had especially delegated Jimmie to attend to this matter, a task which just suited the Italian as it gave him ample time to idle about and pretend to be watching. This it was which made the crime all the greater.

On this particular occasion Jimmie had failed to attend to this matter. We had been working on the platform at Williamsbridge, digging a pit for a coal-bin, when a train bearing the general foreman came along. The latter got off at the station especially to examine the work that had been done so far. When the train arrived there was the hole wide open with Rourke below shouting and gesticulating about something, and totally unconscious, of course, that his order had been neglected. The general foreman, who was, by the way, I believe, an admirer of Rourke, came forward, looked down, and said quietly: "This won't do, Rourke. You'll have to keep the work covered when a train is approaching. I've told you that before, you know."

Rourke looked up, so astonished and ashamed that he should have been put in such a position before his superior that he hardly knew what to say. I doubt if any one ever had a greater capacity for respecting his superiors, anyhow. Instead of trying to answer, he merely choked and began to shout for Jimmie, who came running, crying, as he always did, "What's da mat'? What's da mat'?"

"What's da mat'? What's da mat'?" mocked Rourke, fairly seething with a marvelous Irish fury. "What the devil do ye suppose is the mat'? What do ye mane be waalkin' away an' l'avin' the hole uncovered? Didn't I tell ye niver to l'ave a hole when a train's comin'? Didn't I tell ye to attind to that an' naathin' else? An' now what have ye been doin'? Be all the powers, what d'ye mane be l'avin' it? What else arre ye good fer? What d'ye mane be lettin' a thing like that happen, an' Mr. Wilson comin' along here, an' the hole open?"

He was as red as a beet, purple almost, perspiring, apoplectic. During all this tirade Mr. Wilson, a sad, dark, anæmic-looking person, troubled with acute indigestion, I fancy, stood by with an amused, kindly, and yet mock severe expression on his face. I am sure he did not wish to be severe.

Jimmie, dumbfounded, scarcely knew what to say. In the face of Rourke's rage and the foreman's presence, he did his best to remedy his error by covering the hole, at the same time stuttering something about going for a trowel.

"A trowel!" cried Rourke, glaring at him. "A trowel, ye h'athen ginny! What'd ye be doin' lookin' fer a trowel, an' a train comin' that close on ye it could 'a' knocked ye off the thrack? An' the hole open, an' Mr. Wilson right here! Is that what I told ye? Is that what I pay ye fer? Be all the saints! A trowel, is it? I'll trowel ye! I'll break yer h'athen Eyetalian skull, I will. Get thim boards on, an' don't let me ketch ye l'avin' such a place as that open again. I'll get shut av ye, ye blitherin' lunatic."

When it was all over and the train bearing the general foreman had gone, Rourke quieted down, but not without many fulgurous flashes that kept the poor Italian on tenterhooks.

About an hour later, however, another train arrived, and, by reason of some intervening necessity and the idle, wandering mood of the Italian, the hole was open again. Jimmie was away behind the depot somewhere, smoking perhaps, and Rourke was, as usual, down in the hole. This time misfortune trebled itself, however, by bringing, not the general foreman, but the supervisor himself, a grave, quiet man, of whom Rourke stood in the greatest awe. He was so solid, so profound, so severe. I don't believe I ever saw him smile. He walked up to the hole, and looking reproachfully down, said: "Is this the way you leave your excavations, Rourke, when a train is coming? Don't you know better than to do a thing like that?"

"Jimmie!" shouted Rourke, leaping to the surface of the earth with a bound, "Jimmie! Now, be Jasus, where is that bla'guard Eyetalian? Didn't I tell him not to l'ave this place open!" and he began shoving the planks into place himself.

Jimmie, suddenly made aware of this new catastrophe, came running as fast as his short legs would carry him, scared almost out of his wits. He was as pale as a very dark and dirty Italian could be, and so wrought up that his facial expression changed involuntarily from moment to moment. Rourke was in a fairly murderous mood, only he was so excited and ashamed that he could not speak. Here was the supervisor, and here was himself, and conditions—necessity for order, etc.—would not permit him to kill the Italian in the former's presence. He could only choke and wait. To think that he should be made a mark of like this, and that in the face of his great supervisor! His face and neck were a beet-red, and his eyes flashed with anger. He merely glared at his recalcitrant henchman, as much as to say, "Wait!" When this train had departed and the dignified supervisor had been carried safely out of hearing he turned on Jimmie with all the fury of a masterful and excitable temper.

"So ye'll naht cover the hole, after me tellin' ye naht fifteen minutes ago, will ye?" he shouted. "Ye'll naht cover the hole! An' what'll ye be tellin' me ye was doin' now?"

"I carry da waut (water) for da concrete," pleaded Jimmie weakly.

"Waut fer the concrete," almost moaned Rourke, so great was his fury, his angry face shoved close to the Italian's own. "Waut fer the concrete, is it? It's a pity ye didn't fall into yer waut fer the concrete, ye damned nagur, an' drown! Waut fer the concrete, is it, an' me here, an' Mr. Mills steppin' off an' lookin' in on me, ye black-hearted son of a Eyetalian, ye! I'll waut fer the concrete ye! I'll crack yer blitherin' Eyetalian skull with a pick, I will! I'll chuck ye in yer waut fer the concrete till ye choke, ye flat-footed, leather-headed lunatic! I'll tache ye to waalk aaf an' l'ave the hole open, an' me in it. Now, be Jasus, get yer coat an' get out av this. Get—I'm tellin' ye! I'll have no more thruck with ye! I'll throuble no more with ye. Ye're no damned good. Out with ye! An' niver show me yer face again!" And he made a motion as if he would grab him and rend him limb from limb.

Jimmie, well aware of his dire position, was too clever, however, to let Rourke seize him. During all this conversation he had been slowly backing away, always safely beyond Rourke's reach, and now ran—an amazing feat for him. He had evidently been through many such scenes before. He retreated first behind the depot, and then when Rourke had gone to work once more down in his hole, came back and took a safe position on guard over the hitherto sadly neglected opening. When the next train came he was there to shove the boards over before it neared the station, and nothing more was said about the matter. Rourke did not appear to notice him. He did not even seem to see that he was there. The next morning, however, when the latter came to work as usual, it was, "Come, Matt! Come, Jimmie!" just as if nothing had happened. I was never more astonished in my life.

An incident, even more ridiculous, but illustrative of the atmosphere in which Rourke dwelt, occurred at Highbridge one frosty October Sunday morning, where because of seepage from a hill which threatened to undermine some tracks, Rourke was ordered to hurry and build a drain—a thing which, because the order came on Saturday afternoon, required Sunday labor, a most unusual thing in his case. But in spite of the order, Rourke, who was a good Catholic, felt impelled before coming to go to at least early mass, and in addition—a regular Sunday practice with him, I presume—to put on a long-skirted Prince Albert coat, which I had never seen before and which lent to his stocky figure some amusing lines. It was really too tight, having been worn, I presume, every Sunday regularly since his wedding day. In addition, he had donned a brown derby hat which, to me at least, gave him a most unfamiliar look.

I, being curious more than anything else and wishing to be out of doors as much as possible, also went up, arriving on the scene about nine. Rourke did not arrive until ten. In the meantime, I proceeded to build myself a fire on the dock, for we were alongside the Harlem River and a brisk wind was blowing. Then Rourke came, fresh from church, smiling and genial, in the most cheerful Sunday-go-to-meeting frame of mind, but plainly a little conscious of his grand garb.

"My," I said, surveying him, "you look fine. I never saw you dressed up before."

"L'ave aaf with yer taalk," he replied. "I know well enough how I look—good enough."

Then he bestirred himself about the task of examining what had been done so far. But I could see, in spite of all the busy assurance with which he worked, that he was still highly conscious of his clothes and a little disturbed by what I or others might think. His every-day garb plainly suited his mood much better.

Everything went smoothly until noon, not a cloud in the sky, when, looking across the tracks at that hour, I beheld coming toward us with more or less uncertain step another individual, stocky of figure and evidently bent on seeing Rourke—an Irishman as large as Rourke, younger, and, if anything, considerably coarser in fiber. He was very red-faced, smooth shaven, with a black derby hat pulled down over his eyes and wearing a somewhat faded tight-fitting brown suit. He was drunk, or nearly so, that was plain from the first. From the moment Rourke beheld him he seemed beside himself with anger or irritation. His expression changed completely and he began to swell, as was customary with him when he was angry, as though suffering from an internal eruption of some kind.

"The bla'guard!" I heard him mutter. "Now, be gob, what'll that felly be waantin'?" and then as the stranger drew nearer, "Who was it tould him I was here? Maybe some waan at the ahffice."

Regardless of his speculations on this score, the stranger picked his way across the tracks and came directly to him, his face and manner indicating no particularly friendly frame of mind.

"Maybe ye'll be lettin' me have that money now," he began instanter, and when Rourke made no reply, merely staring at him, he added, "I'll be waantin' to know now, when it is ye're goin' to give me the rest av me time fer that Scarborough job. I've been waitin' long enough."

Rourke stirred irritably and aggressively before he spoke. He seemed greatly put out, shamed, to think that the man should come here so, especially on this peaceful Sabbath morning.

"I've tould ye before," he replied defiantly after a time, "that ye've had aall ye earned, an' more. Ye left me without finishin' yer work, an' ye'll get no more time from me. If ye waant more, go down to the ahffice an' see if they'll give it to ye. I have no money fer ye here," and he resumed a comfortable position before the fire, his hands behind his back.

"It's siven dollars ye still owe me," returned the other, ignoring Rourke's reply, "an' I waant it now."

"Well, ye'll naht get it," replied my boss. "I've naathin' fer ye, I'm tellin' ye. I owe ye naathin'."

"Is that so?" returned the other. "Well, we'll see about that. Ye'll be after givin' it to me, er I'll get it out of ye somehow. It's naht goin' to be ch'ated out av me money I am."

"I'm owin' ye naathin'," insisted Rourke. "Ye may as well go away from here. Ye'll get naathin'. If ye waant anything more, go an' see the ahffice," and now he strode away to where the Italians were, ignoring the stranger completely and muttering something about his being drunk. The latter followed him, however, over to where he stood, and continued the dispute. Rourke ignored him as much as possible, only exclaiming once, "L'ave me be, man. Ye're drunk."

"I'm naht drunk," returned the other. "Once an' fer all now, I'm askin' ye, arre ye goin' to give me that money?"

"No," replied Rourke, "I'm naht."

"Belave me," said the stranger, "I'll get it out av ye somehow," but for the moment he made no move, merely hanging about in an uncertain way. He seemed to have no definite plan for collecting the money, or if he had he had by now abandoned it.

Without paying any more attention to him, Rourke, still very irritated and defiant, returned to the fire. He tried to appear calm and indifferent, but the ex-workman, a non-union mason, I judged, followed after, standing before him and staring in the defiant, irritating way a drunken man will, not quite able to make up his mind what else to do. Presently Rourke, more to relieve the tedium of an embarrassing situation than anything else (a number of accusatory remarks having been passed), turned and began poking at the blaze, finally bending over to lay on a stick of wood. On the instant, and as if seized by sudden inspiration, whether because the tails of Rourke's long coat hung out in a most provoking fashion and suggested the thing that followed or not, I don't know, but now the red-faced intruder jumped forward, and seizing them in a most nimble and yet vigorous clutch, gave an amazing yank, which severed them straight up the back, from seat to nape, at the same time exclaiming:

"Ye'll naht pay me, will ye? Ye'll naht, will ye?"

On the instant a tremendous change came over the scene. It was as swift as stage play. Instantly Rourke was upright and faced about, shouting, "Now, be gob, ye've torn me coat, have ye! Now I'll tache ye! Now I'll show ye! Wait! Get ready, now. Now I'll fix ye, ye drunken, thavin' loafer," and at the same time he began to move upon the enemy in a kind of rhythmic, cryptic circle (some law governing anger and emotion, I presume), the while his hands opened and shut and his eyes looked as though they would be veiled completely by his narrowing lids. At the same time the stranger, apparently seeing his danger, began backing and circling in the same way around Rourke, as well as around the fire, until it looked as though they were performing a war dance. Round and round they went like two Hopi bucks or Zulu warriors, their faces displaying the most murderous cunning and intention to slay—only, instead of feathers and beads, they had on their negligible best. All the while Rourke was calling, "Come on, now! Get ready, now! I'll show ye, now! I'll fix ye, now! It's me coat ye'll rip, is it? Come on, now! Get ready! Make yerself ready! I'm goin' to give ye the lickin' av yer life! Come on, now! Come on, now! Come on, now!"

It was as though each had been secreted from the other and had to be sought out in some mysterious manner and in a circle. In spite of the feeling of distress that an impending struggle of this kind gives one, I could not help noting the comic condition of Rourke's back—the long coat beautifully ripped straight up the back, its ends fluttering in the wind like fans, and exposing his waistcoat and Sunday boiled white shirt—and laying up a laugh for the future. It was too ridiculous. The stranger had a most impressive and yet absurd air of drunken sternness written in his face, a do-or-die look.

Whether anything serious would really have happened I was never permitted to learn, for now, in addition to myself and the Italians, all of them excited and ready to defend their lord and master, some passengers from the nearby station and the street above as well as a foreman of a section gang helping at this same task, a great hulking brute of a man who looked quite able to handle both Rourke and his opponent at one and the same time, came forward and joined in this excited circle. Considerable effort was made on the part of the latter to learn just what the trouble was, after which the big foreman interposed with:

"What's the trouble here? Come, now! What's all this row, Rourke? Ye wouldn't fight here, would ye? Have him arrested, er go to his home—ye say ye know him—but don't be fightin' here. Supposin' waan av the bosses should be comin' along now?" and at the same time he interposed his great bulk between the two.

Rourke, quieted some by this interruption but still sputtering with rage and disgrace, shouted, "Lookit me coat! Lookit what he done to me coat! See what he done to me coat! Man alive, d'ye think I'm goin' to stand fer the likes av that? It's naht me that can be waalked on by a loafer like that—an' me payin' him more than ever he was worth, an' him waalkin' aaf an' l'avin' the job half done. I'll fix him this time. I'll show him. I'll tache him to be comin' around an' disturbin' a man when he's at his work. I'll fix him now," and once more he began to move. But the great foreman was not so easily to be disposed of.

"Well then, let's caall the police," he argued in a highly conciliatory mood. "Ye can't be fightin' him here. Sure, ye don't waant to do that. What'll the chafe think? What is it ye'll think av yerself?"

At the same time he turned to find the intruder and demand to know what he meant by it, but the latter had already decamped. Seeing the crowd that had and was gathering, and that he was likely to encounter more forms of trouble than he had anticipated, he had started down the track toward Mott Haven.

"I'll fix ye!" Rourke shouted when he saw him going. "Ye'll pay fer this. I'll have ye arrested. Wait! Ye'll naht get aaf so aisy this time."

But just the same the storm was over for the present, anyhow, the man gone, and in a little while Rourke left for his home at Mount Vernon to repair his tattered condition. I never saw a man so crestfallen, nor one more determined to "have the laa on him" in my life. Afterwards, when I inquired very cautiously what he had done about it—this was a week or two later—

he replied, "Shewer, what can ye do with a loafer like that? He has no money, an' lockin' him up won't help his wife an' children any."

Thus ended a perfect scene out of Kilkenny.

It was not so very long after I arrived that Rourke began to tell me of a building which the company was going to erect in Mott Haven Yard, one of its great switching centers. It was to be an important affair, according to him, sixty by two hundred feet in breadth and length, of brick and stone, and was to be built under a time limit of three months, an arrangement by which the company hoped to find out how satisfactorily it could do work for itself rather than by outside contract, which it was always hoping to avoid. From his manner and conversation, I judged that Rourke was eager to get this job, for he had been a contractor of some ability in his day before he ever went to work for the company, and felt, I am sure, that fate had done him an injustice in not allowing him to remain one. In addition, he felt a little above the odds and ends of masonry that he was now called on to do, where formerly he had done so much more important work. He was eager to be a real foreman once more, a big one, and to show the company that he could erect this building and thus make a little place for himself in the latter's good graces, although to what end I could not quite make out. He would never have made a suitable general foreman. At the same time, he was a little afraid of the clerical details, those terrible nightmares of reports, o.k.s and the like.

"How arre ye feelin', Teddy, b'y?" he often inquired of me during this period, with a greater show of interest in my troublesome health than ever before. I talked of leaving, I suppose, from time to time because sheer financial necessity was about to compel it.

"Fine, Rourke," I would say, "never better. I'm feeling better every day."

"That's good. Ye're the right man in the right place now. If ye was to sthay a year er two at this work it would be the makin' av ye. Ye're too thin. Ye need more chist," and he would tap my bony chest in a kindly manner. "I niver have a sick day, meself."

"That's right, Rourke," I replied pleasantly, feeling keenly the need of staying by so wonderful a lamp of health. "I intend to stick at it as long as I can."

"Ye ought to; it'll do ye good. If we get the new buildin' to build, it'll be better yet for ye. Ye'll have plenty to do there to relave yer mind."

"Relieve, indeed!" I thought, but I did not say so. On the contrary I felt so much sympathy for this lusty Irishman and his reasonable ambitions that I desired to help him, and urged him to get it. I suggested indirectly that I would see him through, which touched him greatly. He was a grateful creature in his way, but so excitable and so helplessly self-reliant that there was no way of aiding him without doing it in a secret or rather self-effacing manner. He would have much preferred to struggle along alone and fail, though I doubt whether real failure could have come to Rourke so essentially capable was he.

In another three weeks the work was really given him to do, and then began one of the finest exhibitions of Irish domination and self-sufficiency that I have ever witnessed. We moved to Mott Haven Yard, a great network of tracks and buildings, in the center of which this new building was to be erected. Rourke was given a large force of men, whom he fairly gloried in bossing. He had as many as forty Italians, to say nothing of a number of pseudo-carpenters and masons (not those shrewd hawks clever enough to belong to the union, but wasters and failures of another type) who did the preliminary work of digging for the foundation, etc. Handling these, Rourke was in his element. He loved to see so much brisk work going on. He would trot to and fro about the place, beaming in the most angelic fashion, and shouting orders that could be heard all over the neighborhood. It was delicious to watch him. At times he would stand by the long trenches where the men were digging for the foundation, a great line of them, their backs bent over their work, and rub his hands in pleasingly human satisfaction, saying, "We're goin' along fine, Teddy. I can jist see me way to the top av the buildin'," and then he would proceed to harass and annoy his men out of pure exuberance of spirits.

"Ye waant to dig it so, man," or, "Ye don't handle yer pick right; can't ye see that? Hold it this way." Sometimes he would get down in the trench and demonstrate just how it was to be done, a thing which greatly amused some of the workmen. Frequently he would exhibit to me little tricks or knacks of his trade, such as throwing a trowel ten feet so that it would stick in a piece of wood; turning a shovel over with a lump of dirt on it and not dropping the lump, and similar simple acts, always adding, "Ye'll niver be a mason till ye can do that."

When he was tired of fussing with the men outside he would come around to the little wooden shed, where I was keeping the mass of orders and reports in shape and getting his material ready for him, and look over the papers in the most knowing manner. When he had satisfied himself that everything was going right, he would exclaim, "Ye're jist the b'y fer the place, Teddy. Ye'd made a good bookkeeper. If ever I get to be Prisident, I'll make ye me Sicretary av State."

But the thing which really interested and enthralled Rourke was the coming of the masons—those hardy buccaneers of the laboring world who come and go as they please, asking no favors and brooking no interference. Plainly he envied them their reckless independence at the same time that he desired to control their labor in his favor—a task worthy of the shrewdest diplomat. Never in my life have I seen such a gay, ruthless, inconsiderate point of view as these same union masons represented, a most astounding lot. They were— are, I suppose I should say—our modern buccaneers and Captain Kidds of the laboring world, demanding, if you please, their six a day, starting and stopping almost when they please, doing just as little as they dare and yet face their own decaying conscience, dropping any task at the most critical and dangerous point, and in other ways rejoicing in and disporting themselves in such a way as to annoy the representatives of any corporation great or small that suffered the sad compulsion of employing them. Seriously, I am not against union laborers. I like them. They spell rude, blazing life. But when you have to deal with them!

Plainly, Rourke anticipated endless rows. Their coming promised him the opportunity he inmostly desired, I suppose, of once more fussing and fuming with real, strong, determined and pugnacious men like himself, who would not take his onslaughts tamely but would fight him back, as he wished strong men to do. He was never weary of talking of them.

"Wait till we have thirty er forty av thim on the line," he once observed to me in connection with them, "every man layin' his six hundred bricks a day, er takin' aaf his apron! Thim's the times ye'll see what excitement manes, me b'y. Thim's the times."

"What'll I see, Rourke?" I asked interestedly.

"Throuble enough. Shewer, they're no crapin' Eyetalians, that'll let ye taalk to thim as ye pl'ase. Indade not. Ye'll have to fight with them fellies."

"Well, that's a queer state of affairs," I remarked, and then added, "Do you think you can handle them, Rourke?"

"Handle thim!" he exclaimed, his glorious wrath kindling in anticipation of a possible conflict. "Handle thim, an' the likes av a thousand av thim! I know them aall, every waan av thim, an' their thricks. It's naht foolin' me they'll be. But, me b'y," he added instructively, "it's a fine job ye'll have runnin' down to the ahffice gettin' their time." (This is the railroad man's expression for money due, or wages.) "Ye'll have plenty av that to do, I'm tellin' ye."

"You don't mean to say that you're going to discharge them, Rourke, do you?" I asked.

"Shewer!" he exclaimed authoritatively. "Why shouldn't I? They're jist the same as other min. Why shouldn't I?" Then he added, after a pause, "But it's thim that'll be comin' to me askin' fer their time instid av me givin' it to thim, niver fear. They're not the kind that'll let ye taalk back to thim. If their work don't suit ye, it's 'give me me time.' Wait till they'll be comin' round half drunk in the mornin', an' not feelin' just right. Thim's the times ye'll find out what masons arre made av, me b'y."

I confess this probability did not seem as brilliant to me as it did to him, but it had its humor. I expressed wonder that he would hire them if they were such a bad lot.

"Where else will ye get min?" he demanded to know. "The unions have the best, an' the most av thim. Thim outside fellies don't amount to much. They're aall pore, crapin' creatures. If it wasn't fer the railroad bein' against the union I wouldn't have thim at aall, and besides," he added thoughtfully, and with a keen show of feeling for their point of view, "they have a right to do as they pl'ase. Shewer, it's no common workmen they arre. They can lay their eight hundred bricks a day, if they will, an' no advice from any waan. If ye was in their place ye'd do the same. There's no sinse in allowin' another man to waalk on ye whin ye can get another job. I don't blame thim. I was a mason wanst meself."

"You don't mean to say that you acted as you say these men are going to act?"

"Shewer!"

"Well, I shouldn't think you'd be very proud of it."

"I have me rights," he declared, flaring up. "What kind av a man is it that'll let himself be waalked on? There's no sinse in it. It's naht natchral. It's naht intinded that it should be so."

"Very well," I said, smoothing the whole thing over, and so that ended.

Well, the masons came, and a fine lot of pirates they surely were. Such independence! Such defiance! Such feverish punctilio in regard to their rights and what forms and procedures they were entitled to! I stared in amazement. For the most part they were hale, healthy, industrious looking creatures, but so obstreperously conscious of their own rights, and so proud of their skill as masons, that there was no living with them. Really, they would have tried the patience of a saint, let alone a healthy, contentious Irish foreman-mason. "First off," as the railroad men used to say, they wanted to know whether there were any non-union men on the job, and if so, would they be discharged instanter?—if not, no work—a situation which gave Rourke several splendid opportunities for altercations, which he hastened to improve, although the non-union men *went*, of course. Then they wanted to know when, where, and how they were to get their money, whether on demand at any time they chose, and this led to more trouble, since the railroad paid only once a month. However, this was adjusted by a special arrangement being made whereby the building department stood ready to pay them instantly on demand, only I had to run down to the division office each time and get their pay for them at any time that they came to ask for it! Then came an argument (or many of them) as to the number of bricks they were to lay an hour; the number of men they were to carry on one line, or wall; the length of time they were supposed to work, or had worked, or would work—all of which was pure food and drink to Rourke. He was in his element at last, shouting, gesticulating, demanding that they leave or go to——. After all these things had been adjusted, however, they finally consented to go to work, and then of course the work flew. It was a grand scene, really inspiring—forty or fifty masons on the line, perhaps half as many helpers or mixers, the Italians carrying bricks, and a score of carpenters now arriving under another foreman to set the beams and lay the joists as the walls rose upward.

Rourke was about all the time now, arguing and gesticulating with this man or that, fighting with this one or the other, and calling always to some mason or other to "come down" and get his "time." "Come down! Come down!" I would hear, and then would see him rushing for the office, a defiant and even threatening mason at his heels; Rourke demanding that I make out a time-check at once for the latter and go down to the "ahffice" and get the money, the while the mason hung about attempting to seduce other men to a similar point of view. Once in a while, but only on rare occasions, Rourke would patch up a truce with a man. As a rule, the mason was only too eager to leave and spend the money thus far earned, while Rourke was curiously indifferent as to whether he went or stayed. "'Tis to drink he waants," he would declare amusedly. To me it was all like a scene out of comic opera.

Toward the last, however, a natural calm set in, the result no doubt of weariness and a sense of surfeit, which sent the building forward apace. During this time Rourke was to be seen walking defiantly up and down the upper scaffolding of the steadily rising walls, or down below on the ground in front of his men, his hands behind his back, his face screwed into a quizzical expression, his whole body bearing a look of bristling content and pugnacity which was too delicious for words. Since things were going especially well he could not say much, but still he could look his contentiousness, and did. Even now he would occasionally manage to pick a quarrel with some lusty mason or other, which resulted in the customary descent to the office, but not often.

But one cold December day, about three weeks later, when I was just about to announce that I could no longer delay my departure, seeing that my health was now as good, or nearly so, as my purse was lean, and that, whether I would or no, I must arrange to make more money, that a most dreadful accident occurred. It appeared that Rourke and a number of Italians, including Matt and Jimmie, were down in the main room of the building, now fast nearing completion, when the boiler of the hoisting engine, which had been placed inside the building and just at the juncture of three walls, blew up and knocked out this wall and the joists of the second and third floors loose, thus precipitating all of fifteen thousand bricks, which had been placed on the third floor, into this room below. For a few moments there had been a veritable hurricane of bricks and falling timber; and then, when it was over, it was found that the mighty Rourke and five Italians were embedded in or under them, and all but Jimmie more or less seriously injured or killed. Two Italians were killed outright. A third died later. Rourke, in particular, was unfortunately placed and terribly injured. His body from the waist down was completely buried by a pile of bricks, and across his shoulder lay a great joist pressing where it had struck him, and cutting his neck and ear. He was a pathetic sight when we entered, bleeding and pain-wrenched yet grim and undaunted, as one might have expected.

"I'm tight fast, me lad," he said when he could speak. "It's me legs that's caught, not me body. But give a hand to the min, there. The Eyetalians are underneath."

Disregarding his suggestion, however, we began working about him, every man throwing away bricks like a machine; but he would not have it.

"'Tind to the min!" he insisted with all of his old firmness. "The Eyetalians are under there—Matt an' Jimmie. Can't ye see that I'll be all right till ye get thim out? Come, look after the min!"

We fell to this end of the work, although by now others had arrived, and soon there was a great crowd assisting—men coming from the yard and the machine shop. Although embedded in this mass of material and most severely injured, there was no gainsaying him, and he still insisted on directing us as best he could. But now he was so picturesque, so much nobler, really, than he had been in his healthier, uninjured days. A fabled giant, he seemed to me, half-god, half-man, composed in part of flesh, in part of brick and stone, gazing down on our earthly efforts with the eye of a demi-god.

"Come, now—get the j'ists from aaf the end, there. Take the bricks away from that man. Can't ye see? There's where his head is—there. There! Jasus Christ—theyer!"

You would have thought we were Italians ourselves, poor wisps of nothing, not his rescuers, but slaves, compelled to do his lordly bidding.

After a time, however, we managed to release him and all his five helpers— two dead, as I say, and Matt badly cut about the head and seriously injured, while Jimmie, the imperturbable, was but little the worse for a brick mark on one shoulder. He was more or less frightened, of course, and comic to look at, even in this dread situation. "Big-a smash," he exclaimed when he recovered himself. "Like-a da worl' fall. Misha Rook! Misha Rook! Where Misha Rook?"

"Here I am, ye Eyetalian scalawag," exclaimed the unyielding Rourke genially, who was still partially embedded when Jimmie was released. There was, however, a touch of sorrow in his voice as he added weakly, "Arre ye hurted much?"

"No, Misha Rook. Help Misha Rook," replied Jimmie, grabbing at bricks himself, and so the rescue work of "Rook" went on.

Finally he was released, although not without deprecating our efforts the while (this wonderful and exceptional fuss over him), and exclaiming at one point as we tugged at joists and beams rather frantically, "Take yer time. Take yer time. I'm naht so bad fixed as aall that. Take yer time. Get that board out o' the way there, Jimmie."

But he was badly "fixed," and "hurted" unto death also, as we now found, and as he insisted he was not. His hip was severely crushed by the timbers and his legs broken, as well as his internal organs disarranged, although we did not know how badly at the time. Only after we had removed all the weight did he collapse and perhaps personally realize how serious was his plight. He was laid on a canvas tarpaulin brought by the yard-master and spread on the chip-strewn ground, while the doctors from two ambulances worked over him. While they were examining his wounds he took a critical and quizzical interest in what they were doing, and offered one or two humorous suggestions. Finally, when they were ready to move him he asked how he was, and on being told that he was all right, looked curiously about until he caught my eye. I could see that he realized how critical it was with him.

"I'd like to see a priest, Teddy," he whispered, "and, if ye don't mind, I'd like ye to go up to Mount Vernon an' tell me wife. They'll be after telegraphin' her if ye don't. Break it aisy, if ye will. Don't let 'er think there's anything serious. There's no need av it. I'm naht hurted so bad as aall that."

I promised, and the next moment one of the doctors shot a spray of cocaine into his hip to relieve what he knew must be his dreadful pain. A few moments later he lost consciousness, after which I left him to the care of the hospital authorities and hurried away to send the priest and to tell his wife.

For a week thereafter he lingered in a very serious condition and finally died, blood-poisoning having set in. I saw him at the hospital a day or two before, and, trying to sympathize with his condition, I frequently spoke of what I deemed the dreadful uncertainty of life and the seeming carelessness of the engineer in charge of the hoisting engine. He, however, had no complaint to make.

"Ye must expect thim things," was his only comment. "Ye can't aalways expect to go unhurted. I niver lost a man before, nor had one come to haarm. 'Tis the way av things, ye see."

Mighty Rourke! You would have thought the whole Italian population of Mount Vernon knew and loved him, the way they turned out at his funeral. It was a state affair for most of them, and they came in scores, packing the little brick church at which he was accustomed to worship full to overflowing. Matt was there, bandaged and sore, but sorrowful; and Jimmie, artful and scheming in the past, but now thoroughly subdued. He was all sorrow, and sniveled and blubbered and wept hot, blinding tears through the dark, leathery fingers of his hands.

"Misha Rook! Misha Rook!" I heard him say, as they bore the body in; and when they carried it out of the church, he followed, head down. As they lowered it to the grave he was inconsolable.

"Misha Rook! Misha Rook! I work-a for him fifteen year!"

A Mayor and His People

Here is the story of an individual whose political and social example, if such things are ever worth anything (the moralists to the contrary notwithstanding), should have been, at the time, of the greatest importance to every citizen of the United States. Only it was not. Or was it? Who really knows? Anyway, he and his career are entirely forgotten by now, and have been these many years.

He was the mayor of one of those dreary New England mill towns in northern Massachusetts—a bleak, pleasureless realm of about forty thousand, where, from the time he was born until he finally left at the age of thirty-six to seek his fortune elsewhere, he had resided without change. During that time he had worked in various of the local mills, which in one way and another involved nearly all of the population. He was a mill shoe-maker by trade, or, in other words, a factory shoe-hand, knowing only a part of all the processes necessary to make a shoe in that fashion. Still, he was a fair workman, and earned as much as fifteen or eighteen dollars a week at times—rather good pay for that region. By temperament a humanitarian, or possibly because of his own humble state one who was compelled to take cognizance of the difficulties of others, he finally expressed his mental unrest by organizing a club for the study and propagation of socialism, and later, when it became powerful enough to have a candidate and look for political expression of some kind, he was its first, and thereafter for a number of years, its regular candidate for mayor. For a long time, or until its membership became sufficient to attract some slight political attention, its members (following our regular American, unintellectual custom) were looked upon by the rest of the people as a body of harmless kickers, filled with fool notions about a man's duty to his fellowman, some silly dream about an honest and economical administration of public affairs—their city's affairs, to be exact. We are so wise in America, so interested in our fellowman, so regardful of his welfare. They were so small in number, however, that they were little more than an object of pleasant jest, useful for that purpose alone.

This club, however, continued to put up its candidate until about 1895, when suddenly it succeeded in polling the very modest number of fifty-four votes—double the number it had succeeded in polling any previous year. A year later one hundred and thirty-six were registered, and the next year six hundred. Then suddenly the mayor who won that year's battle died, and a special election was called. Here the club polled six hundred and one, a total and astonishing gain of one. In 1898 the perennial candidate was again nominated and received fifteen hundred, and in 1899, when he ran again, twenty-three hundred votes, which elected him.

If this fact be registered casually here, it was not so regarded in that typically New England mill town. Ever study New England—its Puritan, self-defensive, but unintellectual and selfish psychology? Although this poor little snip of a mayor was only elected for one year, men paused astounded, those who had not voted for him, and several of the older conventional political and religious order, wedded to their church and all the routine of the average puritanic mill town, actually cried. No one knew, of course, who the new mayor was, or what he stood for. There were open assertions that the club behind him was anarchistic—that ever-ready charge against anything new in America—and that the courts should be called upon to prevent his being seated. And this from people who were as poorly "off" commercially and socially as any might well be. It was stated, as proving the worst, that he was, or had been, a mill worker!—and, before that a grocery clerk—both at twelve a week, or less!! Immediate division of property, the forcing of all employers to pay as much as five a day to every laborer (an unheard-of sum in New England), and general constraint and subversion of individual rights (things then unknown in America, of course), loomed in the minds of these conventional Americans as the natural and immediate result of so modest a victory. The old-time politicians and corporations who understood much better what the point was, the significance of this straw, were more or less disgruntled, but satisfied that it could be undone later.

An actual conversation which occurred on one of the outlying street corners one evening about dusk will best illustrate the entire situation.

"Who is the man, anyway?" asked one citizen of a total stranger whom he had chanced to meet.

"Oh, no one in particular, I think. A grocery clerk, they say."

"Astonishing, isn't it? Why, I never thought those people would get anything. Why, they didn't even figure last year."

"Seems to be considerable doubt as to just what he'll do."

"That's what I've been wondering. I don't take much stock in all their talk about anarchy. A man hasn't so very much power as mayor."

"No," said the other.

"We ought to give him a trial, anyway. He's won a big fight. I should like to see him, see what he looks like."

"Oh, nothing startling. I know him."

"Rather young, ain't he?"

"Yes."

"Where did he come from?"

"Oh, right around here."

"Was he a mill-hand?"

"Yes."

The stranger made inquiry as to other facts and then turned off at a corner.

"Well," he observed at parting, "I don't know. I'm inclined to believe in the man. I should like to see him myself. Good-night."

"Good-night," said the other, waving his hand. "When you see me again you will know that you are looking at the mayor."

The inquirer stared after him and saw a six-foot citizen, of otherwise medium proportions, whose long, youthful face and mild gray eyes, with just a suggestion of washed-out blue in them, were hardly what was to be expected of a notorious and otherwise astounding political figure.

"He is too young," was the earliest comments, when the public once became aware of his personality.

"Why, he is nothing but a grocery clerk," was another, the skeptical and condemnatory possibilities of which need not be dilated upon here.

And he was, in his way—nothing much of a genius, as such things go in politics, but an interesting figure. Without much taste (or its cultivated shadow) or great vision of any kind, he was still a man who sensed the evils of great and often unnecessary social inequalities and the need of reorganizing influences, which would tend to narrow the vast gulf between the unorganized and ignorant poor, and the huge beneficiaries of unearned (yes, and not even understood) increment. For what does the economic wisdom of the average capitalist amount to, after all: the narrow, gourmandizing hunger of the average multi-millionaire?

At any rate, people watched him as he went to and fro between his office and his home, and reached the general conclusion after the first excitement had died down that he did not amount to much.

When introduced into his office in the small but pleasant city hall, he came into contact with a "ring," and a fixed condition, which nobody imagined a lone young mayor could change. Old-time politicians sat there giving out contracts for street-cleaning, lighting, improvements and supplies of all kinds, and a bond of mutual profit bound them closely together.

"I don't think he can do much to hurt us," these individuals said one to another. "He don't amount to much."

The mayor was not of a talkative or confiding turn. Neither was he cold or wanting in good and natural manners. He was, however, of a preoccupied turn of mind, "up in the air," some called it, and smoked a good many cigars.

"I think we ought to get together and have some sort of a conference about the letting of contracts," said the president of the city council to him one morning shortly after he had been installed. "You will find these gentlemen ready to meet you half-way in these matters."

"I'm very glad to hear that," he replied. "I've something to say in my message to the council, which I'll send over in the morning."

The old-time politician eyed him curiously, and he eyed the old-time politician in turn, not aggressively, but as if they might come to a very pleasant understanding if they wanted to, and then went back to his office.

The next day his message was made public, and this was its key-note:

"All contract work for the city should be let with a proviso, that the workmen employed receive not less than two dollars a day."

The dissatisfied roar that followed was not long in making itself heard all over the city.

"Stuff and nonsense," yelled the office jobbers in a chorus. "Socialism!" "Anarchy!" "This thing must be put down!" "The city would be bankrupt in a year." "No contractor could afford to pay his ordinary day laborers two a day. The city could not afford to pay any contractor enough to do it."

"The prosperity of the city is not greater than the prosperity of the largest number of its component individuals," replied the mayor, in a somewhat altruistic and economically abstruse argument on the floor of the council hall. "We must find contractors."

"We'll see about that," said the members of the opposition. "Why, the man's crazy. If he thinks he can run this town on a goody-good basis and make everybody rich and happy, he's going to get badly fooled, that's all there is to that."

Fortunately for him three of the eight council members were fellows of the mayor's own economic beliefs, individuals elected on the same ticket with him. These men could not carry a resolution, but they could stop one from being carried over the mayor's veto. Hence it was found that if the contracts could not be given to men satisfactory to the mayor they could not be given at all, and he stood in a fair way to win.

"What the hell's the use of us sitting here day after day!" were the actual words of the leading members of the opposition in the council some weeks later, when the fight became wearisome. "We can't pass the contracts over his veto. I say let 'em go."

So the proviso was tacked on, that two a day was the minimum wage to be allowed, and the contracts passed.

The mayor's followers were exceedingly jubilant at this, more so than he, who was of a more cautious and less hopeful temperament.

"Not out of the woods yet, gentlemen," he remarked to a group of his adherents at the reform club. "We have to do a great many things sensibly if we expect to keep the people's confidence and 'win again.'"

Under the old system of letting contracts, whenever there was a wage rate stipulated, men were paid little or nothing, and the work was not done. There was no pretense of doing it. Garbage and ashes accumulated, and papers littered the streets. The old contractor who had pocketed the appropriated sum thought to do so again.

"I hear the citizens are complaining as much as ever," said the mayor to this individual one morning. "You will have to keep the streets clean."

The contractor, a robust, thick-necked, heavy-jawed Irishman, of just so much refinement as the sudden acquisition of a comfortable fortune would allow, looked him quizzically over, wondering whether he was "out" for a portion of the appropriation or whether he was really serious.

"We can fix that between us," he said.

"There's nothing to fix," replied the mayor. "All I want you to do is to clean the streets."

The contractor went away and for a few days after the streets were really clean, but it was only for a few days.

In his walks about the city the mayor himself found garbage and paper uncollected, and then called upon his new acquaintance again.

"I'm mentioning this for the last time, Mr. M——," he said. "You will have to fulfill your contract, or resign in favor of some one who will."

"Oh, I'll clean them, well enough," said this individual, after five minutes of rapid fire explanation. "Two dollars a day for men is high, but I'll see that they're clean."

Again he went away, and again the mayor sauntered about, and then one morning sought out the contractor in his own office.

"This is the end," he said, removing a cigar from his mouth and holding it before him with his elbow at right angles. "You are discharged from this work. I'll notify you officially to-morrow."

"It can't be done the way you want it," the contractor exclaimed with an oath. "There's no money in it at two dollars. Hell, anybody can see that."

"Very well," said the mayor in a kindly well-modulated tone. "Let another man try, then."

The next day he appointed a new contractor, and with a schedule before him showing how many men should be employed and how much profit he might expect, the latter succeeded. The garbage was daily removed, and the streets carefully cleaned.

Then there was a new manual training school about to be added to the public school system at this time, and the contract for building was to be let, when the mayor threw a bomb into the midst of the old-time jobbers at the city council. A contractor had already been chosen by them and the members were figuring out their profits, when at one of the public discussions of the subject the mayor said:

"Why shouldn't the city build it, gentlemen?"

"How can it?" exclaimed the councilmen. "The city isn't an individual; it can't watch carefully."

"It can hire its own architect, as well as any contractor. Let's try it."

There were sullen tempers in the council chamber after this, but the mayor was insistent. He called an architect who made a ridiculously low estimate. Never had a public building been estimated so cheaply before.

"See here," said one of the councilmen when the plans were presented to the chamber—"This isn't doing this city right, and the gentlemen of the council ought to put their feet down on any such venture as this. You're going to waste the city's money on some cheap thing in order to catch votes."

"I'll publish the cost of the goods as delivered," said the mayor. "Then the people can look at the building when it's built. We'll see how cheap it looks then."

To head off political trickery on the part of the enemy he secured bills for material as delivered, and publicly compared them with prices paid for similar amounts of the same material used in other buildings. So the public was kept aware of what was going on and the cry of cheapness for political purposes set at naught. It was the first public structure erected by the city, and by all means the cheapest and best of all the city's buildings.

Excellent as these services were in their way, the mayor realized later that a powerful opposition was being generated and that if he were to retain the interest of his constituents he would have to set about something which would endear him and his cause to the public.

"I may be honest," he told one of his friends, "but honesty will play a lone hand with these people. The public isn't interested in its own welfare very much. It can't be bothered or hasn't the time. What I need is something that will impress it and still be worth while. I can't be reëlected on promises, or on my looks, either."

When he looked about him, however, he found the possibility of independent municipal action pretty well hampered by mandatory legislation. He had promised, for instance, to do all he could to lower the exorbitant gas rate and to abolish grade crossings, but the law said that no municipality could do either of these things without first voting to do so three years in succession—a little precaution taken by the corporation representing such things long before he came into power. Each vote must be for such contemplated action, or it could not become a law.

"I know well enough that promises are all right," he said to one of his friends, "and that these laws are good enough excuses, but the public won't take excuses from me for three years. If I want to be mayor again I want to be doing something, and doing it quick."

In the city was a gas corporation, originally capitalized at $45,000, and subsequently increased to $75,000, which was earning that year the actual sum of $58,000 over and above all expenses. It was getting ready to inflate the capitalization, as usual, and water its stock to the extent of $500,000, when it occurred to the mayor that if the corporation was making such enormous profits out of a $75,000 investment as to be able to offer to pay six per cent on $500,000 to investors, and put the money it would get for such stocks into its pocket, perhaps it could reduce the price of gas from one dollar and nineteen cents to a more reasonable figure. There was the three years' voting law, however, behind which, as behind an entrenchment, the very luxurious corporation lay comfortable and indifferent.

The mayor sent for his corporation counsel, and studied gas law for awhile. He found that at the State capital there was a State board, or commission, which had been created to look after gas companies in general, and to hear the complaints of municipalities which considered themselves unjustly treated.

"This is the thing for me," he said.

Lacking the municipal authority himself, he decided to present the facts in the case and appeal to this commission for a reduction of the gas rate.

When he came to talk about it he found that the opposition he would generate would be something much more than local. Back of the local reduction idea was the whole system of extortionate gas rates of the State and of the nation; hundreds of fat, luxurious gas corporations whose dividends would be threatened by any agitation on this question.

"You mean to proceed with this scheme of yours?" asked a prominent member of the local bar who called one morning to interview him. "I represent the gentlemen who are interested in our local gas company."

"I certainly do," replied the mayor.

"Well," replied the uncredentialed representative of private interests, after expostulating a long time and offering various "reasons" why it would be more profitable and politically advantageous for the new mayor not to proceed, "I've said all I can say. Now I want to tell you that you are going up against a combination that will be your ruin. You're not dealing with this town now; you're dealing with the State, the whole nation. These corporations can't afford to let you win, and they won't. You're not the one to do it; you're not big enough."

The mayor smiled and replied that of course he could not say as to that.

The lawyer went away, and that next day the mayor had his legal counsel look up the annual reports of the company for the consecutive years of its existence, as well as a bulletin issued by a firm of brokers, into whose hands the matter of selling a vast amount of watered stock it proposed to issue had been placed. He also sent for a gas expert and set him to figuring out a case for the people.

It was found by this gentleman that since the company was first organized it had paid dividends on its capital stock at the rate of ten per cent per annum, for the first thirty years; had made vast improvements in the last ten, and notwithstanding this fact, had paid twenty per cent, and even twenty-five per cent per annum in dividends. All the details of cost and expenditure were figured out, and then the mayor with his counsel took the train for the State capitol.

Never was there more excitement in political circles than when this young representative of no important political organization whatsoever arrived at the State capitol and walked, at the appointed time, into the private audience room of the commission. Every gas company, as well as every newspaper and every other representative of the people, had curiously enough become interested in the fight he was making, and there was a band of reporters at the hotel where he was stopping, as well as in the commission chambers in the State capitol where the hearing was to be. They wanted to know about him—why he was doing this, whether it wasn't a "strike" or the work of some rival corporation. The fact that he might foolishly be sincere was hard to believe.

"Gentlemen," said the mayor, as he took his stand in front of an august array of legal talent which was waiting to pick his argument to pieces in the commission chambers at the capitol, "I miscalculated but one thing in this case which I am about to lay before you, and that is the extent of public interest. I came here prepared to make a private argument, but now I want to ask the privilege of making it public. I see the public itself is interested, or should be. I will ask leave to postpone my argument until the day after tomorrow."

There was considerable hemming and hawing over this, since from the point of view of the corporation it was most undesirable, but the commission was practically powerless to do aught but grant his request. And meanwhile the interest created by the newspapers added power to his cause. Hunting up the several representatives and senators from his district, he compelled them to take cognizance of the cause for which he was battling, and when the morning of the public hearing arrived a large audience was assembled in the chamber of representatives.

When the final moment arrived the young mayor came forward, and after making a very simple statement of the cause which led him to request a public hearing and the local condition which he considered unfair begged leave to introduce an expert, a national examiner of gas plants and lighting facilities, for whom he had sent, and whose twenty years of experience in this line had enabled him to prepare a paper on the condition of the gas-payers in the mayor's city.

The commission was not a little surprised by this, but signified its willingness to hear the expert as counsel for the city, and as his statement was read a very clear light was thrown upon the situation.

Counsel for the various gas corporations interrupted freely. The mayor himself was constantly drawn into the argument, but his replies were so simple and convincing that there was not much satisfaction to be had in stirring him. Instead, the various counsel took refuge in long-winded discussions about the methods of conducting gas plants in other cities, the cost of machinery, labor and the like, which took days and days, and threatened to extend into weeks. The astounding facts concerning large profits and the present intentions of not only this but every other company in the State could not be dismissed. In fact the revelation of huge corporation profits everywhere became so disturbing that after the committee had considered and re-considered, it finally, when threatened with political extermination, voted to reduce the price of gas to eighty cents.

It is needless to suggest the local influence of this decision. When the mayor came home he received an ovation, and that at the hands of many of the people who had once been so fearful of him, but he knew that this enthusiasm would not last long. Many disgruntled elements were warring against him, and others were being more and more stirred up. His home life was looked into as well as his past, his least childish or private actions. It was a case of finding other opportunities for public usefulness, or falling into the innocuous peace which would result in his defeat.

In the platform on which he had been elected was a plank which declared that it was the intention of this party, if elected, to abolish local grade crossings, the maintenance of which had been the cause of numerous accidents and much public complaint. With this plank he now proposed to deal.

In this of course he was hampered by the law before mentioned, which declared that no city could abolish its grade crossings without having first submitted the matter to the people during three successive years and obtained their approval each time. Behind this law was not now, however, as in the case of the gas company, a small $500,000 corporation, but all the railroads which controlled New England, and to which brains and legislators, courts and juries, were mere adjuncts. Furthermore, the question would have to be voted on at the same time as his candidacy, and this would have deterred many another more ambitious politician. The mayor was not to be deterred, however. He began his agitation, and the enemy began theirs, but in the midst of what seemed to be a fair battle the great railway company endeavored to steal a march. There was suddenly and secretly introduced into the lower house of the State legislature a bill which in deceptive phraseology declared that the law which allowed all cities, by three successive votes, to abolish grade crossings in three years, was, in the case of a particular city mentioned, hereby abrogated for a term of four years. The question might not even be discussed politically.

When the news of this attempt reached the mayor, he took the first train for the State capitol and arrived there just in time to come upon the floor of the house when the bill was being taken up for discussion. He asked leave to make a statement. Great excitement was aroused by his timely arrival. Those who secretly favored the bill endeavored to have the matter referred to a committee, but this was not to be. One member moved to go on with the consideration of the bill, and after a close vote the motion carried.

The mayor was then introduced.

After a few moments, in which the silent self-communing with which he introduced himself impressed everyone with his sincerity, he said:

"I am accused of objecting to this measure because its enactment will remove, as a political issue, the one cause upon which I base my hope for reëlection. If there are no elevated crossings to vote for, there will be no excuse for voting for me. Gentlemen, you mistake the temper and the intellect of the people of our city. It is you who see political significance in this thing, but let me assure you that it is of a far different kind from that which you conceive. If the passing of this measure had any significance to me other than the apparent wrong of it, I would get down on my knees and urge its immediate acceptance. Nothing could elect me quicker. Nothing could bury the opposition further from view. If you wish above all things to accomplish my triumph you will only need to interfere with the rights of our city in this arbitrary manner, and you will have the thing done. I could absolutely ask nothing more."

The gentlemen who had this measure in charge weighed well these assertions and trifled for weeks with the matter, trying to make up their minds.

Meanwhile election time approached, and amid the growing interest of politics it was thought unwise to deal with it. A great fight was arranged for locally, in which every conceivable element of opposition was beautifully harmonized by forces and conceptions which it is almost impossible to explain. Democrats, republicans, prohibitionists, saloon men and religious circles, all were gathered into one harmonious body and inspired with a single idea, that of defeating the mayor. From some quarter, not exactly identified, was issued a call for a civic committee of fifty, which should take into its hands the duty of rescuing the city from what was termed a "throttling policy of commercial oppression and anarchy." Democrats, republicans, liquor and anti-liquorites, were invited to the same central meeting place, and came. Money was not lacking, nor able minds, to prepare campaign literature. It was openly charged that a blank check was handed in to the chairman of this body by the railway whose crossings were in danger, to be filled out for any amount necessary to the destruction of the official upstart who was seeking to revolutionize old methods and conditions.

As may be expected, this opposition did not lack daring in making assertions contrary to facts. Charges were now made that the mayor was in league with the railroad to foist upon the city a great burden of expense, because the law under which cities could compel railroads to elevate their tracks declared that one-fifth of the burden of expense must be borne by the city and the remaining four-fifths by the railroad. It would saddle a debt of $250,000 upon the taxpayers, they said, and give them little in return. All the advantage would be with the railroad. "Postpone this action until the railroad can be forced to bear the entire expense, as it justly should," declared handbill writers, whose services were readily rendered to those who could afford to pay for them.

The mayor and his committee, although poor, answered with handbills and street corner speeches, in which he showed that even with the extravagantly estimated debt of $250,000, the city's tax-rate would not be increased by quite six cents to the individual. The cry that each man would have to pay five dollars more each year for ten years was thus wholesomely disposed of, and the campaign proceeded.

Now came every conceivable sort of charge. If he were not defeated, all reputable merchants would surely leave the city. Capital was certainly being scared off. There would be idle factories and empty stomachs. Look out for hard times. No one but a fool would invest in a city thus hampered.

In reply the mayor preached a fair return by corporations for benefits received. He, or rather his organization, took a door-to-door census of his following, and discovered a very considerable increase in the number of those intending to vote for him. The closest calculations of the enemy were discovered, the actual number they had fixed upon as sufficient to defeat him. This proved to the mayor that he must have three hundred more votes if he wished to be absolutely sure. These he hunted out from among the enemy, and had them pledged before the eventual morning came.

The night preceding election ended the campaign, for the enemy at least, in a blaze of glory, so to speak. Dozens of speakers for both causes were about the street corners and in the city meeting room.

Oratory poured forth in streams, and gasoline-lighted band-wagons rattled from street to street, emitting song and invective. Even a great parade was arranged by the anti-mayoral forces, in which horses and men to the number of hundreds were brought in from nearby cities and palmed off as enthusiastic citizens.

"Horses don't vote," a watchword handed out by the mayor, took the edge off the extreme ardor of this invading throng, and set to laughing the hundreds of his partisans, who needed such encouragement.

Next day came the vote, and then for once, anyhow, he was justified. Not only was a much larger vote cast than ever, but he thrashed the enemy with a tail of two hundred votes to spare. It was an inspiring victory from one point of view, but rather doleful for the enemy. The latter had imported a carload of fireworks, which now stood sadly unused upon the very tracks which, apparently, must in the future be raised. The crowning insult was offered when the successful forces offered to take them off their hands at half price.

For a year thereafter (a mayor was elected yearly there), less was heard of the commercial destruction of the city. Gas stood, as decided, at eighty cents a thousand. A new manual training school, built at a very nominal cost, a monument to municipal honesty, was also in evidence. The public waterworks had also been enlarged and the rates reduced. The streets were clean.

Then the mayor made another innovation. During his first term of office there had been a weekly meeting of the reform club, at which he appeared and talked freely of his plans and difficulties. These meetings he now proposed to make public.

Every Wednesday evening for a year thereafter a spectacle of municipal self-consciousness was witnessed, which those who saw it felt sure would redound to the greater strength and popularity of the mayor. In a large hall, devoted to public gatherings, a municipal meeting was held. Every one was invited. The mayor was both host and guest, an individual who chose to explain his conduct and his difficulties and to ask advice. There his constituents gathered, not only to hear but to offer counsel.

"Gentlemen," so ran the gist of his remarks on various of these occasions, "the present week has proved a most trying one. I am confronted by a number of difficult problems, which I will now try to explain to you. In the first place, you know my limitations as to power in the council. But three members now vote for me, and it is only by mutual concessions that we move forward at all."

Then would follow a detailed statement of the difficulties, and a general discussion. The commonest laborer was free to offer his advice. Every question was answered in the broadest spirit of fellowship. An inquiry as to "what to do" frequently brought the most helpful advice. Weak and impossible solutions were met as such, and shown to be what they were. Radicals were assuaged, conservatives urged forward. The whole political situation was so detailed and explained that no intelligent person could leave, it was thought, with a false impression of the mayor's position or intent.

With five thousand or more such associated citizens abroad each day explaining, defending, approving the official conduct of the mayor, because they understood it, no misleading conceptions, it was thought, could arise. Men said that his purpose and current leaning in any matter was always clear. He was thought to be closer to his constituency than any other official within the whole range of the Americas and that there could be nothing but unreasoning partisan opposition to his rule.

After one year of such service a presidential campaign drew near, and the mayor's campaign for reëlection had to be contested at the same time. No gas monopoly evil was now a subject of contention. Streets were clean, contracts fairly executed; the general municipal interests as satisfactorily attended to as could be expected. Only the grade crossing war remained as an issue, and that would require still another vote after this. His record was the only available campaign argument.

On the other side, however, were the two organizations of the locally defeated great parties, and the railroad. The latter, insistent in its bitterness, now organized these two bodies into a powerful opposition. Newspapers were subsidized; the national significance of the campaign magnified; a large number of railroad-hands colonized. When the final weeks of the campaign arrived a bitter contest was waged, and money triumphed. Five thousand four hundred votes were cast for the mayor. Five thousand four hundred and fifty for the opposing candidate, who was of the same party as the successful presidential nominee.

It was a bitter blow, but still one easily borne by the mayor, who was considerable of a philosopher. With simple, undisturbed grace he retired, and three days later applied to one of the principal shoe factories for work at his trade.

"What? You're not looking for a job, are you?" exclaimed the astonished foreman.

"I am," said the mayor.

"You can go to work, all right, but I should think you could get into something better now."

"I suppose I can later," he replied, "when I complete my law studies. Just now I want to do this for a change, to see how things are with the rank and file." And donning the apron he had brought with him he went to work.

It was not long, however, before he was discharged, largely because of partisan influence anxious to drive him out of that region. It was said that this move of seeking a job in so simple a way was a bit of "grand standing"—insincere—that he didn't need to do it, and that he was trying to pile up political capital against the future. A little later a local grocery man of his social faith offered him a position as clerk, and for some odd reason—humanitarian and sectarian, possibly—he accepted this. At any rate, here he labored for a little while. Again many said he was attempting to make political capital out of this simple life in order to further his political interests later, and this possibly, even probably, was true. All men have methods of fighting for that which they believe. So here he worked for a time, while a large number of agencies pro and con continued to denounce or praise him, to ridicule or extol his so-called Jeffersonian simplicity. It was at this time that I encountered him—a tall, spare, capable and interesting individual, who willingly took me into his confidence and explained all that had hitherto befallen him. He was most interesting, really, a figure to commemorate in this fashion.

In one of the rooms of his very humble home—a kind of office or den, in a small house such as any clerk or working-man might occupy—was a collection of clippings, laudatory, inquiring, and abusive, which would have done credit to a candidate for the highest office in the land. One would have judged by the scrap-books and envelopes stuffed to overflowing with long newspaper articles and editorials that had been cut from papers all over the country from Florida to Oregon, that his every movement at this time and earlier was all-essential to the people. Plainly, he had been watched, spied upon, and ignored by one class, while being hailed, praised and invited by another. Magazine editors had called upon him for contributions, journalists from the large cities had sought him out to obtain his actual views, citizens' leagues in various parts of the nation had invited him to come and speak, and yet he was still a very young man in years, not over-intelligent politically or philosophically, the ex-mayor of a small city, and the representative of no great organization of any sort.

In his retirement he was now comforted, if one can be so comforted, by these memories, still fresh in his mind and by the hope possibly for his own future, as well as by a droll humor with which he was wont to select the sharpest and most willful slur upon his unimpeachable conduct as an offering to public curiosity.

"Do you really want to know what people think of me?" he said to me on one occasion. "Well, here's something. Read this." And then he would hand me a bunch of the bitterest attacks possible, attacks which pictured him as a sly and treacherous enemy of the people—or worse yet a bounding anarchistic ignoramus. Personally I could not help admiring his stoic mood. It was superior to that of his detractors. Apparent falsehoods did not anger him. Evident misunderstandings could not, seemingly, disturb him.

"What do you expect?" he once said to me, after I had made a very careful study of his career for a current magazine, which, curiously, was never published. I was trying to get him to admit that he believed that his example might be fruitful of results agreeable to him in the future. I could not conclude that he really agreed with me. "People do not remember; they forget. They remember so long as you are directly before them with something that interests them. That may be a lower gas-rate, or a band that plays good music. People like strong people, and only strong people, characters of that sort—good, bad or indifferent—I've found that out. If a man or a corporation is stronger than I am, comes along and denounces me, or spends more money than I do (or can), buys more beers, makes larger promises, it is 'all day' for me. What has happened in my case is that, for the present, anyhow, I have come up against a strong corporation, stronger than I am. What I now need to do is to go out somewhere and get some more strength in some way, it doesn't matter much how. People are not so much interested in me or you, or your or my ideals in their behalf, as they are in strength, an interesting spectacle. And they are easily deceived. These big fighting corporations with their attorneys and politicians and newspapers make me look weak—puny. So the people forget me. If I could get out, raise one million or five hundred thousand dollars and give the corporations a good drubbing, they would adore me—for awhile. Then I would have to go out and get another five hundred thousand somewhere, or do something else."

"Quite so," I replied. "Yet *Vox populi, vox dei.*"

Sitting upon his own doorstep one evening, in a very modest quarter of the city, I said:

"Were you very much depressed by your defeat the last time?"

"Not at all," he replied. "Action, reaction, that's the law. All these things right themselves in time, I suppose, or, anyhow, they ought to. Maybe they don't. Some man who can hand the people what they really need or ought to have will triumph, I suppose, some time. I don't know, I'm sure. I hope so. I think the world is moving on, all right."

In his serene and youthful face, the pale blue, philosophical eyes, was no evidence of dissatisfaction with the strange experiences through which he had passed.

"You're entirely philosophical, are you?"

"As much as any one can be, I suppose. They seem to think that all my work was an evidence of my worthlessness," he said. "Well, maybe it was. Self-interest may be the true law, and the best force. I haven't quite made up my mind yet. My sympathies of course are all the other way. 'He ought to be sewing shoes in the penitentiary,' one paper once said of me. Another advised me to try something that was not above my intelligence, such as breaking rock or shoveling dirt. Most of them agreed, however," he added with a humorous twitch of his large, expressive mouth, "that I'll do very well if I will only stay where I am, or, better yet, get out of here. They want me to leave. That's the best solution for them."

He seemed to repress a smile that was hovering on his lips.

"The voice of the enemy," I commented.

"Yes, sir, the voice of the enemy," he added. "But don't think that I think I'm done for. Not at all. I have just returned to my old ways in order to think this thing out. In a year or two I'll have solved my problem, I hope. I may have to leave here, and I may not. Anyhow, I'll turn up somewhere, with something."

He did have to leave, however, public opinion never being allowed to revert to him again, and five years later, in a fairly comfortable managerial position in New York, he died. He had made a fight, well enough, but the time, the place, the stars, perhaps, were not quite right. He had no guiding genius, possibly, to pull him through. Adherents did not flock to him and save him. Possibly he wasn't magnetic enough—that pagan, non-moral, non-propagandistic quality, anyhow. The fates did not fight for him as they do for some, those fates that ignore the billions and billions of others who fail. Yet are not all lives more or less failures, however successful they may appear to be at one time or another, contrasted, let us say, with what they hoped for? We compromise so much with everything—our dreams and all.

As for his reforms, they may be coming fast enough, or they may not. *In medias res.*

But as for him...?

W.L.S.

Life's little ironies are not always manifest. We hear distant rumbling sounds of its tragedies, but rarely are we permitted to witness the reality. Therefore the real incidents which I am about to relate may have some value.

I first called upon W.L.S———, Jr., in the winter of 1895. I had known of him before only by reputation, or, what is nearer the truth, by seeing his name in one of the great Sunday papers attached to several drawings of the most lively interest. These drawings depicted night scenes of the city of New York, and appeared as colored supplements, eleven by eighteen inches. They represented the spectacular scenes which the citizen and the stranger most delight in—Madison Square in a drizzle; the Bowery lighted by a thousand lamps and crowded with "L" and surface cars; Sixth Avenue looking north from Fourteenth Street.

I was a youthful editor at the time and on the lookout for interesting illustrations of this sort, and when a little later I was in need of a colored supplement for the Christmas number I decided to call upon S———. I knew absolutely nothing about the world of art save what I had gathered from books and current literary comment of all sorts, and was, therefore, in a mood to behold something exceedingly bizarre in the atmosphere with which I should find my illustrator surrounded.

I was not disappointed. It was at the time when artists—I mean American artists principally—went in very strongly for that sort of thing. Only a few years before they had all been going to Paris, not so much to paint as to find out and imitate how artists *do* and live. I was greeted by a small, wiry, lean-looking individual arrayed in a bicycle suit, whose countenance could be best described as wearing a perpetual look of astonishment. He had one eye which fixed you with a strange, unmoving solemnity, owing to the fact that it was glass. His skin was anything but fair, and might be termed sallow. He wore a close, sharp-pointed Vandyke beard, and his gold-bridge glasses sat at almost right angles upon his nose. His forehead was high, his good eye alert, his hair sandy-colored and tousled, and his whole manner indicated thought, feeling, remarkable nervous energy, and, above all, a rasping and jovial sort of egotism which pleased me rather than otherwise.

I noticed no more than this on my first visit, owing to the fact that I was very much overawed and greatly concerned about the price which he would charge me, not knowing what rate he might wish to exact, and being desirous of coming away at least unabashed by his magnificence and independence.

"What's it for?" he asked, when I suggested a drawing.

I informed him.

"You say you want it for a double-page center?"

"Yes."

"Well, I'll do it for three hundred dollars."

I was taken considerably aback, as I had not contemplated paying more than one hundred.

"I get that from all the magazines," he added, seeing my hesitation, "wherever a supplement is intended."

"I don't think I could pay more than one hundred," I said, after a few moments' consideration.

"You couldn't?" he said, sharply, as if about to reprove me.

I shook my head.

"Well," he said, "let's see a copy of your publication."

The chief value of this conversation was that it taught me that the man's manner was no indication of his mood. I had thought he was impatient and indifferent, but I saw now that he was not so, rather brusque merely. He was simply excitable, somewhat like the French, and meant only to be businesslike. The upshot of it all was that he agreed to do it for one hundred and fifty, and asked me very solemnly to say nothing about it.

I may say here that I came upon S—— in the full blush of his fancies and ambitions, and just when he was verging upon their realization. He was not yet successful. A hundred and fifty dollars was a very fair price indeed. His powers, however, had reached that stage where they would soon command their full value.

I could see at once that he was very ambitious. He was bubbling over with the enthusiasm of youth and an intense desire for recognition. He knew he had talent. The knowledge of it gave him an air and an independence of manner which might have been irritating to some. Besides, he was slightly affected, argue to the contrary as he would, and was altogether full of his own hopes and ambitions.

The matter of painting this picture necessitated my presence on several occasions, and during this time I got better acquainted with him. Certain ideas and desires which we held in common drew us toward each other, and I soon began to see that he was much above the average in insight and skill. He talked with the greatest ease upon a score of subjects—literature, art, politics, music, the drama, and history. He seemed to have read the latest novels; to have seen many of the current plays; to have talked with important people. Theodore Roosevelt, previously Police Commissioner but then

Governor, often came to his studio to talk and play chess with him. A very able architect was his friend. He had artist associates galore, many of whom had studios in the same building or the immediate vicinity. And there were literary and business men as well, all of whom seemed to enjoy his company, and who were very fond of calling and spending an hour in his studio.

I had only called the second time, and was going away, when he showed me a steamship he had constructed with his own hands—a fair-sized model, complete in every detail, even to the imitation stokers in the boiler-room, and which would run by the hour if supplied with oil and water. I soon learned that his skill in mechanical construction was great. He was a member of several engineering societies, and devoted some part of his carefully organized days to studying and keeping up with problems in mechanics.

"Oh, that's nothing," he observed, when I marveled at the size and perfection of the model. "I'll show you something else, if you have time some day, which may amuse you."

He then explained that he had constructed several model warships, and that it was his pleasure to take them out and fight them on a pond somewhere out on Long Island.

"We'll go out some day," he said when I showed appropriate interest, "and have them fight each other. You'll see how it's done!"

I waited some time for this outing, and finally mentioned it.

"We'll go tomorrow," he said. "Can you be around here by ten o'clock?"

Ten the next morning saw me promptly at the studio, and five minutes later we were off.

When we arrived at Long Island City we went to the first convenient arm of the sea and undid the precious fighters, in which he much delighted.

After studying the contour of the little inlet for a few moments he took some measurements with a tape-line, stuck up two twigs in two places for guide posts, and proceeded to fire and get up steam in his war-ships. Afterwards he set the rudders, and then took them to the water-side and floated them at the points where he had placed the twigs.

These few details accomplished, he again studied the situation carefully, headed the vessels to the fraction of an inch toward a certain point of the opposite shore, and began testing the steam.

"When I say ready, you push this lever here," he said, indicating a little brass handle fastened to the stern-post. "Don't let her move an inch until you do that. You'll see some tall firing."

He hastened to the other side where his own boat was anchored, and began an excited examination. He was like a school-boy with a fine toy.

At a word, I moved the lever as requested, and the two vessels began steaming out toward one another. Their weight and speed were such that the light wind blowing affected them not in the least, and their prows struck with an audible crack. This threw them side by side, steaming head on together. At the same time it operated to set in motion their guns, which fired broadsides in such rapid succession as to give a suggestion of rapid revolver practice. Quite a smoke rose, and when it rolled away one of the vessels was already nearly under water and the other was keeling with the inflow of water from the port side. S—lost no time, but throwing off his coat, jumped in and swam to the rescue.

Throughout this entire incident his manner was that of an enthusiastic boy who had something exceedingly novel. He did not laugh. In all our acquaintance I never once heard him give a sound, hearty laugh. Instead he cackled. His delight apparently could only express itself in that way. In the main it showed itself in an excess of sharp movements, short verbal expressions, gleams of the eye.

I saw from this the man's delight in the science of engineering, and humored him in it. He was thereafter at the greatest pains to show all that he had under way in the mechanical line, and schemes he had for enjoying himself in this work in the future. It seemed rather a recreation for him than anything else. Like him, I could not help delighting in the perfect toys which he created, but the intricate details and slow process of manufacture were brain-racking. For not only would he draw the engine in all its parts, but he would buy the raw material and cast and drill and polish each separate part.

Upon my second visit I was deeply impressed by the sight of a fine passenger engine, a duplicate of the great 999 of the New York Central, of those days. It stood on brass rails laid along an old library shelf that had probably belonged to the previous occupant of the studio. This engine was a splendid object to look upon, strong, heavy, silent-running, with the fineness and grace of a perfect sewing-machine. It was duly trimmed with brass and nickel, after the manner of the great "flyers," and seemed so sturdy and powerful that one could not restrain the desire to see it run.

"How do you like that?" S—— exclaimed when he saw me looking at it.

"It's splendid," I said.

"See how she runs," he exclaimed, moving it up and down. "No noise about that."

He fairly caressed the mechanism with his hand, and went off into a most careful analysis of its qualities.

"I could build that engine," he exclaimed at last, enthusiastically, "if I were down in the Baldwin Company's place. I could make her break the record."

"I haven't the slightest doubt in the world," I answered.

This engine was a source of great expense to him, as well as the chief point in a fine scheme. He had made brass rails for it—sufficient to extend about the four sides of the studio—something like seventy feet. He had made most handsome passenger-cars with full equipment of brakes, vestibules, Pintsch gas, and so on, and had painted on their sides "The Great Pullman Line." One day, when we were quite friendly, he brought from his home all the rails, in a carpet-bag, and gave an exhibition of his engine's speed, attaching the cars and getting up sufficient steam to cause the engine to race about the room at a rate which was actually exciting. He had an arrangement by which it would pick up water and stop automatically. It was on this occasion that he confided what he called his great biograph scheme, the then forerunner of the latter day moving pictures. It was all so new then, almost a rumor, like that of the flying machine before it was invented.

"I propose to let the people see the photographic representation of an actual wreck—engine, cars, people, all tumbled down together after a collision, and no imitation, either—the actual thing."

"How do you propose to do it?" I asked.

"Well, that's the thing," he said, banteringly. "Now, how do you suppose I'd do it?"

"Hire a railroad to have a wreck and kill a few people," I suggested.

"Well, I've got a better thing than that. A railroad couldn't plan anything more real than mine will be."

I was intensely curious because of the novelty of the thing at that time. The "Biograph" was in its infancy.

"This is it," he exclaimed suddenly. "You see how realistic this engine is, don't you?"

I acknowledged that I did.

"Well," he confided, "I'm building another just like it. It's costing me three hundred dollars, and the passenger-cars will cost as much more. Now, I'm going to fix up some scenery on my roof—a gorge, a line of woods, a river, and a bridge. I'm going to make the water tumble over big rocks just above the bridge and run underneath it. Then I'm going to lay this track around these rocks, through the woods, across the bridge and off into the woods again.

"I'm going to put on the two trains and time them so they'll meet on the bridge. Just when they come into view where they can see each other, a post on the side of the track will strike the cabs in such a way as to throw the firemen out on the steps just as if they were going to jump. When the engines take the bridge they'll explode caps that will set fire to oil and powder under the cars and burn them up."

"Then what?" I asked.

"Well, I've got it planned automatically so that you will see people jumping out of the cars and tumbling down on the rocks, the flames springing up and taking to the cars, and all that. Don't you believe it?" he added, as I smiled at the idea. "Look here," and he produced a model of one of the occupants of the cars. He labored for an hour to show all the intricate details, until I was compelled to admit the practicability and novelty of the idea. Then he explained that instantaneous photography, as it was then called, was to be applied at such close range that the picture would appear life size. The actuality of the occurrence would do the rest.

Skepticism still lingered with me for a time, but when I saw the second train growing, the figures and apparatus gradually being modeled, and the correspondence and conferences going on between the artist and several companies which wished to gain control of the result, I was perfectly sure that his idea would some day be realized.

As I have said, when I first met S—— he had not realized any of his dreams. It was just at that moment that the tide was about to turn. He surprised me by the assurance, born of his wonderful virility, with which he went about all things.

"I've got an order from the *Ladies' Home Journal*," he said to me one day. "They came to me."

"Good," I said. "What is it?"

"Somebody's writing up the terminal facilities of New York."

He had before him an Academy board, on which was sketched, in wash, a midnight express striking out across the Jersey meadows with sparks blazing from the smoke stacks and dim lights burning in the sleepers. It was a vivid thing, strong with all the strength of an engine, and rich in the go and enthusiasm which adhere to such mechanisms.

"I want to make a good thing of this," he said. "It may do me some good."

A little later he received his first order from Harper's. He could not disguise that he was pleased, much as he tried to carry it off with an air. It was just before the Spanish war broke out, and the sketches he was to do related to the navy.

He labored at this order with the most tireless enthusiasm. Marine construction was his delight anyhow, and he spent hours and days making studies about the great vessels, getting not only the atmosphere but the mechanical detail. When he made the pictures they represented all that he felt.

"You know those drawings?" he said the day after he delivered them.

"Yes."

"I set a good stiff price on them and demanded my drawings back when they were through."

"Did you get them?"

"Yep. It will give them more respect for what I'm trying to do," he said.

Not long after he illustrated one of Kipling's stories.

He was in high feather at this, but grim and repressed withal. One could see by the nervous movements of his wiry body that he was delighted over it.

At this time Kipling came to his studio. It was by special arrangement, but S—— received him as if he were—well, as artists usually receive authors. They talked over the galley proofs, and the author went away.

"It's coming my way now," he said, when he could no longer conceal his feelings. "I want to do something good on this."

Through all this rise from obscurity to recognition he lived close to his friends—a crowd of them, apparently, always in his studio jesting, boxing, fencing—and interested himself in the mechanics I have described. His drawing, his engine-building, his literary studies and recreations were all mixed, jumbled, plunging him pell-mell, as it were, on to distinction. In the first six months of his studio life he had learned to fence, and often dropped his brush to put on the mask and assume the foils with one of his companions.

As our friendship increased I found how many were the man's accomplishments and how wide his range of sympathies. He was an expert bicyclist, as well as a trick rider, and used a camera in a way to make an amateur envious. He could sing, having a fine tenor voice, which I heard the very day I learned that he could sing. It so happened that it was my turn to buy the theater tickets, and I invited him to come with me that especial evening.

"Can't do it," he replied.

"All right," I said.

"I'm part of an entertainment tonight, or I would," he added apologetically.

"What do you do?" I inquired.

"Sing."

"Get out!" I said.

"So be it," he answered. "Come up this evening."

To this I finally agreed, and was surprised to observe the ease with which he rendered his solo. He had an exquisitely clear and powerful voice and received a long round of applause, which he refused to acknowledge by singing again.

The influence of success is easily observable in a man of so volatile a nature. It seems to me that I could have told by his manner, day by day, the inwash of the separate ripples of the inrolling tide of success. He was all alive, full of plans, and the tale of his coming conquests was told in his eye. Sometime in the second year of our acquaintance I called at his studio in response to a card which he had stuck under my office door. It was his habit to draw an outline head of himself, something almost bordering upon a caricature, writing underneath it "I called," together with any word he might have to say. This day he was in his usual good spirits, and rallied me upon having an office which was only a blind. He had a roundabout way of getting me to talk about his personal affairs with him, and I soon saw that he had something very interesting, to himself, to communicate. At last he said,—

"I'm going to Europe next summer."

"Is that so?" I replied. "For pleasure?"

"Well, partly."

"What's up outside of that?" I asked.

"I'm going to represent the American Architectural League at the international convention."

"I didn't know you were an architect," I said.

"Well, I'm not," he answered, "professionally. I've studied it pretty thoroughly."

"Well, you seem to be coming up, Louis," I remarked.

"I'm doing all right," he answered.

He went on working at his easel as if his fate depended upon what he was doing. He had the fortunate quality of being able to work and converse most entertainingly at the same time. He seemed to enjoy company under such circumstances.

"You didn't know I was a baron, did you?" he finally observed.

"No," I answered, thinking he was exercising his fancy for the moment. "Where do you keep your baronial lands, my lord?"

"In Germany, kind sir," he replied, banteringly.

Then in his customary excitable mood he dropped his brushes and stood up.

"You don't believe me, do you?" he exclaimed, looking over his drooping glasses.

"Why, certainly I believe you, if you are serious. Are you truly a baron?"

"It was this way," he said. "My grandfather was a baron. My father was the younger of two brothers. His brother got the title and what was left of the estate. That he managed to go through with, and then he died. Now, no one has bothered about the title—"

"And you're going back to claim it?"

"Exactly."

I took it all lightly at first, but in time I began to perceive that it was a serious ambition. He truly wanted to be Baron S—— and add to himself the luster of his ancestors.

With all this, the man was really not so much an aristocrat in his mood as a seeker after life and new experiences. Being a baron was merely a new experience, or promised to be. He had the liveliest sympathies for republican theories and institutions—only he considered his life a thing apart. He had a fine mind, philosophically and logically poised. He could reason upon all things, from the latest mathematical theorem to Christian Science. Naturally, being so much of an individualist, he was not drifting toward any belief in the latter, but was never weary of discussing the power of mind—a universal mind even—its wondrous ramifications and influences. Also he was a student of the English school of philosophy, and loved to get up mathematical and mechanical demonstrations of certain philosophic truths. Thus he worked out by means of a polygon, whose sides were of unequal lengths, a theory of friendship which is too intricate to explain here.

From now on I watched his career with the liveliest interest. He was a charming and a warm friend, and never neglected for a moment the obligations which such a relationship demands.

I heard from him frequently in many and various ways, dined with him regularly every second or third week, and rejoiced with him in his triumphs, now more and more frequent. One spring he went to Europe and spent the summer in tracing down his baronial claims, looking up various artists and scientists and attending several scientific meetings here and there at the same time. He did the illustrations for one of Kipling's fast express stories which one of the magazines published, and came back flushed and ready to try hard for a membership in the American Water-Color Society.

I shall never forget his anxiety to get into that mildly interesting body. He worked hard and long on several pictures which should not only be hung on the line but enlist sufficient interest among the artists to gain him a vote of admission. He mentioned it frequently and fixed me with his eyes to see what I thought of him.

"Go ahead," I said; "you have more right to membership perhaps than many another I know. Try hard."

He painted not one, but four, pictures, and sent them all. They were very interesting after their kind. Two were scenes from the great railroad terminal yards; the others, landscapes in mist or rain. Three of these pictures were passed and two of them hung on the line. The third was *skyed*, but he was admitted to membership.

I was delighted for his sake, for I could see, when he gave me the intelligence, that it was a matter which had keyed up his whole nervous system.

Not long after this we were walking on Broadway, one drizzly autumn evening, on our way to the theater. Life, ambition, and our future were the *small* subjects under discussion. The street, as usual, was crowded. On every hand blazed the fire signs. The yellow lights were beautifully reflected in the wet sidewalks and gray wet cobblestones glistening with water.

When we reached Greeley Square (at that time a brilliant and almost sputtering spectacle of light and merriment), S—— took me by the arm.

"Come over here," he said. "I want you to look at it from here."

He took me to a point where, by the intersection of the lines of the converging streets, one could not only see Greeley Square but a large part of Herald Square, with its then huge theatrical sign of fire and its measure of store lights and lamps of vehicles. It was a kaleidoscopic and inspiring scene. The broad, converging walks were alive with people. A perfect jam of vehicles marked the spot where the horse and cable cars intersected.

Overhead was the elevated station, its lights augmented every few minutes by long trains of brightly lighted cars filled with changing metropolitan crowds—crowds like shadows moving in a dream.

"Do you see the quality of that? Look at the blend of the lights and shadows in there under the L."

I looked and gazed in silent admiration.

"See, right here before us—that pool of water there—do you get that? Now, that isn't silver-colored, as it's usually represented. It's a prism. Don't you see the hundred points of light?"

I acknowledged the variety of color, which I had scarcely observed before.

"You may think one would skip that in viewing a great scene, but the artist mustn't. He must get all, whether you notice it or not. It gives feeling, even when you don't see it."

I acknowledged the value of this ideal.

"It's a great spectacle," he said. "It's got more flesh and blood in it than people usually think. It's easy to make it too mechanical and commonplace."

"Why don't you paint it?" I asked.

He turned on me as if he had been waiting for the suggestion.

"That's something I want to tell you," he said. "I am. I've sketched it a half-dozen times already. I haven't got it yet. But I'm going to."

I heard more of these dreams, intensifying all the while, until the Spanish-American war broke out. Then he was off in a great rush of war work. I scarcely saw him for six weeks, owing to some travels of my own, but I saw his name. One day in Broadway I stopped to see why a large crowd was gathered about a window in the Hoffman House. It was one of S——'s drawings of our harbor defenses, done as if the artist had been sitting at the bottom of the sea. The fishes, the green water, the hull of a massive war-ship—all were there—and about, the grim torpedoes. This put it into my head to go and see him. He was as tense and strenuous as ever. The glittering treasure at the end of the rainbow was more than ever in his eye. His body was almost sore from traveling.

"I am in now," he said, referring to the war movement. "I am going to Tampa."

"Be gone long?" I asked.

"Not this first time. I'll only be down there three weeks."

"I'll see you then."

"Supposing we make it certain," he said. "What do you say to dining together this coming Sunday three weeks?"

I went away, wishing him a fine trip and feeling that his dreams must now soon begin to come true. He was growing in reputation. Some war pictures, such as he could do, would set people talking. Then he would paint his prize pictures, finish his wreck scheme, become a baron, and be a great man.

Three weeks later I knocked at his studio door. It was a fine springlike day, though it was in February. I expected confidently to hear his quick aggressive step inside. Not a sound in reply. I knocked harder, but still received no answer. Then I went to the other doors about. He might be with his friends, but they were not in. I went away thinking that his war duties had interfered, that he had not returned.

Nevertheless there was something depressing about that portion of the building in which his studio was located. I felt as if it should not be, and decided to call again. Monday it was the same, and Tuesday.

That same evening I was sitting in the library of the Salmagundi Club, when a well-known artist addressed me.

"You knew S——, didn't you?" he said.

"Yes; what of it?"

"You knew he was dead, didn't you?"

"What!" I said.

"Yes, he died of fever, this morning."

I looked at him without speaking for a moment.

"Too bad," he said. "A clever boy, Louis. Awfully clever. I feel sorry for his father."

It did not take long to verify his statement. His name was in the perfunctory death lists of the papers the next morning. No other notice of any sort. Only a half-dozen seemed to know that he had ever lived.

And yet it seemed *to me* that a great tragedy had happened—he was so ambitious, so full of plans. His dreams were so near fulfillment.

I saw the little grave afterward and the empty studio. His desks revealed several inventions and many plans of useful things, but these came to nothing. There was no one to continue the work.

My feeling at the time was as if I had been looking at a beautiful lamp, lighted, warm and irradiating a charming scene, and then suddenly that it had been puffed out before my eyes, as if a hundred bubbles of iridescent hues had been shattered by a breath. We toil so much, we dream so richly, we hasten so fast, and, lo! the green door is opened. We are through it, and its grassy surface has sealed us forever from all which apparently we so much crave— even as, breathlessly, we are still running.

Milton Keynes UK
Ingram Content Group UK Ltd.
UKHW030837021124
450589UK00006B/723

9 789362 511195